Triune Eternality

Triune Eternality

God's Relationship to Time in the Theology of Karl Barth

Daniel M. Griswold

Fortress Press
Minneapolis

TRIUNE ETERNALITY
God's Relationship to Time in the Theology of Karl Barth

Copyright © 2015 Fortress Press. All rights reserved. Except for brief quotations in critical articles or reviews, no part of this book may be reproduced in any manner without prior written permission from the publisher. Visit http://www.augsburgfortress.org/copyrights/ or write to Permissions, Augsburg Fortress, Box 1209, Minneapolis, MN 55440.

Cover design: Alisha Lofgren

Library of Congress Cataloging-in-Publication Data
Hardcover ISBN: 978-1-4514-9967-4
Paperback ISBN: 978-1-4514-7930-0
eBook ISBN: 978-1-4514-9656-7

The paper used in this publication meets the minimum requirements of American National Standard for Information Sciences — Permanence of Paper for Printed Library Materials, ANSI Z329.48-1984.

Manufactured in the U.S.A.

This book was produced using PressBooks.com, and PDF rendering was done by PrinceXML.

Contents

	Acknowledgements	vii
1.	Introduction	1
2.	The Conceptual Context Traditional Reflections on God and Time	21
3.	Aside Reflections on Eternity after Barth	83
4.	The Developmental Context	117
5.	The Doctrinal Context	157
6.	Eternity and Time in the Church Dogmatics	195
7.	Conclusion	235
	Bibliography	251
	Index	261

Acknowledgements

> The youth gets together the materials to build a bridge to the moon, or perchance a palace or temple on the earth, and at length the middle-aged man concludes to build a woodshed with them.[1]

I feel great resonance with Thoreau's words, surely because of the long gestation period enjoyed by the dissertation that led to this book. Through the many years from its conception to its completion, I received the help and encouragement of many people, some indeed who did not know they were helping me in this peculiar labor. So it is that I mention a few of those who were part of my work, who encouraged it, helped refine it, or blessedly and momentarily distracted me from it for a greater purpose.

The congregations of Hope Reformed Church (Carrollton, Texas), the Reformed Church in Plano, and Trinity Reformed Church (Rochester, New York) helped me embrace the vocation that now fills a good number of my God-given moments, and granted me time for study and writing.

Numerous scholars have been part of my journey and deserve thanks. Space permits my naming only a few. It was the late Allen Verhey who, by his pedagogy, scholarship, and artistry with the

---

1. Henry David Thoreau, cited by Annie Dillard, *The Writing Life* (New York: Harper & Row, 1989), 5.

written word, inspired me in my sophomore year at Hope College to consider the path that I have taken. Allen, more than any other single person, is why I am both a minister and a scholar. His support, reflections, and gentle urging through the years were a great gift. Michael Bush, who has been my friend since our start at Union Seminary in Virginia almost thirty years ago, was steadfast and lovingly irksome in his encouragement. Daniel Meeter provided valuable and generous assistance at an important time. Few friends volunteer to read another's dissertation; that Daniel did, and offered such outstanding comments, is evidence of his love and talent.

I owe the members of my dissertation committee special acknowledgment: William Babcock, George Hunsinger, and Charles Wood. They each played an important part in the genesis and development of the dissertation, and my debt to them is more than I can repay. I count it as a great honor that they agreed to help me and persisted to the end. Prof. Wood stands out among all others. His wise and perceptive counsel was invaluable, always offered with patience, encouragement, humor, and simple delight in the subject. I will be happy if his virtues are reflected in this book.

Last, I name the members of my family, aware that simply naming them is not nearly enough. My children, Bethany, Jonathan, and Christopher, have lived with this project lurking in the background all their lives, or at least as long as they can remember. That they regard it as simply what I do in addition to other things is a priceless gift, freely and joyfully given, because it reminds me that we are not the work we do, or fail to do. Such grace they have learned, no doubt, from their mother and my wife, Tammi. Her constant love and supportive care for me is among the greatest of temporal gifts, a sign that time, in God's grace, can be much more than burden, but truly blessing.

1

Introduction

How is God related to time? What is the proper theological way of expressing that relationship, and why? Such questions may appear to many to be precisely the kind of abstract, irrelevant speculation that relegates theological discourse as a whole off to the margins of so-called real life. What difference *does* it make, one may ask, *how* God is related to time, whether God is temporal or atemporal?

Behind this book lies the conviction that it does matter. The question of God's relationship to time bears on almost every theological doctrine, in some places only implicitly, yet elsewhere quite prominently. The meaning and efficacy of prayer; the doctrines of creation, providence, and last things: all are quite readily affected by how one answers this question.[1] For if God is atemporal, then

---

1. Stump and Kretzmann put it well in a different context: "The concept of eternity makes a significant difference in the consideration of a variety of issues in the philosophy of religion, including, for instance, the apparent incompatibility of divine omniscience with human freedom, of divine immutability with the efficacy of petitionary prayer, and of divine omniscience with divine immutability." Eleonore Stump and Norman Kretzmann, "Eternity," *Journal of Philosophy* 78 (1981): 429. This article is also printed in Thomas V. Morris, ed., *The Concept of God* (New York: Oxford University Press, 1987). It is now available (although with

does that make our prayers ineffectual? If God is temporal, does that make God dependent upon, and thus subject to, time? Does Christian hope depend on a concept of time running to a definite end? Other doctrines even more central to Christian faith (such as election, prophecy, eschatology, or the freedom of the will) are likewise impacted by theological judgments regarding God's temporality or atemporality, and although these effects may be less obvious, they are nonetheless genuine. For surely the incarnation, to name one such central doctrine, is a doctrine about, among other things, a unique event of historical time interrupted by God. Insofar as the connection between that event and the being of God is in view, any doctrine of the incarnation takes up, if only implicitly, the question of how God and all time are related.

Now, none of this is to say that how one decides the issue of divine eternality determines all other doctrines in one's theological system. This issue is neither the *Grundfrage* nor the Rosetta Stone of all doctrinal theology.[2] In any theological scheme, some elements are primary and others are derived, some doctrines are central and others are peripheral. The question of God's relationship to time bears an unusual relationship to other doctrines. It is not central or foundational, nor is it really peripheral either, because, as we have seen, it touches on so many other doctrines. Rather, I will suggest that decisions concerning God's relationship to time reflect prior theological judgments. For Barth, these judgments concern, to name only a few, the being of God, the doctrine of the Trinity, the nature of theological language, and the proper use of philosophy in

---

different pagination) on the web site of St. Louis University (where Prof. Stump is on the faculty) at https://sites.google.com/site/stumpep/Eternity.pdf?attredirects=0.

2. It is not here denied that one could construct a systematic theology in which divine eternality or temporality exercised such a fundamental role. However, it seems to me that such a construction would be rather odd chiefly because, to my knowledge, no religious tradition (Christian or otherwise) places at the center of its doctrines a particular concept of God's relationship to time.

theology—thus this question intersects or interpenetrates decidedly central or foundational doctrines.

The twentieth century saw a great deal of ferment surrounding the question of time. Theoretical physics may have been the first area of inquiry to see such changes, as the work of Albert Einstein led to a profound alteration in our understanding of time. Einstein's special and general theories of relativity have rendered quaint the idea that time is a uniform constant, and quantum theory has pushed that project even further, sometimes with intriguing (and even whimsical) results.[3] In philosophy, Martin Heidegger took up a phenomenological analysis of time, reviving by means of existentialism an approach reminiscent of St. Augustine (albeit with very different results);[4] since then, certain philosophers, such as Stephen Toulmin, approach the problem of time with the tools of analytic philosophy.[5]

Accompanying this rejuvenated focus on time was a renewed interest in how we ought to understand the relationship between time and God. Much of this attention may be described as a discussion over what sense there can be made of the claim, deeply embedded in the Christian tradition, that God is eternal. Many participants in the discussion argued that God's relationship to time is not rightly construed as that of an atemporal eternity, but rather as an everlasting existence in and throughout time. From a variety of voices came a trenchant criticism of the traditional understanding of God's relationship to time.

---

3. Two examples that readily suggest themselves are the Schroediger's cat thought experiment, and an entertaining essay, David Deutsch and Michael Lockwood, "The Quantum Physics of Time Travel," *Scientific American* (1994): 68–74.
4. Martin Heidegger, *Being and Time* (San Francisco: Harper & Row, 1962).
5. Stephen Toulmin and June Goodfield, *The Discovery of Time* (New York: Harper Torchbooks, 1965.)

Among theologians, two obvious examples of those who accepted this criticism are Robert Jenson[6] (in whose work the criticism is explicit) and Thomas Torrance[7] (where it is more implicit). I believe that one can make the case that Eberhard Jüngel and Jürgen Moltmann assume the validity of the criticism, and incorporate it into their work.[8] In addition, many philosophers and philosophers of religion have argued against the traditional understanding of God's eternity,[9] so many, indeed, that it would be accurate to describe the position as dominant in philosophical theology.

For all of these who take this tack, theologians and philosophers alike, their arguments amount to a conscious rejection of the conception of God's relationship to time that had until relatively recently dominated the Christian tradition and indeed all of Western philosophical thought. This traditional conception holds that God is not in time, but exists outside of time; that is, God always exists, but cannot be temporally located and thus confined, and furthermore is

---

6. Robert W. Jenson, *God after God: The God of the Past and the God of the Future, Seen in the Work of Karl Barth* (New York: The Bobbs-Merrill Company, 1969); Robert W. Jenson, "Does God Have Time? The Doctrine of the Trinity and the Concept of Time in the Physical Sciences," *CTNS Bulletin* 11 (1991): 1–6; Robert W. Jenson, *Unbaptized God: The Basic Flaw in Ecumenical Theology* (Minneapolis: Fortress Press, 1992).
7. Thomas F. Torrance, *Space, Time and Incarnation* (New York: Oxford University Press, 1969).
8. Jürgen Moltmann, *Theologie der Hoffnung* (München: Chr. Kaiser Verlag, 1965); Jürgen Moltmann, *Theology of Hope: On the Ground and the Implications of a Christian Eschatology* (London: SCM Press, 1967); Eberhard Jüngel, *Gottes Sein ist im Werden: verantwortliche Rede vom Sein Gottes bei Karl Barth: eine Paraphrase*, 4th ed. (Tübingen: Mohr Siebeck, 1986); Eberhard Jüngel, *God's Being Is in Becoming: The Trinitarian Being of God in the Theology of Karl Barth*, trans. John Webster (T. & T. Clark, 2001).
9. It should be sufficient to cite a few representative works: Charles Hartshorne and William L. Reese, *Philosophers Speak of God* (Chicago: University of Chicago Press, 1953); W. C. Kneale, "Time and Eternity in Theology," *Proceedings of the Aristotelian Society* 61 (1961): 87–108; Martha Kneale, "Eternity and Sempiternity," *Proceedings of the Aristotelian Society* 69 (1969): 223–38; Anthony Kenny, "Divine Foreknowledge and Human Freedom," in *Aquinas: A Collection of Critical Essays*, ed. Anthony Kenny (Garden City, NY: Doubleday-Anchor, 1969), 255–70; Nicholas Wolterstorff, "God Everlasting," in *God and the Good*, ed. Clifton J. Orlebeke and Lewis M. Smedes (Grand Rapids: Eerdmans, 1975), 181–203; Alan G. Padgett, *God, Eternity, and the Nature of Time* (New York: St. Martin's Press, 1992).

not subject to the limitations and burdens of time to which temporal creatures are subject.

The traditional conception also has its defenders, some of whom, beginning in the early 1980s, joined the conversation to challenge the challengers.[10] The new defenders of divine timeless eternity have creatively thought anew about the traditional concept of eternity, so as to draw on its benefits and correct its shortcomings. I am convinced that they pose a significant challenge to those for whom the literal temporality of God has become an unquestioned article of faith.

Approaching the Question through Barth's Theology

These mid- to late- twentieth-century developments marked a new phase for the question of God's relationship to time. To be sure, those developments were stimulating, showing (for example) a refreshing openness to the post-Einsteinian physics. However, I will argue (throughout, although mainly in chapters 3 and 4) that the apparent disregard for the Western theological tradition of reflection on eternity in these developments is unwarranted. In a number of theologians who accept the modern view of God's temporality (again, I see Robert Jenson as an important example) I find a curious stance that, when it comes to the question of God and time, the past has nothing of value to contribute but must be entirely rejected. Yet we impoverish ourselves if we regard earlier answers as negligible. We have a twofold opportunity: to allow the old answers to speak to our modern questions, and to use our contemporary perspective to gain insight on historic contributions.

---

10. The following would count as able representatives: Stump and Kretzmann, "Eternity"; Paul Helm, *Eternal God: A Study of God without Time* (Oxford: Oxford University Press, 1988); Brian Leftow, *Time and Eternity* (Ithaca, NY: Cornell University Press, 1991).

The burden of this project is to show that this twofold opportunity is present in the theology of Karl Barth. On the question of God's relationship to time, on the puzzle over the nature of eternity, the contributions may surely run in both directions. Barth has a position that deserves our attention. Furthermore, a perspective shaped by the discussions over the last forty years enables one to explore Barth's position in ways not possible before. In Barth's mature theology, we find a full, rich, and fascinating understanding of God's relationship to time. Not surprisingly, Barth's is a thoroughly *theological* answer to the question. It is theological in that (again, not surprisingly) it is intimately connected with Barth's doctrine of the Trinity and with his doctrine of revelation. For that reason, Barth's statements about God, time, and eternity are sometimes difficult to follow. Indeed, to some they often seem contradictory.[11]

Yet it is precisely at this point that Barth's work provides us with the twofold opportunity I wish to pursue. Barth has, it will be shown, a deeply theological, complex, and often metaphorical understanding of time and eternity. That understanding can provide some guidance for us in the contemporary, paradoxical age of quantum theory, analytic philosophy, deconstructionism, and postmodernity try to think about God and time. But today's conversations, particularly the philosophical conversation about divine atemporal eternity, may in turn give us a new opportunity to understand Barth afresh, for they can provide an important conceptual context in which to understand Barth's ideas about God and time.

It is surely the case that Barth deserves to be understood afresh. For on the question of God, time, and eternity, until recently Barth has not been given the careful attention he deserves. Many who have actually read Barth have, furthermore, interpreted his views

---

11. William C. Placher, *Narratives of a Vulnerable God: Christ, Theology, and Scripture* (Louisville: Westminster/John Knox Press, 1994), 36.

on God and time in a less than satisfactory way. In particular, the common practice seems to be for theologians to make much of Barth's statements about God's temporality, God's time, God's historicity, in addition to Barth's expressed antipathy to more Platonic conceptions of God. So far, so good. But then these statements are usually read as giving explicit support to a theological conception of God's absolute temporality, such that no distinction from creaturely temporality seems to remain.[12] What is missing in these interpretations is acknowledgment that Barth also found much that was theologically necessary in the traditional conception of eternity. More importantly, also missing is an awareness of the all-important doctrinal context of Barth's statements.[13]

Such a reading of Barth is common among his admirers. Among others, however, the tendency is to notice Barth's genuine interest in a more or less traditional concept of eternity, but to judge such interest as evidence of conceptual incoherence[14] or of theological inadequacy.[15]

The latter tendency is clear in the work of Richard Roberts. Roberts sees the whole of the *Church Dogmatics* as a monolithic and totalitarian theological system that is closed off from real life, and posits the dialectic of time and eternity to be the key to the *Dogmatics*, assessing it as the fuel that drives the system's isolation. Roberts's criticisms are important because they point to a significant issue:[16]

---

12. Although such an approach seems common, I have in mind particularly Jenson, *God after God* and Jenson, *Unbaptized God*, chapters 8 and 10.
13. Neglect of this data also seems to play into the tendency of these interpreters of Barth to overemphasize the distinction between the early Barth and the later Barth, particularly between the second edition of *Römerbrief* and the *Kirchliche Dogmatik*. We will return to this point in chapter 4.
14. One representative of this stance is Padgett, *God, Eternity, and the Nature of Time*.
15. See Oscar Cullmann, *Christ and Time: The Primitive Christian Conception of Time and History* (London: SCM Press, 1962); and Richard H. Roberts, *A Theology on Its Way? Essays on Karl Barth* (Edinburgh: T. & T. Clark, 1991).
16. However, Barth himself was concerned about this issue.

our understanding of God and time should not carry implications that deny all freedom to God or human beings. Yet Roberts's work represents a seriously flawed interpretation of Barth, for it fails to see the genuine openness of the *Dogmatics*. It furthermore perpetuates the long-standing yet fruitless attempt to seek one concept, in this case the dialectic of time and eternity, that alone provides coherence to the whole of the *Church Dogmatics*, an attempt that has since been discredited by the work of George Hunsinger.[17]

The Thesis of This Work

For these reasons, a new look at Karl Barth on the question of God's eternity is needed, not only to move beyond flawed interpretations, and not simply to achieve a better understanding of Barth's theology, but also to gain greater insight into the issue itself by means of Barth's work. In this book I propose just such a new look. The thesis to be pursued has, to some small extent, already been implied, but I now state it explicitly.

Karl Barth's understanding of God's relationship to time, of God's eternity, is thoroughly theological (that is, both its subject matter and its method of development arise from reflection on the being and works of God). Consequently, it can be comprehended only if one understands the *doctrinal context* out of which his ideas on time and eternity develop. Furthermore, Barth's theological judgments about the meaning of time and eternity and their relationship to each other are not well understood unless one understands the *conceptual context* out of which his judgments grew and, in part, against which they reacted. Finally, Barth's understanding of time and eternity evolved over time; yet, within that growth and development, continuity is

---

17. George Hunsinger, *How to Read Karl Barth: The Shape of His Theology* (New York: Oxford University Press, 1991).

far more important than discontinuity.[18] Consequently, Barth is not well understood on the question before us unless one understands the *developmental context* of Barth's views.

When we pay attention to each of these three contexts, we come away with the following picture. For Barth, God is not determined or confined by time as human beings are, but neither is God completely alien to time. In different senses, God is neither temporal nor atemporal, and, in yet still different senses, God is both temporal and atemporal. One cannot express Barth's understanding of God's eternity by saying simply and without qualification that for Barth God is temporal.[19]

Through critical appropriation of classical understandings of God's eternity, particularly those developed by Augustine, Boëthius, and Anselm, Barth expresses this radically other relationship to time by creative use of three Christian doctrines, from which two major patterns emerge. The three principal doctrines he uses are the doctrines of the Trinity, revelation, and the person of Jesus Christ. The two patterns derived from these doctrines, which weave themselves throughout the entire *Church Dogmatics* and are used as structuring devices or rhetorical tools (and thus are not simply restatements of their originating doctrines), are the pattern of God's threefold eternality, and the pattern of the distinction and the connection between God's being in God's own self (God's being *ad*

---

18. Such a point is one of the many significant things to be learned from McCormack's groundbreaking work on Barth's early theological development. His influence is found in those sections dealing with the developmental context. Bruce L. McCormack, *Karl Barth's Critically Realistic Dialectical Theology: Its Genesis and Development, 1909–1936* (New York: Oxford University Press, 1995); Bruce L. McCormack, "A Scholastic of a Higher Order: The Development of Karl Barth's Theology, 1921–31" (PhD diss., Princeton Theological Seminary, 1989).
19. Nor, for that matter, can one adequately convey Barth's position by saying without further explication that, for Barth, God is atemporal. However, it appears that the oversimplification stated above is by far the more common one.

intra, the ontic Trinity) and God's being as revealed toward the world (God's economy or God's being *ad extra*, the noetic Trinity).

The first pattern, that of God's threefold eternality, is an exceedingly important piece of Barth's thought. Barth portrayed divine eternity as a living relationality structured as God's pretemporality, supratemporality, and posttemporality. That is, God is the origin of all time, God accompanies or contains all time, and God is there after time as its goal and hope.

In so structuring his concept of divine eternity, Barth sought to express a distinction and yet a positive *relationship* between eternity and time. Eternity is described not as merely atemporality, but rather, in this threefold way, with each aspect, pre-, supra-, and post*temporality, having time in view*. The terms by which Barth defines eternity (*Vorzeitlichkeit, Überzeitlichkeit, Nachzeitlichkeit*) point to a conception of eternity that is oriented to time rather than alienated from it. However, as a temporality that is before, above, and after time, in Barth eternity is clearly distinct from time as it is typically understood and experienced. The temporal cast to Barth's construction notwithstanding, eternity is not the same as time.

The importance of this first pattern is seen in another, more doctrinal, matter. In giving eternity this threefold structure, Barth thereby connects eternity with his doctrine of the Trinity. The connection is demonstrated not simply because he had a threefold understanding of eternity. The mere occurrence of a pattern of three does not a trinity make. Rather, the connection of Barth's concept of eternity with his doctrine of the Trinity is seen in a much more substantive, and doctrinal, focus. This conception of eternity, with its threefold cast, is understood *perichoretically*.

The doctrine of *perichoresis* in traditional dogmatics is a means of describing the relations between the persons of the Trinity. Those relations, the doctrine insists, are mutual and cooperative, unified yet distinct. Father, Son, and Holy Spirit exist and work together in such a way that they are both united with and distinct from each other. To say that Barth's threefold conception of eternity is perichoretic is to say that the relations among the three aspects of eternity are construed in analogy with the relations among the persons of the Trinity. Pre-, post-, and supratemporality are to be understood as describing divine realities that may be distinguished but not ultimately separated from one another, and that must be understood in their relation to each other.

We see this threefold pattern throughout the *Dogmatics*, not only as a structuring device, and not only as reflecting the doctrine of the Trinity, but put to use in Barth's Christology. For Barth, Jesus is the Lord of time,[20] because the risen Lord reveals to us the unity of his past life, death, and resurrection; his presence with us; and his future coming, such unity mirroring the eternal being of God, for whom past, present, and future are one, to whom the entire divine life is present.

The second major pattern that emerges from Barth's doctrinal formulation of divine eternality is one I will call the pattern of revelation. It is, as Hunsinger might describe it, a pattern of dialectical inclusion.[21] It is a pattern reflected in the very distinction and relation between time and eternity Barth is careful to draw. Fundamentally, or rather, with regard to the most basic doctrines of the faith, this pattern is found in the distinction and relation that Barth draws between the economy and the being of God, that is, between God in God's works and God in God's self. For Barth, in express opposition to Schleiermacher, the doctrine of the Trinity is not a doctrine of

---

20. Barth, *Church Dogmatics*, trans. Geoffrey Bromiley et al. (Edinburgh: T. & T. Clark, 1956–69), III/2, §47.1. Hereafter *CD*.
21. Hunsinger, *How to Read Karl Barth*, e.g., 107.

an *economic* Trinity only, saying only how God appears to us, but a doctrine of an *immanent* Trinity as well, indicating who God really is. Barth believed that it is only through the economy that we know God, and that the God thus known is the real God. For Barth, revelation is a real making known *of* God *by* God, a self-disclosure of the inner life of God. Yet what God reveals is revealed through God's works; we know God only through them. We know God *ad intra* or *a se* by means of God *ad extra* or *pro nobis*. Yet Barth is careful never to collapse the two into each other, for God's freedom and mystery prevent a simple identification of our knowledge of God with the inner being of God. However, the revelational dialectic of God's veiling and unveiling, of God's being and act, expresses Barth's conviction that we can know something true about God, while it also preserves the mystery and freedom of God. This very significant pattern pervades the entirety of the *Church Dogmatics*.

The dialectic of the economy and the being of God determines a parallel dialectic of time and eternity. Many times throughout the *Church Dogmatics* we find Barth speaking of time and eternity. These many instances could give the impression (as it apparently does for Roberts) that this dialectic is itself a fundamental key to the whole of the *Church Dogmatics*. Yet that would be a mistake. It is very important to notice that the time-eternity dialectic in the *Church Dogmatics* is used as a shorthand for a more fundamental dialectic of revelation: the economy and the being of God—God for us and God in God's own being. As Karl-Hinrich Manzke puts it, "The relationship of time and eternity is for Barth an essential means for bringing into effect the subject of theology as a whole."[22]

---

22. "Die Relation von Zeit und Ewigkeit ist für Barth ein wesentliches Mittel, um das Thema der Theologie insgesamt zur Ausführung zu bringen." Karl Hinrich Manzke, *Ewigkeit und Zeitlichkeit: Aspekte für eine theologische Deutung der Zeit* (Göttingen: Vandenhoeck und Ruprecht, 1992), 490.

Terms and Scope

Before we turn to the investigation that lies before us, allow me to clarify a few items. First, throughout I frequently use the word *eternality*.[23] I do this quite intentionally. My purpose in using this uncommon word is to suggest that for Barth, God's eternity is not a thing separate from God's own being, such as a place in which God exists, but is rather a perfection[24] of God's being, an integral aspect of God's nature, which, because of divine simplicity,[25] is connected with all of God's other perfections. As George Hunsinger puts it so well, "Eternity for Barth is not the container in which God lives. It is a predicate of God's triune being."[26] Gotthard Oblau nicely speaks of eternity for Barth being God's "form of existence": "Eternity and time are thus related to each other analogically: As time is the form of existence for human beings, so eternity is the form of existence for God. As time is the formal principle of human history, so eternity is the formal principle of history in the divine being."[27]

In other, perhaps more philosophical, contexts, eternality might be called a *mode of God's being* or a *mode of existence*. But in the context of interpreting Barth, this expression could be misleading, since Barth uses *modes of being* to describe the persons of the divine Trinity. Also, one might mistakenly infer from the phrase that God may or may not exist in that mode at a given moment, that, essentially, such a "mode" is not intrinsic to God's being. In short, the important thing here is

---

23. It is likewise used frequently by Stump and Kretzmann.
24. *Perfections* is Barth's preferred word for the divine attributes.
25. The doctrine of divine simplicity holds that God does not have parts but is a whole.
26. Hunsinger, "*Mysterium Trinitatis*: Karl Barth's Conception of Eternity," in *Disruptive Grace: Studies in the Theology of Karl Barth* (Grand Rapids: Eerdmans, 2000), 189.
27. "Die Ewigkeit und die Zeit stehen also zueinander im Verhältnis der Analogie: Wie die Zeit die Daseinsform des Menschen ist, so ist die Ewigkeit die Daseinsform Gottes. Wie die Zeit das formale Prinzip der Geschichte der Menschen ist, so ist die Ewigkeit das formale Prinzip der Geschichte im göttlichen Dasein." Gotthard Oblau, *Gotteszeit und Menschenzeit: Eschatologie in der Kirchlichen Dogmatik von Karl Barth* (Neukirchen-Vluyn: Neukirchener Verlag, 1988), 120.

that, for the purposes of this book, eternity/eternality is not a thing separate from God, but is an aspect of the very being of God.

Second, I wish to make clear the specific meaning of the word *doctrine* as I use it here. In the context of Karl Barth's theological work, a doctrine is the articulation of a dogma of the church. It describes a fundamental theological reality to which the Christian faith points and that may be considered basic to the faith. For Barth, there are several doctrines, but not everything is a doctrine. Among those that are would be the doctrine of the Trinity and the doctrine of Jesus Christ. Barth's work contains other items that, although significant, are not doctrines in this sense, although they grow out of his treatment of doctrines. Barth's scriptural hermeneutics may be one: it is a significant piece of Barth's work, it grows out of his understanding of the doctrines of revelation and Scripture, but he does not raise it to the level of a doctrine. Something similar may be said about Barth's understanding of eternity. It is a very important feature of Barth's theology, it grows out of his doctrinal exposition of several church dogmas, but it is itself not a doctrine. For this reason, I am careful throughout this book to speak of Barth's concept or teaching of time and eternity, but not of his doctrine of time and eternity.

I should also make clear the scope of this investigation. I have excluded, perhaps quite noticeably for some, significant exploration of two areas. The first of these is the relationship between theology and science. I have chosen to keep that area of inquiry out of this book for reasons that flow from my stated objectives above: to move beyond flawed interpretations of Barth, to understand more adequately Barth's contribution on this matter, and to gain better understanding of the underlying theological issue of the nature of God's relationship to time. Certainly with regard to the first two of these, but also, in this context, with regard to the third, the extension of our inquiry into scientific cosmology or theoretical physics would yield very little benefit. Not to be too simplistic, but I find it pretty clear that Barth's working out of the question of time and eternity is a matter of systematic theology and perhaps, as an ancillary discipline, of philosophy. Questions of physics and quantum mechanics, although very important in other contexts, recede in importance within the context of explicating Barth's thought. Even with regard to that third goal, using Barth's theological understanding of God's relationship to time, I see little benefit from expanding the scope of this thesis to include the work of theoretical physics.

Such is by no means universally accepted. Thomas Torrance wrote quite often of the connections between science and theology,[28] and did so in some cases as an interpretation of Barth. At least one relatively recent dissertation has drawn on Barth and the natural sciences in order to propose a Christian theological concept of time and eternity.[29] Such explorations of scientific connections have no doubt been interesting, and even productive in certain ways. But I am convinced that what is needed is a careful interpretation of Barth on eternity and time; and, specifically, such an interpretation must keep the scientific questions and interconnections in the wings, for they are not immediately relevant to the interpretive task. To exclude these questions is not to say that they are unimportant. Rather, they are excluded here only for the sake of keeping the path clear for our main task.

---

28. Torrance, *Space, Time and Incarnation; Theological Science* (New York: Oxford University Press, 1978); *Belief in Science and in Christian Life: The Relevance of Michael Polanyi's Thought for Christian Faith and Life* (Edinburgh: Handsel Press, 1980); *Christian Theology and Scientific Culture* (New York: Oxford University Press, 1981); *Reality and Scientific Theology* (Edinburgh: Scottish Academic Press, 1985).
29. Duane Howard Larson, "The Temporality of the Trinity: A Christian Theological Concept of Time and Eternity in View of Contemporary Physical Theory" (PhD diss., Graduate Theological Union, 1993).

Indeed, there is some warrant to be found for this decision in Barth's own statements. He had great respect for other forms of inquiry. Yet he believed that theology had its own contribution to make, and must speak on its own terms. When discussing the nature of time, under the heading "Man in His Time" (§47), he has this to say:

> It is obvious that the problem of time, too, is a problem of all anthropology. We cannot, therefore, ignore the attempts and conclusions of other non-theological understandings of being. But this should not debar us from approaching the problem from our own particular standpoint, the theological; and therefore from noting what is revealed to us in this respect by the Word of God.[30]

Yet there is another, more substantive reason for excluding discussion of science. Scientific discussions describe time as particles, waves, quantum phenomena, light cones, and the movements of the heavenly bodies. Barth describes time doctrinally, that is, in the context of the covenant, Christology, the doctrine of the Trinity, and revelation. Barth will even, to make a point, speak of time phenomenologically, that is, by describing how human beings, particularly *fallen* human beings, experience time. Certainly, the scientific, doctrinal, and phenomenological are all quite appropriate fields of discourse for the subject of time. Yet it must be emphasized that they are not the *same* fields of discourse. A pronouncement in one field may not be transferred uncritically over to another. We see such uncritical transference frequently in theology, where scientific statements about time are turned into phenomenological statements, and phenomenological statements are placed into a scientific context, without reflection or qualification.

---

30. *CD* III/2, 439.

For this reason also, I intend here to keep the scientific material at bay, even in those sections that are more constructive rather than interpretive, so as to prevent the uncritical transference between fields of discourse that causes so many problems in works that seek to connect science and theology. Certainly, this work now bears the burden of having to demonstrate that it has not unreflectively transferred statements from a doctrinal or theological sphere into a phenomenological sphere, or vice versa. The possibility of such transference, however, parallels the problem of the relationship between theology and philosophy, a problem with which almost every page of this work is concerned.

The scope of this work is thus delineated, in one respect, by the exclusion of scientific questions. The second area I have chosen to limit (likewise perhaps to the surprise of some) is exegesis of Scripture. In some theological works on time, extensive discussions of Scripture find a prominent place.[31] It will be noticed that this work does not engage in lengthy exegesis of scriptural texts. Such absence has several reasons. First, this book is primarily an interpretation of Karl Barth's theological reflections on time. While his exegesis of scriptural passages undoubtedly informs his theological judgments about the nature of time and God's bearing toward time, his exegesis is not what is in view here, but rather the theological conclusions that were the result of his reflection on the witness of Scripture.

A second, more substantive, reason would relate to any constructive objective achieved in this work, as well as the interpretive objectives. In short, one must ask what kind of insight

---

31. Most obvious in this regard are Cullmann, *Christ and Time*; J. Marsh, *The Fulness of Time* (London: Nisbet & Co., 1952); John A. T. Robinson, *In the End, God . . . : A Study of the Christian Doctrine of the Last Things* (New York: Harper & Row, 1968). These three works in particular were criticized quite extensively by James Barr in *The Semantics of Biblical Language* (Oxford: Oxford University Press, 1961) and *Biblical Words for Time*, Studies in Biblical Theology 33 (London: SCM, 1962). Padgett, *God, Eternity, and the Nature of Time*, draws on Barr's criticisms, but, in my view, draws faulty conclusions from them.

into the nature of time and of eternity one hopes to gain from Scripture. Although the witness of Scripture, in whatever unity it has, may have implications regarding time and eternity, it is rather too much to say that the Bible, in all its literary diversity, has a single understanding of time and eternity. Certainly, the problem of the unity and the diversity of Scripture is far beyond the scope of this book. It should be clear that I am taking for granted that Scripture is diverse, and that the obviously difficult task is to discern the unity therein.[32]

James Barr made the point very forcefully that Scripture does not have a single concept of time, or of eternity, and that it is quite illegitimate to analyze the lexical stocks found in biblical texts in order to discern fundamental concepts underlying the psyches of the peoples whom the biblical authors represent. In short, it is quite risky to go looking in the Bible for one biblical concept of time. Indeed, as Barr has shown quite clearly and thoroughly, the question "What is the nature of time and eternity in biblical thought? is a question for which the Bible itself gives no precedent, and one for the answering of which it affords so little material that [the] appeal [of a writer such as Cullmann] has to be one to the lexical stock of the Bible rather than to its actual statements."[33] Moreover, there is a "very serious shortage within the Bible of the kind of *actual statement* about time or eternity which could form a sufficient basis for a Christian philosophical-theological view of time. It is the lack of actual statements about what time is like, more than anything else, that has forced exegetes into trying to get a view of time out of the *words* themselves."[34] For these reasons, Barr suggests that the question should be handled much

---

32. A conversation with George Hunsinger was instructive on this matter.
33. James Barr, *Biblical Words for Time*, 150.
34. Ibid., 131–32. Also cited in Helm, *Eternal God*, 5f.

more frankly and more completely within the area of philosophical theology.[35]

What Barr meant precisely by the term *philosophical theology* is perhaps open to different readings, but there is little reason to suppose that he would wish to exclude an approach that was thoroughly a work of dogmatic or systematic theology. With regard to interpretation of Barth, I am convinced that whatever Barth sought in Scripture, he was not seeking some one biblical view of time and eternity with which to be (naively) in correspondence.[36]

With these reasons I hope to have made clear why I have focused my task as I have. The path I will take throughout is as follows. I will first explore each of the three formative contexts of Barth's understanding of God and time: the conceptual, the developmental, and the doctrinal. After looking at each of those contexts, I will pursue a more specific analysis of time and eternity in the *Church Dogmatics*. I will conclude with some critical and constructive observations.

---

35. Barr, *Biblical Words for Time*, 151.
36. Oblau says that Barth's view of time more likely corresponds to the biblical view of time (der biblischen Anschauung von der Zeit). Oblau, *Gotteszeit und Menschenzeit*, 37. I find this inadequate from an interpretive and a theological point of view.

2

The Conceptual Context

Traditional Reflections on God and Time

Barth did not produce his mature understanding of divine eternality in a vacuum. He did not come up with his concepts all on his own. Rather, he incorporated, modified, and rejected various understandings of time and eternity that are represented throughout the history of Western thought. Some of those came from theologians, while some came from figures who would more properly be described as philosophers. In either case, these ideas and the figures who promoted them are significant in the history of ideas, even if Barth had never written a word about them. A discussion of the concept of eternity in Western thought would need to address most if not all of them, even if Barth's name were never mentioned. Of course, Barth did draw on these figures, and so, one may better understand Barth's theological expression of God's eternality if one considers the conceptual approaches that may have influenced Barth, either positively or negatively, implicitly or explicitly. Furthermore, considering such figures and the options they proposed enables us to approach Barth's own proposal better informed.

Our investigation in this section will thus attend to various figures, six of them in all, whose influence in one way or another may be seen in Barth's understanding of time and eternity. In the next chapter, we will review several theological and philosophical approaches to the problem that have arisen since Barth. The purpose shared by both chapters is to introduce several important concepts and themes that will prove significant for the rest of the book.

Augustine

Augustine of Hippo (354–430) is perhaps the one figure in the Western Christian tradition whose reflections on the nature of time are read more than any other. In book 11 of his *Confessions*, we find an eloquent and searching inquiry into time, which has exercised a profound hold over the thoughts of many subsequent theologians and philosophers. That hold has not always been welcome. Augustine's reflections on time raise a number of apparent problems. Many subsequent thinkers take issue with what they see as Augustine's main conclusion about time, namely, that time may well be unreal, or at any rate nothing but a product of the human mind. Further, the Neoplatonic categories in which Augustine's discussion is cast are difficult for people of later periods to understand, let alone to accept.

These difficulties can be rightly evaluated, however, only when we have rightly understood Augustine's handling of the problem of time, a task to which we now turn. The context of Augustine's exploration of time in the *Confessions* must be kept in mind, for without that context much appears strange and abstract. The entire *Confessions*, clearly, is in the form of a lengthy prayer, through which Augustine undertakes an exploration of the self before God. In book

9, Augustine finishes the narrative about his life up to his conversion, and in book 10 he explores the mystery of human memory, which he describes as a storehouse from which he could retrieve his experiences in order to narrate them. Then, in book 11, Augustine turns to one of his present burdens as a bishop and thus as a leader of the Christian faithful: an exegesis of Scripture (moreover, an anti-Manichaen exegesis), in particular of Genesis chapter 1.[1]

Exposition: Eternity in the *Confessions*

The concern out of which book 11 develops, then, is the right interpretation of Scripture. Evidence for this claim is not difficult to find. The book begins in transition, as Augustine asks why he lays out such an "ordered account" of his life (the content of books 1 through 10). Since God's "vision of occurrences in time is not temporally conditioned," why engage in this extended prayer to a God from whom nothing is hidden? The answer, for Augustine, is that his prayers are for his own edification, rather than for God's.[2] But Augustine wants to be able to edify not only himself, but others as well. "When shall I be capable of proclaiming by 'the tongue of my pen' (Ps. 44:2) all your exhortations and all your terrors and consolations and directives, by which you brought me to preach your word and dispense your sacrament to your people?" Indeed, Augustine's deepest desire at this point in his life is to "meditate

---

1. A division between books 9 and 10 is easily recognized, as, e.g., in Ulrich Duchrow, "Der sogenannte psychologische Zeitbegriff Augustins im Verhältnis zur physikalischen und geschichtlichen Zeit," *Zeitschrift für Theologie und Kirche* 63, no. 3 (1966): 267–88. He describes the two parts of the *Confessions* as the "pietas-Stufe" (1–9) and the "scientia-Stufe" (10–12).
2. *Conf.* 11.1.1. All quotations from the *Confessions* herein are from Saint Augustine, *The Confessions*, trans. Henry Chadwick (New York: Oxford University Press, 1991). Note that "the Bible text used by Augustine was the Old Latin version made from the Greek of both Old and New Testaments during the second century," and the numbering of the Psalms is in some places significantly different from the numbering of English translations. I have decided to leave those references to the Psalms unaltered. See Chadwick's note on this, xxvi.

in [God's] law," that is, to study Scripture, not simply for his own benefit, but for others as well.[3] "Lord my God, 'hear my prayer' (Ps. 60:2), may your mercy attend to my longing which burns not for my personal advantage but desires to be of use in love to the brethren. . . . May your scriptures be my pure delight, so that I am not deceived in them and do not lead others astray in interpreting them."[4]

Yet the task is not easy, nor is it readily open to the creature. That we exist in time makes Augustine's quest too fragile for him to attempt on his own, because Augustine finds that he simply does not have the time to pursue this quest to his satisfaction. For that reason he prays for divine assistance in understanding Scripture. "At your nod the moments fly by. From them grant us space for our meditations on the secret recesses of your law, and do not close the gate to us as we knock."[5] Augustine plainly needs help, and so he makes his plea for understanding, "so that to me as I knock (Matt. 7:7) may be opened the hidden meaning of your words," through the mediation of Jesus Christ. "I make my prayer through our Lord Jesus Christ your Son, 'the man of your right hand, the Son of man whom you have strengthened' (Ps. 18:15) to be mediator between yourself and us. . . . I make my prayer to you through him 'who sits at your right hand and intercedes to you for us' (Rom. 8:34)." Yet Christ is not only the mediator of this prayer, but is also the one in whom the treasures of Scripture are hidden and hence the one in whom those treasures must be sought. "'In him are hidden all the treasures of wisdom and knowledge' (Col. 2:3). For those treasures I search in your books."[6]

At this point let me make clear several important aspects of these first few paragraphs of book 11. Book 11 is concerned from the outset

---

3. *Conf.* 11.2.2.
4. Ibid., 11.2.3.
5. Ibid.
6. Ibid., 11.2.4.

with the interpretation of Scripture. Augustine understands proper interpretation of Scripture to be grounded in Christ's mediation between God and humanity. In this we find an important aspect of Augustine's implicit understanding of eternity: God's perspective on temporal events is not itself temporally conditioned. Here time and eternity are separate realms, at least in the manner in which those who exist in those realms know temporal events. Finally, time for Augustine is in itself fragile and fleeting, and yet it is ultimately a gift from God; for this reason Augustine prays that God give this gift for the exploration of the treasures of Scripture.

Augustine then turns to the task of exegesis, as he asks concerning the very first verse of Genesis, "May I hear and understand how in the beginning you made heaven and earth."[7] Augustine's interpretation of these words about creation emphasizes quite strongly the difference between creation and Creator by highlighting the contrast between change and changelessness. For Augustine, creation "suffer[s] change and variation. . . . To be what once was not the case is to be subject to change and variation." Such characteristics are set in contrast to God, who does not change, for the "beauty and goodness and being" of creation are deficient when compared to God.[8] Thus Scripture's testimony that God created heaven and earth points Augustine to the profound contrast between changing creatures and the changeless God.

Yet God's very *manner* of creating is also quite different from our own. God created the heavens and the earth simply by speaking.[9] But such speaking, too, surely differs from how we creatures speak. For when we speak, one word follows another in time, and each word comes into existence and dies before the next one. But God did not

---

7. Ibid., 11.3.5.
8. Ibid., 11.4.6.
9. Ibid., 11.5.7.

create by speaking in this manner, for nothing in God is transient. When God created by means of speaking, it was not with "words which sound and pass away," for such a way of speaking is that of the creature, and not of the Creator, and thus God would have spoken the words that brought creation into existence through the mediation of a temporal creature. Yet that is clearly absurd, for it implies that there was a "creation" before creation.[10]

What, then, is God's speech of creation? It is the Eternal Word: Christ, the Second person of the Trinity, that is "the Word, God who is with you God (John 1:1). That word is spoken eternally, and by it all things are uttered eternally." Christ is God's Word by which God speaks, yet without a succession of finite words uttered one after another. Indeed, through the Word "everything is said in the simultaneity of eternity" (*simul ac sempiterne*). This Word is not a creature, subject to change or decay, but is of the very essence of the Father, that is, eternal. "No element of your word yields place or succeeds to something else, since it is truly immortal and eternal."[11] This Word, furthermore, is the "Beginning" of which Genesis speaks, the "Beginning" in which God created the heavens and the earth, indeed, the true source of all truth and of our very being, the point of constancy to which we may return from error. Incarnate, this Word is God's eternality communicated to us temporal creatures.[12]

But if in Christ God created the heavens and the earth, what was God doing before creation? If there was a time when there was no creation, and then there was a time when there was, it seems to imply a change in God. "For if in God any new development took place and any new intention, so as to make a creation which he had never made before, how then can there be a true eternity in which a will, not

---

10. Ibid., 11.6.8.
11. Ibid., 11.7.9.
12. Ibid., 11.8.10, 11.9.11.

there previously, comes into existence?" Yet God's will is not, says. Augustine, a created thing, but is identical with God's own substance. So God eternally willed creation. "But if it was God's everlasting will that the created order exist, why is not the creation also everlasting?"[13]

Such a question, however, belies a profound misunderstanding of the difference between time and eternity. For Augustine, "No comparison is possible" between eternity and "temporal successiveness which never has any constancy."[14] It is this successiveness that determines the fundamental and profound difference between time and eternity. "A long time is long only because constituted of many successive movements which cannot be simultaneously extended. Thus in the eternal, nothing is transient, but the whole is present. But no time is wholly present." Time, then, is characterized by successiveness, change, and createdness,[15] whereas God's unchanging eternity is entirely present to God: it is all "today" for God. "All [God's] 'years' subsist in simultaneity, because they do not change; those going away are not thrust out by those coming in."[16]

The eternal, then, is the source of the temporal, but not in such a way that the eternal is not truly eternal. God is "the originator and creator of all ages.... You have made time itself. Time did not elapse before you made time.... There was no 'then' when there was not time."[17] Yet "it is not in time that you precede times. Otherwise you would not precede all times. In the sublimity of an eternity which is always in the present, you are before all things past and transcend all things future, because they are still to come, and when they have

---

13. Ibid., 11.10.12.
14. Ibid., 11.11.13.
15. Ibid., 11.13.15.
16. Ibid., 11.13.16.
17. Ibid., 11.13.15.

come they are past."[18] In short, Augustine insists that God created all time while remaining eternal.

Out of this conviction of time's creation by God, Augustine undertakes a lengthy consideration of time. Such an investigation, Augustine admits, is very difficult if pursued with the resources normally at our disposal. The initial difficulty seems to lie in our language, which insists on speaking in past and future tenses as if the past and future events to which they refer actually exist at that moment. They do not now exist, for the past has passed into nonbeing, and the future has not yet come into being. Indeed, time seems to have very little existence at all, for past and future do not properly exist. "The cause of [time's] being is that it will cease to be. So indeed we cannot truly say that time exists except in the sense that it tends toward non-existence."[19] This judgment is confirmed when Augustine considers what normal parlance means by "lengths" of time. When we speak of lengths of past or future time, such talk seems quite empty, for these times exist no longer or not yet. Even to speak of the length of present time is improper, for every length of time, such as years, months, days, hours, minutes, and seconds, seems to be divisible into smaller and smaller quanta that make up the unit, among which some will be past, as already gone, and others future, as not yet arrived, and only one is left to designate as the infinitesimally small "present." "If we can think of some bit of time which cannot be divided into even the smallest instantaneous moments, that alone is what we can call 'present.'"[20] Left with that one tiny dot to call "the present," Augustine concludes that "the present occupies no space."[21]

Yet if the present has no extension, the past exists no longer, and the future does not yet exist, how, then, do we measure time?[22]

18. Ibid., 11.13.16.
19. Ibid., 11.14.17.
20. Ibid., 11.15.20.
21. Ibid.

Whence does the future come, and whither goes the past? The solution is not to be found in defining time as the movement of heavenly bodies, for any physical object would do, and the response does not solve the problem of how we are able to discern that one length of time is longer than another.[23] Indeed, "it follows that a body's movement is one thing, the period by which we measure is another," and only the latter is rightly called "time."[24]

Augustine is thus led to suspect "that time is simply a distension . . . of the mind itself."[25] The mind measures time in the memory,[26] by means of a painful stretching out or distension of the memory in two directions: in anticipation of the future, and in remembering the past.[27] Yet to speak of "a distension . . . of the mind itself" is ambiguous.[28] The words *of the mind* could be taken either as a subjective or as an objective genitive. If *of the mind* is read as a subjective genitive, the phrase would mean that time is a distension *by* the mind itself, an operation in which the mind itself distends reality and thus produces time, which then has no other form of existence. On the other hand, if *of the mind* is understood as an objective genitive, the phrase would mean that time, as an ongoing passing

---

22. Ibid., 11.21.27.
23. Ibid., 11.23.29.
24. Ibid., 11.24.31. Of course, Augustine could not have anticipated the position offered by modern physics, for which the standard reference for time is, more or less, the "movement" of a "heavenly body," that is, the speed of light; nor could he have anticipated its other component, the affirmation that there is no absolute time. See, however, n30 below.
25. Ibid., 11.26.33.
26. Ibid., 11.27.35.
27. Ibid., 11.28.37, 38.
28. I would suggest that such ambiguity gives rise to interpretations of Augustine's view of time as psychological or even solipsistic. A different tack in addressing this misconception is pursued by Duchrow: "Not until one sees that Augustine did not simply factor out the question of physical and historical time in favor of a 'psychological' concept of time, but that even in connection to his Confessions it inevitably presides over the problems abandoned with it, can one appreciate his historical and objective attempts at an answer. But then one can also ask critically whether the correlation of physical, historical and psychological time is successful for him." Duchrow, "Der sogenannte psychologische Zeitbegriff Augustins im Verhältnis zur physikalischen und geschichtlichen Zeit," 269–70, my translation.

of moments, is an experience in which the mind itself is distended, stretched out, even painfully, and indeed, problematically.

That the second reading is to be preferred is shown by how Augustine himself views the results of his investigation. He measures (not creates) periods of time in his mind, and he measures by means of a distension, in memory and anticipation. Yet for Augustine, this distension of the soul is a painful experience, from which he prays to God to be liberated.

> "Because your mercy is more than lives" (Ps. 62:4), see how my life is a distension in several directions. . . . But now "my years pass in groans" (Ps. 30:11) and you, Lord, are my consolation. You are my eternal Father, but I am scattered in times whose order I do not understand. The storms of incoherent events tear to pieces my thoughts, the inmost entrails of my soul, until that day when, purified and molten by the fire of your love, I flow together to merge into you.[29]

Even more problematic is Augustine's seeming equation of time with this mental operation: "Time *is simply* . . . a distension of the mind itself." Does this mean that Augustine believes that time has no reality apart from his thinking about it? The answer is a qualified yes and no. We might paraphrase him as follows. Time, as we look at it and experience it, has no substantial reality. If we try to grab onto it, it passes through our fingers. It has no extension nor duration: the past is gone, the future is not yet, and the present is an infinitesimal point having no length. How then can we speak of time's reality? How can we measure it? We cannot, other than in our minds marking the changes brought about over time by remembering and storing the past and anticipating the future. Things that exist in time have some substance, but time *itself* is measured and known and experienced only in the minds that (sometimes painfully) are stretched out in the act of grappling with time.[30]

---

29. *Conf.* 11.29.39.

Augustine's discussion of time, then, ends in his confession of his need for salvation from the distension of time, a salvation only God can deliver, for the eternal God suffers no distension: "You are unchangeably eternal, that is the truly eternal Creator of minds. Just as you knew heaven and earth in the beginning without that bringing any variation into your knowing, so you made heaven and earth in the beginning without that meaning a tension between past and future in your activity."[31]

Summary of Augustine's Concept of Eternity

Having walked through book 11 of Augustine's *Confessions*, we are now in a position to state some major features of his understanding of eternity. What is surely obvious is that time and eternity are contrasted along lines precisely parallel to the contrast between creature and Creator, and to that of change and changelessness. Those contrasts are religiously very significant, for time as experienced and thus explored by Augustine is a very fragile reality, one that makes the human condition very problematic and begs for a solution that in the end only God can provide.

For that reason I believe that Gotthard Oblau is mistaken when he concludes that for Augustine, "the time that arises in the activity of the human mind is unproblematic: he undoubtedly has it, he masters

---

30. Here we can see connections with modern existential understandings of time characteristic of Heidegger and others. But one might also note a correspondence with the judgments of modern physics, in that Augustine likewise seems close to rejecting the idea of a universal time, in the sense that the measuring of time is so dependent on the minds that measure it. See n24 above.
31. *Conf.* 11.31.41. "The eleventh Book, in point of fact, neither begins nor ends with the self. It begins, as it ends, with God." Robert Jordan, "Time and Contingency in St. Augustine," in *Augustine: A Collection of Critical Essays*, ed. R. A. Markus (Garden City, NY: Anchor Books, Doubleday & Co., 1972), 263–64.

and commands it."³² Rather, the result of Augustine's task is truly described by Robert Jordan as follows:

> Augustine's investigation of time is a study in contingency, finiteness, creatureliness, dependency, incompleteness, imperfection, a study of the limitation of being that characterizes *any* finite entity, that entity which *is*, but which is not He Who Is. Time exists because there are existent things in the universe which are just so much reality, but no more.³³

Oblau is of course referring to a passage from *Die kirkliche Dogmatik* (*KD*) I/2 (51), where Barth offers a critique of Augustine. But Barth is not making precisely the same point Oblau interprets Barth to make. Indeed, Oblau goes far beyond Barth, first by insisting that Augustine held that time was unproblematic for human experience, and, second by asserting that Barth's description of time in §47.2 ("Given Time") constitutes a *rejoinder* to Augustine and the whole *existentiell Zeitbegriff*. We will return to Barth's interpretation of Augustine soon, but for now let me simply describe Oblau's interpretation of Augustine as a mistake and his evidence for Barth's massive disagreement with Augustine as unconvincing.

Time for Augustine is in origin God's gift, yet mediately, from the perspective of human experience, a painful distending of the soul, and ultimately, something from which Augustine seeks salvation. For time as analyzed is a succession of infinitely small quanta, a rushing stream of moments that hurtle by, from nonexistence to brief existence to nonexistence.³⁴ The present is what we arbitrarily call one of the many quanta that happens to pass by. The present, for us,

---

32. "Die im Akt des menschlichen Geistes entstehende Zeit ist für den Menschen unproblematisch: Er hat sie unangefochten, er meistert und beherrscht sie." Gotthard Oblau, *Gotteszeit und Menschenzeit: Eschatologie in der Kirchlichen Dogmatik von Karl Barth* (Neukirchen-Vluyn: Neukirchener Verlag, 1988), 37.
33. Jordan, "Time and Contingency in St. Augustine," 256.
34. "Augustine's image of the historical process is that of a flowing river or rivers, with many stormy cataracts. Underlying this passage is the language of Plotinus (6. 6. 1. 5) about the fall away from the One as a scattering and an extending. Temporal successiveness is an experience

is thus a vanishingly small item that comes into and out of experience, and is held onto, if it is, only by anticipation and memory. Eternity, however, is quite different. Not by change or succession, but rather by permanence and simultaneity is eternity characterized. "No times are coeternal with you since you are permanent. . . . You say all that you say in the simultaneity of eternity."[35]

Yet such a characterization may rightly strike us as odd. For *permanence* and *simultaneity* are temporal terms.[36] In what sense does Augustine mean these terms in their new, atemporal, context? Such "category breaking" is not even limited to these terms, nor to the two cited passages. For Augustine also speaks of God's *present*: "Your Today is eternity," prays Augustine.[37] Yet what Augustine means is that God has a "present" that does not disappear into the past, a "present" that is not characterized by successively fleeting "present moments." Let us return to a passage we considered earlier:

> In the sublimity of an eternity which is always in the present, you are before all things past and transcend all things future, because they are still to come, and when they have come they are past. "But you are the same and your years do not fail" (Ps. 101:28). Your "years" neither go nor come. Ours come and go so that all may come in succession. All your "years" subsist in simultaneity, because they do not change; those going away are not thrust out by those coming in. But the years which are ours will not all be until all years have ceased to be. Your "years" are "one day" (Ps. 89:4; 2 Peter 3:8), and your "day" is not any and every day but Today, because your Today does not yield to a tomorrow, nor did it follow on a yesterday.[38]

---

of disintegration; the ascent to divine eternity is a recovery of unity." Chadwick, in *Confessions*, 244n31.
35. *Conf.* 11.13.17, 11.7.9.
36. I thank Prof. William Babcock for first making me aware of this problem. The question is also raised by Paul Helm, *Eternal God: A Study of God without Time* (Oxford: Oxford University Press, 1988), particularly in the second chapter, "What Is Divine Eternity?," 23–40.
37. *Conf.* 11.13.16.
38. Ibid.

Augustine is surely aware that he is using, or even misusing, terms native to a temporal context to express something about the divine reality in its eternality. His awareness is signaled by the way in which he qualifies his use of "temporal" words to speak of eternity. For he does not simply speak of God's *years*, or *present*, or *today*; rather, he describes a fundamental contrast between the significance of such terms in their normal, creaturely context, and their significance when applied to God. Indeed, Augustine seems to affirm (if only implicitly) the principle later articulated by Pseudo-Dionysius the Areopagite: "Regarding things divine, negations are true and affirmations inadequate."[39] Furthermore, Augustine uses *simultaneity* to clarify further the distinction between creaturely and divine reality, and thus this use is a further indication of his awareness that none of these terms (*years, present, today, simultaneity, permanence*) are used univocally in both creaturely and divine contexts.

Why, then, does he use these terms, besides to emphasize the contrast between Creator and creature? First, he does so in order to take up the language of Scripture, which speaks of God's *years*, God's *day*, and God's *today*. Quite simply, it is a controlling feature of the literary context of these terms. We do well to recall that in this part of the *Confessions* Augustine is pursuing a commentary on Scripture.

Second, Augustine's use of these terms suggests that even for Augustine, as Neoplatonic as he was, God's eternity was not construed merely as "timeless," or rather "timeless" in the way a mathematical equation is timeless,[40] but was construed as a fundamental aspect of God's living being. Eternity, for Augustine, is

---

39. Dionysius the Areopagite, *De coel. hier.* 2.3. Cited in Wolfgang Beinert and Francis Schüssler Fiorenza, *Handbook of Catholic Theology* (New York, NY: Crossroad, 1995), 5.
40. Such a meaning of *timeless* I find suggested by the historical examples to which the Kneales draw attention. W. C. Kneale, "Time and Eternity in Theology," *Proceedings of the Aristotelian Society* 61 (1961): 87–108; Martha Kneale, "Eternity and Sempiternity," *Proceedings of the Aristotelian Society* 69 (1969): 223–38.

not a timeless and thus contentless point, and for that reason neutral and irrelevant, but rather it envelops our past and future, because God is "before all things past and transcend[s] all things future."[41] Such a point is made clearer by the way in which Augustine specifies the word *simul*. In a passage quoted above from book 11, Augustine says that God speaks through the divine Word *simul ac sempiterne*. The force of this, I suggest, cross-clarifies *simul* and *sempiterne*. For *simul* has the sense of things happening at the same time, but with no sense of duration, while *sempiterne* implies everlasting duration, but of a kind that normally means succession. By using *simul* and *sempiterne* together, Augustine defines eternity as a duration that is nonsuccessive, a present that is much more than infinitesimal.

Third, by using the various temporal terms to speak of eternity, Augustine implies, not merely *via negationis* but indeed *via eminentiae*, that God possesses that which alone makes time real, the present, and possesses it in an infinite manner. The difference between the divine and the human present is that God's present is immense, or rather, infinite.

Barth's Interaction with Augustine

Such will have to suffice as an exposition of Augustine's understanding of time and eternity, as he expresses this in book 11 of the *Confessions*. What then does this have to do with Karl Barth?

---

41. It may even be said that whereas human beings *have* a present (if only the most fragile of senses), only God *is* God's own present. In putting it this way I am indebted to Sarah Heaner Lancaster, who makes a similar point concerning Augustine's understanding of the Trinity: "In Book XV [of *de Trinitate*] Augustine says that though we can begin to understand the Trinity through the image of the Trinity that is in us, even our perfected image falls short of the Trinity that God is. A human is not the same as memory, understanding, and will. One can say 'I *have* these three,' but not, 'I *am* these three.' With supreme simplicity, though, God *is* Trinity." Sarah Heaner Lancaster, "Three-Personed Substance: The Relational Essence of the Triune God in Augustine's De Trinitate," *The Thomist* 60, no. 1 (1996): 138.

Quite a bit. For Barth did explicitly refer to Augustine, indeed, in order to criticize him. He also alluded to Augustine, but in doing so, I will argue, Barth signals his agreement, albeit limited, with Augustine.

It is true that Barth criticizes Augustine's view of time. Yet what Barth criticizes is not a view of time in general, but the inadequacy of that view for understanding a quite specific time, the time of revelation.[42]

> If by the statement, "God reveals Himself" is meant the revelation attested in Holy Scripture, it is a statement about the occurrence of an event. That means it also includes an assertion about a time *proper to revelation*. If stated with reference to this, it is equivalent to the statement, "God has time for us." The time God has for us is just this time of His revelation, the time that is real in His revelation, revelation time. Moreover in the interpretation of the concept of this time, which is now our task, we shall not have to take as a basis any time concept gained independently of revelation itself.[43]

Barth's criticisms of Augustine[44] are thus strictly concerned with one very specific theological question: whether Augustine's concept of humanity's experience of time is theologically helpful and appropriate for understanding another kind of time, which Barth calls "revelation time," that is, God's time for us. "If we are to understand the time of God's revelation, then our possession of time must be made comprehensible as God's possession of it for us, overcoming the difficulties of our possession of it."[45] Indeed, Barth finds Augustine's understanding of time as experienced by the human subject quite an acceptable way of understanding one particular kind of time, namely,

---

42. Oblau does not appear to recognize this important distinction.
43. Barth, *Church Dogmatics*, trans. Geoffrey Bromiley et al. (Edinburgh: T. & T. Clark, 1956–69), I/2, 45; *Die kirchliche Dogmatik* (Munich: Chr. Kaiser, 1932, and Zurich: EVZ, 1938–65), I/2, 50. Emphasis added.
44. And Heidegger, whom he considers with Augustine.
45. *CD* I/2, 46; *KD* I/2, 51.

what he calls, with intentional irony, "our" time, which might be described as fallen time or (as he calls it later) lost time.

> The time we think we know and possess, "our" time, is by no means the time God created. Between our time and God-created time as between our existence and the existence created by God there lies the Fall. "Our" time, as Augustine and Heidegger in their own ways quite correctly inform us, is the time produced by us, that is by the fallen human being.[46]

We see more of Barth's limited acceptance of Augustine's understanding of time in *CD* III/2, in the subsection titled "Given Time." Here he gives expression to the problematic aspect of human temporality, the *in extremis* aspect of humanly experienced temporality.

> That man is in time means at its simplest that he always is now, i.e., that he is always crossing the frontier between past and future which one moment is just ahead and the next just behind, only to be ahead again, to have to be recrossed, and again to be behind. If man really is in his time, if he really has time, it is always now, in the crossing of this frontier. Every conception of human being, life and activity (even when ostensibly concerned with the past or future) has to do concretely with this step from the past to the future.[47]

And again:

> It is true, of course, that nothing is more impressive and palpable than our being in the present. How many sceptics have thought they could take refuge in the boast, "I am"! And what structures of assurance have been erected on the foundation of this boast! But what does this boast mean on the lips of man and as an expression of his conviction that he really exists in the present and therefore in time? The insecurity of our being in the present is no less impressive and palpable. For the present is merely the frontier between past and future, and our being in it is

---

46. *CD* I/2, 47; *KD* I/2, 52. Trans. revised.
47. *CD* III/2, 527.

merely the crossing of this frontier. *The present is without duration or extension.* What then do we mean by being in the present?[48]

That Barth points to the terror to be found in time understood in this way is not to be taken as a criticism of this concept of time in and of itself. For we recall that Augustine's description of time as experienced is a description of a *problem*, a problem whose solution is found only in God. Although their solutions are different, Barth too uses this Augustinian motif, by way of contrast, to point to God. "Primarily . . . it is not we who are now but God who is now."[49] Humanly experienced time, *for Barth as well as for Augustine*, is problematic, not only existentially, but also religiously.

Not only does Barth pick up elements of Augustine's understanding of time, but the same is also true for Augustine's understanding of eternity. It is true, of course, that there are great differences. The Platonic contrast between the unchanging God and changing creatures is a theme for which Barth has little use. And although Barth accepted Augustine's negative contrast between time and eternity,[50] he felt that this was not enough.[51] Yet at this stage we must insist that there were points of agreement. For even as he insisted that the antithesis between time and eternity must not be the final word, he did agree that this word must indeed be spoken. At particular stages in his argument, furthermore, his description of eternity sounds very Augustinian. Eternity "is the simultaneity and coinherence of past, present and future. Thus eternity is the dimension of God's own life, the life in which He is self-positing, self-existent and self-sufficient as Father, Son and Holy Ghost. It is

---

48. *CD* III/2, 528. Emphasis added.
49. *CD* III/2, 529.
50. *CD* II/1, 608.
51. *CD* II/1 610.

this in contrast to time as the dimension of our life—the dimension in which past, present and future follow in succession."[52]

There is much in this passage that begs to be unpacked. This task must wait until later. Let me simply flag the following points. 1) Here Barth not only brings in the Augustinian (and, as we will see, Boëthian) notion of *simultaneity*, he also adds specificity to it with the term *coinherence*, thus implying a relationship between divine eternity and the doctrine of the Trinity. 2) Barth insists that time and eternity are contrasted, yet also that eternity is not timeless. His reasons for this reflect his belief that God and God's attributes are not rightly described either by negating human attributes or raising them to the infinite degree.[53]

We could raise up for scrutiny more points of contrast and convergence between Augustine and Barth on the subjects of time and eternity. We have, however, done enough to describe Augustine's ideas of time and eternity, correct some misunderstandings of Augustine on these topics, and illustrate some points of agreement between Augustine and Barth. To do more would be to get ahead of ourselves. By way of summary, I now reiterate the following key aspects of Augustine's understanding of time and eternity. First, eternity is strictly contrasted with time, in precise parallel with the Christian theological distinction between Creator and creation and with the Platonic distinction between permanence and change. Second, God's eternity is conceived of as a "simultaneity," for which all "moments" of God's experience are equally present; in other words, God's present is infinite and one. Third, time is significantly problematic for Augustine, both existentially and religiously. Fourth, the radical separation between eternity and time, and the very problematic nature of time when

---

52. *CD* III/2, 526.
53. Such an understanding of analogical predication came out of Barth's struggle over Feuerbach.

viewed phenomenologically, is overcome only by Christ, the Word of God.

Boëthius

The next figure of significance in the history of Christian thought on the problem of divine eternity is Boëthius (c. 480–524). His influence on subsequent figures who considered the concept of eternity may well be equal to that of Augustine, in great part because their reflections on the subject stood alone in the early Middle Ages. Brian Leftow describes the historical importance suggestively.

> The history of philosophical theology has the shape of an hourglass. The subject flourished in the academies of late antiquity. With the rest of the humanities, it was caught up in the collapse of Roman civilization and dribbled down to the Middle Ages through comparatively few sources. Later, the field was reborn from these sources and flourished anew. Where the concept of eternity is concerned, Augustine and Boëthius were the hourglass's neck. The study of Augustine as anthologized in Peter Lombard's *Sentences* was the meat of theological education well into the 1300s, and most treatments of eternity for long after that included discussion of Boëthius' definition of the concept.[54]

Such discussion of Boëthius's definition continued indeed long after Lombard, for we find echoes of it in Heinrich Heppe's summary of post-Reformation Reformed theology, *Reformierte Dogmatik*.[55] Much more useful for our purposes, however, is Barth's frequent use of Boëthius's definition. For all these reasons, then, it is essential that we understand Boëthius's conception of divine eternity, as this is

---

54. Brian Leftow, *Time and Eternity* (Ithaca, NY: Cornell University Press, 1991), 112.
55. Heinrich Heppe, *Die Dogmatik der evangelisch-reformierten Kirche, dargestellt und aus den Quellen belegt von Heinrich Heppe*, ed. Ernst Bizer (Neukirchen: K. Moer, 1935); English translation: Heinrich Heppe, *Reformed Dogmatics Set Out and Illustrated from the Sources*, ed. Ernst Bizer, trans. G. T. Thompson (London: Allen & Unwin, 1950).

reflected in the definition he gives it in book 5 of *The Consolation of Philosophy*.[56]

Exposition: *The Consolation of Philosophy*

Boëthius's *Consolation* is cast as a conversation between a distraught Boëthius, imprisoned and facing death, and the comforting Lady Philosophy. Thus the Consolation is a very different text from Augustine's *Confessions*, and the locus of Boëthius's definition, the fifth and final book of this philosophic conversation, draws together the themes of chance, free will, determinism, and providence. As book 5 begins, Boëthius asks Lady Philosophy whether there is such a thing as chance. There is not, responds Lady Philosophy, if by "chance" one means "an event produced by random motion and not by any chain of causes."[57] Indeed, there is a chain of causes, which is ultimately appointed by God, for "God constrains all things into his order."[58] But if by "chance" one means "the unexpected event of concurring causes among things done for some purpose," then Philosophy admits that chance does exist.[59] For such chance is not the occurrence of events outside the chain of causes, but rather of events within the chain of causes unexpected by some of their actors.

Boëthius then asks Philosophy whether such a conception of a chain of causes allows for free will.[60] Philosophy's answer is that God foreknows the free decisions rational beings will make. "That regard of providence which looks forth on all things from eternity, sees this

---

56. The translation used here is from Boethius, *The Theological Tractates & The Consolation of Philosophy*, trans. S. J. Tester, H. F. Stewart, and E. K. Rand (Cambridge, MA: Harvard University Press, 1973). Hereafter referred to as *Cons. Ph.*
57. *Cons. Ph.* 5, prose 1, 18–20.
58. Ibid., 23–24.
59. Ibid., 53–55.
60. Ibid., prose 2.

and disposes all that is predestined to each according to his deserts."⁶¹ The picture drawn for us in verse is quite vivid:

> That Phoebus shining with pure light "Sees all and all things hears," So Homer sings, he of the honeyed voice; Yet even he, with the light of his rays, too weak, Cannot burst through To the inmost depths of earth or ocean. Not thus the Maker of this great universe: Him, viewing all things from his height, no mass of earth obstructs, no night with black cloud thwarts. What is, what has been, and what is to come, In one swift mental stab he sees; Him, since he only all things sees, The true sun could you call.⁶²

Boëthius then asks Philosophy how human freedom is possible if God foreknows all things, for foreknowledge seems to make the free acts of human beings necessary: if God foreknows them, they necessarily must occur.⁶³ Philosophy's response, beginning in book 5, chapter 4, covers the rest of the *Consolation*. First of all, she says, the objects of knowledge are known according to the power of the knower.⁶⁴ Thus there is not just one kind of knowing, determined by the object, but a hierarchy of knowing, depending upon the faculty of knowing that is used. Thus a rose may be "known" through the sense of smell, or the sense of sight or of touch or even taste, or it may be known through the reason, which may take into account and understand all that the other senses are able to discern of the flower. "So it is that that kind of knowledge is better than the rest which of its own nature knows

---

61. Ibid., 27–29.
62. Ibid., poem 2. Clearly, this picture of God emphasizes God's transcendence to such a degree that it implies an unfortunate remoteness. For that reason I believe that Boëthius's help is limited. Nonetheless, as is demonstrated by my exposition, I believe that in spite of this shortcoming Boëthius's *Consolation* is helpful for developing a modern constructive doctrine of God's eternity. Boëthius's picture of a remote God does make somewhat ironic Barth's affirmative use of Boëthius's definition of eternity, which we will describe shortly.
63. Ibid., 3. We see the same question, with a different answer, addressed by Anselm in his *de Concordia*.
64. Ibid., prose 4, 75–77.

not only its own object but the subjects of other kinds of knowledge also."[65]

Having established that, Philosophy then insists we should not make judgments about the divine foreknowledge of contingent events according to standards of human reason. Continuing the analogy, she asks, "What, then, if sense and imagination gainsay reasoning, saying that that universal which reason thinks she perceives, is nothing at all?. . . It is similar when human reason thinks that the divine intelligence does not see future things except in the same manner as she herself knows them."[66]

Rather, Philosophy insists that we must not think of these matters in the manner to which we are accustomed. "Wherefore let us be raised up, if we can, to the height of that highest intelligence; for there reason will see . . . in what way even those things which have no certain occurrence a certain and definite foreknowledge yet does see, [which] neither is that opinion, but rather the simplicity . . . of the highest knowledge."[67] Any clue, then, to the problem of human free will and divine foreknowledge must first recognize how different God's knowledge of events is when compared to human knowledge of events.

How, then, is God's knowledge different? How does God know events? In short, the way God knows things is from eternity. And what is eternity? The passage deserves to be quoted completely and in context.

> Eternity, then, is the whole, simultaneous and perfect possession of boundless life [*Aeternitas igitur est interminabilis vitae tota simul et perfecta possessio*], which becomes clearer by comparison with temporal things. For whatever lives in time proceeds in the present from the past into the future, and there is nothing established in time which can embrace the

---
65. Ibid., prose 5, 19–21.
66. Ibid. 21–24, 39–41.
67. Ibid., 50–56.

whole space of its life equally, but tomorrow surely it does not yet grasp, while yesterday it has already lost. And in this day to day life you live no more than in that moving and transitory moment.[68]

We see here some echoes of themes we noticed in Augustine, yet now they are stated with greater precision. We also see some new themes emerging. For now the theme of simultaneity that we saw in Augustine is linked up with the notion of boundless life. Such a linkage (particularly in the definition "whole, simultaneous and perfect possession of boundless life") points to a peculiar form of existence proper only to God. Unlike that of temporal beings, whose past is no longer and whose future is not yet, God's life is entirely present to and grasped by God, a boundless duration of simultaneity. Even if time had no bounds, no beginning nor end, but was infinite, that would not make it eternal. "For it is one thing to be drawn out through a life without bounds . . . but it is a different thing to have embraced at once the whole presence of boundless life, which it is clear is the property of the divine mind."[69]

Thus what is truly eternal is not simply everlasting, enduring moment by moment throughout time.[70] Rather, it is "whole, simultaneous, and perfect." Nor does the truly eternal exist in such a way that its entire life is present to it, but only in an instantaneous unit, the barest momentary flash; rather, true eternity, for Boëthius, is "boundless life." The eternality that characterizes the divine life, then, is neither the infinity of temporally successive moments, nor the flash of a durationless instant. It is, as some have put it, a kind of duration, but a duration that is not really temporal.[71] "Whatever . . . comprehends and possesses at once the whole fullness of boundless

---

68. Ibid., 6, 9–18.
69. Ibid., 35–38.
70. To exist in such a way would be to exist, as some call it, "sempiternally," rather than "eternally."
71. Such an affirmation is characterissitic of the work found in Leftow, *Time and Eternity*, and Stump and Kretzmann, "Eternity," *Journal of Philosophy* 78 (1981): 429–58.

life, and is such that neither is anything future lacking from it, nor has anything past flowed away, that is rightly held to be eternal, and that must necessarily both always be present to itself, possessing itself in the present, and hold as present the infinity of moving time."[72]

But what sense does it make to talk about a duration that is not temporal? Does not the very meaning of the word *duration* necessarily include *temporality*? Is Boëthius confused? Or does he not rather have an important point to make, when he combines duration with atemporality? This problem has been the focus of numerous critics of Boëthius, who have pointed out the inconsistency of this combination.[73] More recently, however, others have attempted to defend Boëthius and his definition of God's eternity as being far from merely confused. Most significant among these are Eleonore Stump and Norman Kretzmann, and Brian Leftow.[74] All three of them have argued that Boëthius is not simply confused or inconsistent when he speaks of eternity as if it were a duration and yet also as if it were instantaneous. "When Boëthius seems to waffle between talk of a durationless now and talk of everlasting duration, he is actually trying to communicate a single thesis, that eternity is 'atemporal duration.'"[75]

They have different solutions to the problem, and our discussion of them will have to wait until the next chapter, since with that topic we move into recent philosophical developments, and the debate in

---

72. *Cons. Ph.* 5, 6, 25–31.
73. See, e.g., M. Kneale, "Eternity and Sempiternity," 227f. Similarly, W. Kneale focuses his criticism on the combination of timelessness and life: W. Kneale, "Time and Eternity in Theology," 99–100. A similar question might be asked about Augustine, who, as noted above, combined *simul* and *sempiterne* in his understanding of eternity. It seems reasonable to suggest that Augustine's combination of these two concepts serves a function similar to Boëthius's combination of *interminabilis vitae* and *tota simul*. That is, both, in effect, serve to define eternity in such a way that a *form* of duration, yet one lacking successiveness, is in view.
74. Stump and Kretzmann, "Eternity," and "Atemporal Duration: A Reply to Fitzgerald," *Journal of Philosophy* 84 (1987): 214–219; Leftow, *Time and Eternity*.
75. Leftow, *Time and Eternity*, 113.

philosophy and theology that has taken place, in at least two phases, in the last third of the twentieth century.

For now, we note Leftow's suggestion that

> perhaps one must use both point and extension models in thinking about Boëthian eternity. . . . If this is so, it is because eternity is (inter alia) a kind of life that could be enjoyed by a metaphysically simple being. As eternity is a kind of life, it may require us to model it as a way of enduring, or a sort of duration. As eternity is the life of a simple being, it may require us to model it as lacking parts and so pointlike.[76]

Let us now return to the context of Boëthius's definition of eternity. That definition was proposed as a solution to, and in turn has profound implications for, the problem at issue in book 5 of the *Consolation*, the problem of divine (fore-) knowledge and human freedom. Now human beings, as knowers, know things temporally, since they are temporal creatures. Their fundamental temporality determines, to some extent, how we know something. God, on the other hand, is eternal. So, says Boëthius, how would God eternally know something? "Since . . . God has an always eternal and present nature, then his knowledge too, surpassing all movement of time, is permanent in the simplicity of his present, and embracing all the infinite spaces of the future and the past, considers them in his simple act of knowledge as though they were now going on."[77] Thus God's foreknowledge is "not foreknowledge as it were of the future but knowledge of a never-passing instant."[78]

So God's foreknowledge of our free acts takes place within God's present, and so is not really *fore*-knowledge at all; and just as in the case of human beings, for whom knowledge of something in that person's present does not make that event absolutely necessary, so

---

76. Leftow, *Time and Eternity*, 149.
77. *Cons. Ph.* 5, 6, 59, 61–66.
78. Ibid., 67–69.

in God's case, God's knowledge of a free act in the divine present does not make that act necessary. On the contrary, God is able to distinguish between those events that occur out of necessity and those events that occur from the action of freely willing agents.[79] So just as when we observe something happening we can say, "It is necessarily the case that x is occurring simply because it *is* occurring" without hindering the freedom of the freely acting agents who brought about x, so too does God's foreknowledge of free acts, as observations of God's eternal present, make those acts, as it were, only "noetically" necessary.[80]

Barth's Use of Boethius's Concept of Eternity

Let us now summarize Boëthius's concept of eternity. Eternity, for Boëthius, is first of all a quality of the divine life.[81] That is, eternity is not simply a place in which God exists, or some "thing" other than God. It is a form or mode of existence peculiar to God, and thus different from the form or mode of existence that human beings have, which is temporal. Second, Boëthian eternity combines the two concepts of simultaneity and duration,[82] so that God is a being who exists timelessly (unlike sempiternal beings) and yet encompasses all of time (unlike a quantum or speck of time).

These particular aspects of eternity—life and boundless simultaneous duration—are the very ones picked up by Barth:

> In God actual years and days are enumerated before numbers existed

---

79. Ibid., 72–91.
80. Ibid., 115–20. We will see a similar argument at work in Anselm's *de Concordia*, which we will consider below.
81. I do not wish to imply that this or what follows are unique contributions of Boëthius, particularly with regard to Augustine. Rather, I see much of what Boëthius says as implicit in Augustine, only stated in Boëthius with greater clarity, and in a different context.
82. Again, we seem to have here a point on which Boëthius and Augustine are very close.

and when He did not need them. Years and days could not exist if this were not the case, if, without being bound to them, God were not their beginning, succession and end, and did not possess them in Himself. This positive quality of eternity is finely expressed in the definition of Boëthius which is classic for the whole Middle Ages: *aeternitatis est interminabilis vitae tota simul et perfecta possessio.*[83]

What is "this positive quality" that Barth sees in Boëthius's definition? I suggest that it is the conjunction (*simul*) of interminability (*interminabilis*) and life (*vitae*), with the result that God encompasses time, and is the source or ground of all times. In short, Barth sees in Boëthius's definition something quite other than a negative diastasis of time and eternity. God is not merely opposed to time, but comprehends in one *interminabilis vita* all that exists, and does so *tota simul et perfecta*. It is these two together, the *interminabilis* and the *vita*, that are important for Barth, at times with more of an emphasis on *vita*, particularly when Barth turns to a critique of other theologians' views of eternity. Hunsinger may be right in highlighting "interminability" as "strikingly new" from the standpoint of how the definition may connect the notion of eternity with the doctrine of the Trinity.[84] Yet from the standpoint of Barth's argument in the context of his use of Boëthius's definition, it appears that something else is significant. It is not just because God's eternity is interminable that "the definition of eternity does not depend on the negation of time."[85] Rather, it is the concomitant appearance of "life" in the definition that, for Barth, suggests something other than the negation of time. Such an emphasis Barth approvingly finds in Boëthius, even as with regret he finds it lacking in other theologians.

---

83. *CD* II/1, 610.
84. "From this standpoint, the one strikingly new element in the definition is 'interminability.'" George Hunsinger, "*Mysterium Trinitatis*: Karl Barth's Conception of Eternity," in *Disruptive Grace: Studies in the Theology of Karl Barth* (Grand Rapids: Eerdmans, 2000), 199.
85. Hunsinger, "*Mysterium Trinitatis*," 200.

So also in Barth's treatment of time under the doctrine of creation, we find this especially Boëthian phrasing:

> Even the eternal God does not live without time. He is supremely temporal. For his eternity is authentic temporality, and therefore the source of all time. But in his eternity, in the uncreated self-subsistent time which is one of the perfections of His divine nature, present, past and future, yesterday, to-day and to-morrow, are not successive, but simultaneous.[86]

Barth derives another point from Boëthius, namely that eternity is an attribute of *God*: "'Whole, simultaneous and perfect possession of boundless life', this is indeed eternity, provided it is not at all the eternity of being, but the eternity of *God* prior to and after, above and under all being."[87]

Such an emphasis must be understood against the background of and in contrast to idealistic philosophy, particularly Hegel, whom we will discuss in greater detail later in this chapter. The point here, however, is simply that eternity was sometimes defined as a concept of being. In such a view, "eternity" was a characteristic of the world, the flip side, as it were, of our awareness of the permanence of being in general, the permanence collectively behind the impermanence of all individual things. Barth is not disputing that such a definition of "eternity" may in fact correspond to the actual constitution of the world; he is simply denying that such an understanding of "eternity" applies to God. What Barth means by eternity is this very point he sees in Boëthius: that it is an attribute of God.

---

86. *CD* III/2, 437.
87. *KD* II/1, 688–89.; *CD* II/1, 611. Revised translation.

Anselm

We turn now to Anselm of Canterbury (1033–1109), in whose understanding of eternity we find much that echoes Augustine and, even more, Boëthius. In what follows, we will explore the contours of Anselm's theology of eternity and note its similarities to and differences from Boëthius' own view.

Exposition: *Monologium, Prosologion, de Concordia*

As an example of such Boëthian resonance, we can do no better than to turn to the primary locus of Anselm's view of eternity in his *Monologium*. "Hence, if this Being is said to exist always; since, for it, it is the same to exist and to live, no better sense can be attached to this statement, than that it exists or lives eternally, that is, it possesses interminable life, as a perfect whole at once. For its eternity apparently is an interminable life, existing at once as a perfect whole."[88]

Throughout the *Monologium*, Anselm is pursuing a formal logical argument concerning some Being that may rightly be the highest of all beings, and who alone may be called this. Because of this context of medieval formal logic, Anselm frequently uses the third person neuter pronoun *it* in referring to this object of his argument.[89]

The Boëthian language is quite clear in this passage, particularly in the phrase "it possesses interminable life, as a perfect whole at once."

---

88. *Monologium*, 24. The translation is from Anselm, *Saint Anselm: Basic Writings—Proslogium, Monologium, Gaunilon's On Behalf of the Fool, Cur Deus Homo*, trans. Sidney Norton Deane (LaSalle, IL: Open Court, 1962), 83. Further citations from the *Monologium* will be from this translation, and will have the page numbers of that translation in parentheses following the chapter number.
89. Incidentally, Anselm's *Proslogium* instead takes the form of an extended prayer, and God is there consistently addressed and referred to in the second person singular. It thus stands, as it were, between Augustine's *Confessions* and Anselm's *Monologium* in style and method.

Yet Anselm's understanding of divine eternality differs formally from that of Boëthius in two ways. First of all, Anselm's (Boëthian) definition comes at the *end* of his argument concerning divine eternity: it is the conclusion, or rather one of several conclusions, he reaches, and not the premise. Second, Anselm's development of eternity differs from Boëthius's from the start, for it unfolds from and depends expressly on his understanding of the *simplicity of God*.

Although the simplicity of God may also be thematic in Boëthius's treatment, such a theme does not have the programmatic relevance for Boëthius that it does for Anselm. Anselm expressly takes simplicity to be foundational. Whereas Boëthius begins with a consideration of divine knowledge, and its distinction from human knowledge, Anselm actually begins with an emphasis on divine simplicity, and turns to that theme again and again. For Anselm, God's simplicity is described as follows: "Since, then, that [Divine] Nature is by no means composite, and yet is by all means those so many goods, necessarily all these are not more than one, but are one. Any one of them is, therefore, the same as all, whether taken all at once or separately."[90]

In other words, God's "goods" or attributes, even though they may be enumerated as several, are really one. They each imply and contain all the others, for God is not a composite being.

Such an understanding of God's nature provides the immediate backdrop for Anselm's discussion of God's relationship to time and to space. His formal argument develops as follows. This simple divine nature (that is, God), says Anselm, cannot have a beginning or an end caused by itself, because if it were to begin from itself, then the divine nature would consist of at least two parts: the originating or generating part, and the part that is originated or generated by the

---

90. *Monologium*, 17 (p. 67).

other. Furthermore, if God were *willingly* to come to an end, then that will, as a will to end, would not be simply good, for God's existence is good, and the will to end would be the denial of an intrinsic good. Thus divine simplicity precludes the very possibility of the divine Nature coming to an end from itself. Furthermore, the possibility of God's existence having a beginning or an end from outside itself is excluded since God is the supreme being and thus supremely powerful: whatever could bring God into being or cause God to cease to exist would be more powerful than God.[91]

For Anselm, it is clear that the Being under consideration, the Supreme Being, "exists everywhere, and in all things, and through all," and "always has been, and is, and will be." Yet Anselm "perceive[s] a certain murmur of contradiction," which he intends to explore by means of a rigorous multistep argument. He sees, then, three mutually exclusive possibilities. Either God exists (a) everywhere and always, (b) merely at some place and time, or (c) nowhere and never. These alternatives may also be put as follows: God may exist either (a) in every place and at every time; or (b) finitely, in some place and at some time; or (c) in no place and at no time.[92]

---

91. *Monologium*, 18 (pp. 68–69). Certainly, the kind of possibility (and impossibility) in view here is logical possibility (and impossibility). This class of possibility is described well in Raymond Bradley and Norman Swartz, *Possible Worlds: An Introduction to Logic and Its Philosophy* (Indianapolis: Hackett, 1979), especially 6–7. "The class of *logically* possible worlds is the *most inclusive* class of possible worlds. It includes every other kind of possible world as well: all those that are physically possible and many, but not all, that are physically impossible; and it includes all worlds which are technologically possible, i.e., physically possible worlds having the same physical resoucesresources and industrial capacity as the actual world, and many, but not all, which are technologically impossible" (ibid., 7). Anselm is speaking of what the very meaning of divinity allows; the impossibility is not merely contingent, but necessary. "A simple way of describing the relation which holds between two propositions which are contradictories of one another is to say that in each possible world one or other of those propositions is true and the other is false. This description has two immediate consequences. . . . First, note that any contradictory of a contingent proposition is itself a contingent proposition. . . . Second, note that any contradictory of a noncontingent proposition is itself a noncontingent proposition" (ibid., 18, 19).
92. *Monologium* 20 (72).

Anselm rejects option (c), because God is the supreme being, and all things depend upon God's existence.[93] He also rejects option (b), for if God exists only in some place and at some time, then there are places and times at which God does not exist. But nothing can exist without God. So then there would be places and times at which nothing exists. Yet place and time are themselves things, so for option (b) there would be places and times in which nothing, not even places and times, exist. The logical contradiction involved makes this second option impossible. So since these second and third options are ruled out, only option (a) is possible: that God "must exist everywhere and always, that is, in every place and at every time."[94]

Anselm now turns to consider how God may be related to all those times and places. He addresses two possibilities: (a.1) that God "exists in every place and at every time"; and (a.2) that "only a part of God exists" in all places and times, "the other part transcending every place and time."[95]

Anselm rejects (a.2), the second option, because it implies that the divine nature has parts, which contradicts divine simplicity. How, then, should the first option (a.1) be construed? Here there are also two possibilities: either

a.1.α. God exists as a whole with respect to the totality of all places and times, but that the whole is "spread out" over those places and times, so that there are then parts of God that correspond to discrete times and places;

or a.1.β. God "exists as a whole, in individual places and times as well"; that is, for each place and time, God exists as a whole.[96]

The first option (a.1.α), of course, is inadequate because it, too, conflicts with divine simplicity. But how is a.1.β possible? Indeed,

---

93. Ibid. (72–73).
94. Ibid. (73).
95. Ibid., 21 (73).
96. Ibid., (73–74).

it seems that for God to exist as a whole for each time and place "is doubtless impossible, unless [the Supreme Being] either exists at once or at different times in individual places or times."[97]

It is this possibility (a.1.β), of God's existing "at once or at different times in individual places or times," that Anselm will now explore. But note that it is a fairly complex option: God may exist, as a whole it may be added, either (ρ) at once, or (ς) at different times, and that existence is with respect to (x) individual places or (y) individual times. Because of the complexity involved here, Anselm decides to split up the argument, and no longer consider time and place at once. Thus he will first pursue the argument with regard to place, that is whether (ρ) or (ς) is true with respect to (x) [space]. Then he will focus on the temporal option, that is whether (ρ) or (ς) is true with respect to (y) [time].[98]

The spatial argument must be pursued in two steps. First he will consider whether God can exist as a whole in different discrete places simultaneously (ρ-x), and then whether God exists "at different times, in different places"(ς-x).[99]

The first step, again, concerns the possibility of whether God exists as a whole at discrete locations at the same time (ρ-x). The problem, says Anselm, is "If . . . [God] exists as a whole in each individual place, then for each individual place there is an individual whole" that is God. The reason for this is that we take "place" to mean that, for example, if place p and place q are distinct places, and entity u exists as a whole in place p and, at the same time, entity v exists as a whole in place q, then entities u and v cannot be at all a part of each other.[100] Since that is so, then any existing thing that exists entirely in a place at a certain time, cannot have part of it existing outside that

---

97. Ibid., (74).
98. Ibid.
99. Ibid.
100. Ibid., (74–75).

place at the same time. Therefore, how is it possible for existence as a whole in one place to be simultaneous with existence as a whole in a completely different place?[101]

Given this spatial rule, it follows that "for individual places, there are individual wholes, if anything is to exist as a whole in different individual places at once." The result of this line of argument is that if God exists as a whole at each discrete place at the same time, "then there are as many supreme Natures as there can be individual places." This conclusion, of course, makes no sense, so the conclusion must be that God "does not exist, as a whole, at one time in individual places."[102] Option p-x is rejected.

Now for the second possibility (ς-x) concerning space: perhaps God exists as a whole at discrete places nonsimultaneously. This is no better, for any good or existence whatsoever depends on God's existence then and there, and when God (on this supposition) exists at time t at place a, then God does not exist then at place b (assuming that a and b do not intersect); and thus at place b there is no good or existence. But b, as a place, must have existence, and so must be dependent upon the existence of God there and then. So this possibility is rejected, and with it Anselm has dismissed both possibilities concerning God's relationship as a whole to individual places.[103] "If neither at the same time nor at different times does it exist, as a whole, in individual places, it is evident that it does not at all exist, as a whole, in each individual place."[104]

Anselm then addresses how God exists as a whole in individual times. Here as well, there are two possibilities. "We must now examine, then, whether this supreme Nature exists, as a whole, at individual times, either simultaneously or at distinct times for

101. Ibid., (75).
102. Ibid.
103. Ibid., (75–76).
104. Ibid., (76).

individual times." That is, does God exist as a whole simultaneously with each individual time (ρ-y)? Or does God exist as a whole at each distinct time for every temporal moment there is (ς-y)?[105]

The first of these, ρ-y, is immediately problematic. For if anything is to be entirely simultaneous with all individual times, then each one of those times would itself be simultaneous with all the others, destroying the integrity of temporal sequence.[106]

He then immediately moves on to the other possibility, ς-y: God existing as a whole at each temporal moment. God's age, or God's eternity (taking these to be synonyms in the divine case), then, would seem to be distributed in parts along the temporal line.[107] Yet since God's eternity is the same thing as God's being,[108] God would then be divided into parts along the temporal axis. This would introduce past, present, and future into the very being of God.[109] The problem, for Anselm, is that these temporal distinctions indicate compositeness and change, which contradicts Anselm's principle of divine simplicity. God ends up being different things at different times. "By no means, then, is past or future attributable to the creative Being, either its age or its eternity.... But was means past, and will be future. Therefore that Being never was, nor will be." Thus Anselm must reject this possibility, ς-y, that God might exist as a whole at distinct times, just as he rejected the previous one, ρ-y, that God might exist as a whole simultaneously with all times.[110] In short, he has now eliminated a.1.β as a valid possibility.

He thus concludes his exploration of the various possibilities of God's being related as a whole to all times and places (a.1), and he

---

105. Ibid.,
106. Ibid.,
107. Ibid.,
108. This step seems to be based, again, on divine simplicity.
109. *Monologium* 21 (76).
110. Ibid., (77).

reaches the troubling conclusion that they are all invalid, that God "does not in any way exist, as a whole, in every time or place." He has also explored and rejected all the possibilities regarding God's existing in part relative to space and time (a.2). And so the even more troubling conclusion seems to be that God cannot exist "everywhere and always." No construals of option (a) are workable, since to exist everywhere and always requires existence either as a whole or in part. But if God does not exist everywhere and always, then God must exist either finitely or in no place or time. He has already proved that God cannot exist finitely (option [b] from earlier). The only alternative seems to be that God exists in no place or time. For the only alternatives are God existing in every place and time, in some place or time, or in no place or time.[111] Yet this is option (c), which earlier Anselm rejected, on the grounds that it is essential that God, the Supreme Being, must exist, "through itself, and without beginning and without end," for without God's existing nothing at all would exist. So God "must exist everywhere and always."[112] But how?

To reconcile these contradictions, Anselm proposes that God exists in a manner not subject to the normal operation of space and time. Thus God would exist as a whole in different places at the same time without there being several different wholes; and God would exist so God's age "is not distributed among past, present, and future."[113] One might say that God is wholly present both "here" and "there," and so too is God entirely with us both "then" and "now"; and even so, "here" and "there" as well as "then" and "now" remain distinct as places or times. Leftow puts it this way: "For Anselm, God is simultaneously present at discrete, non-simultaneous times, *without*

---

111. Ibid., (77–78).
112. Ibid., (78).
113. Ibid.,22 (78).

wiping out their temporal distinction. Anselm claims, in so many words, that God is present at different times *at once*."[114]

The law of space and time, suggests Anselm, applies only to those creatures "that . . . do not transcend extent of space or duration of time." For other beings "not of this class" the law of space and time does not apply, and thus neither do the conclusions reached above.[115] Place applies only to objects contained by space, and time only to objects contained by time. "Hence, to any being, to whose spatial extent or duration no bound can be set, either by space or time, no place or time is properly attributed." For such a being, "no place is its place, and no time its time." Beings that have no place or time are not subject to the law of place and time. Since God created all things, God is not contained or constrained by any of them, nor by their laws. Space does not "circumscribe . . . the magnitude of truth," nor does "time measure . . . its duration."[116] Only things confined by space or time are bound by their laws. God is not so confined. "Whatever is in no wise confined by the restraint of place or time, is not compelled by any law of places or times to multiplicity of parts, nor is it prevented from being present, as a whole and simultaneously, in more places or times than one."[117]

God must be present, as a whole, to all places and times, in order for those places and times to exist. Further, since the law of space and time doesn't apply to God, God can be present to these spaces and times simultaneously. "For, being it [the divine nature] is present in one place, it is not therefore prevented from being present at the same time, and in like manner in this or that other, place or time." Also, to assert that God was, is, and will be does not imply that God's being is changing with the passing of time, such that part of God is no longer,

---

114. Leftow, *Time and Eternity*, 183.
115. *Monologium* 22 (78).
116. Ibid., (79).
117. Ibid., (79–80).

part having existence, and part not yet. When we say that God exists in space and time, we do not mean quite the same thing as we do when we usually say this. Normally, when we speak of something being in some space and time, we mean that (a) it is present in that time and space, and (b) it is contained by that time and space.[118] But with God, only the first applies. It would seem, then, that it would be better to say that God "exists *with* place or time, than that [God] exists *in* place or time. For the statement that a thing exists *in* another implies that it is *contained*, more than does the statement that it exists *with* another."[119]

So God exists in no place or time, being contained by none. But in a manner unique to God, God does exist in every place and time, because without God no place or time could exist.

> It exists in every place and time, because it is absent from none; and it exists in none, because it has no place or time, and has not taken to itself distinctions of place or time, neither here nor there, nor anywhere, nor then, nor now, nor at any time; nor does it exist in terms of this fleeting present, in which we live, nor has it existed, nor will it exist, in terms of past or future, since these are restricted to things finite and mutable, which it is not.[120]

However, in an admission intriguing and suggestive, Anselm says that temporal properties may rightly be applied to God in some sense, because God is as truly present to times and places as are those things present and circumscribed by those times and places.[121] We may see this view also in Anselm's later work, *de Concordia*:

> For though we can only say that something within eternity does occur, never that it has occurred or will occur, still we do say without contradicting ourselves that a temporal event has occurred or will occur.

---

118. Ibid., (80).
119. Ibid., (81).
120. Ibid.
121. Ibid.

> Accordingly, it is possible to show without inconsistency that a thing which is eternally immutable may sometimes, before it actually occurs, be mutable within time because of free will.[122]

Turning back to his argument in *Monologium*, we may then observe that with his proposal he removes the contradiction at which he previously arrived. It is true that "the highest Being of all exists, everywhere and always, and nowhere and never, that is, in every place and time, and in no place or time." This is not a contradiction because of "the consistent truth of different senses of the terms employed."[123] God exists in all existing things, and not merely in every place.[124] God's being is immutable, ever alike itself, and so different from temporality, which is always changing. So it is better to say that God exists always rather than that God exists at every time. It is a matter of implications.[125]

The end of this long line of formal argumentation in the *Monologium* is the Boëthian definition of eternity, the same passage with which our consideration of Anselm began. "Hence, if this Being is said to exist always . . . no better sense can be attached to this statement, than that it exists or lives eternally, that is, it possesses interminable life, as a perfect whole at once." Additionally, Anselm sees the Boëthian definition proved also by these points: (a) because of divine simplicity, God simply is God's life and is God's eternity; (b) God is interminable; (c) God exists as a perfect whole at once. These all demonstrate the Boëthian definition. Only God, as uncreated and the creator of all other things, could possess true eternity.[126]

---

122. Anselm of Canterbury, "On the Harmony of the Foreknowledge, the Predestination, and the Grace of God with Free Choice (De Concordia Praescientiae et Praedestinationis et Gratiae Dei cum Libero Arbitrio)," in *Theological Treatises, Volume III*, ed. by Jaspear Hopkins and Herbert Richardson, trans. by Douglas Johnson, G. Stanley Kane, Raymond Phyles, and Charles Waldrop (Cambridge: Harvard Divinity School Library, 1967), 58.
123. *Monologium* 22 (81).
124. Ibid., 23 (82).
125. Ibid., 24 (82–83).

Barth on Anselm

There we have the argument concerning God's eternity that Anselm pursues in his *Monologium*. What ought to be said about this with regard to Karl Barth? Barth does consider Anselm in his discussion of divine eternity in *CD* II/1, in two places. Yet the text to which Barth refers is not the *Monologium*, but the *Proslogium*, chapter 11X, from which he quotes the following:

> Thou wast not, then, yesterday, nor wilt thou be to-morrow; but yesterday and to-day and to-morrow thou art; or, rather, neither yesterday nor to-day nor to-morrow thou art; but simply, thou art, outside all time. For yesterday and to-day and to-morrow have no existence, except in time; but thou, although nothing exists without thee, nevertheless dost not exist in space or time, but all things exist in thee.[127]

When Barth quotes this text, very early in his discussion of God's eternity, he does so approvingly and as an example of what he takes to be a positive first step.

> Eternity is not . . . an infinite extension of time both backwards and forwards. Time can have nothing to do with God. The infinity of its extension cannot help it. For even and especially in this extension there is the separation and distance and contradiction which mark it as time and distinguish it from eternity as the creature from the Creator. It is quite correct, as in the older theology, to understand the idea of eternity and therefore God Himself *first of all* in this clear antithesis.[128]

Yet it is clear that Barth does not wish to remain with this first step. In a sequence to which we will give more attention later, Barth insists that "it is a poor and short-sighted view to understand God's eternity

---

126. Ibid., 24 (83).
127. *Proslogium* 19, in Anselm, *Saint Anselm, trans.* Deane, 25. The location of Barth's use of this text is *CD* II/1, 608.
128. *CD* II/1, 608. Emphasis added.

only from the standpoint that it is the negation of time."[129] In the excursus in the immediately subsequent paragraph, Barth suggests that a positive conception of the relationship of time and eternity, one that does not reject the negative first step yet moves beyond it, is to be found in Scripture, and in Boëthius. He does not, however, find it in Anselm's statement, nor in one from Augustine he likewise quotes. "This positive quality," which Barth sees in Boëthius, "goes farther and deeper than the statements of Augustine and Anselm, which are far too occupied with the confrontation of eternity and time."[130]

We have here a rather strange assertion. It shows no awareness that Anselm's fully developed position took Boëthius's definition as the concluding piece—the solution, as it were—to his whole argument in *Monologium* concerning God's relationship to time. Clearly, Barth is rejecting one implication of one statement of Anselm's. Barth uses that statement as an illustration of a necessary yet insufficient first step in defining eternity, a step that must be followed by other steps. Yet none of this indicates that Barth was rejecting Anselm's fully developed position on divine eternity, the position that I have attempted to trace above. Indeed, it is possible that such a position may complement Barth's view.[131]

The full exploration of this possibility would take us off the main track of this project. Facets of it may become clearer through the following chapters. A tentative exploration, however, may be initiated by summarizing Anselm's view, as follows. He conceives eternity as a property of God's being that comprehends all of time, is entirely present to every moment, and yet is not contained or limited by any specific moment. God is not alienated from time, but neither is God constrained by time. *All* of God is present to *every*

---

129. *CD* II/1, 610.
130. Ibid.
131. I wish to thank George Hunsinger for suggesting this possibility to me.

time, without doing violence to the integrity of time or of God's being. God is not measured by time, since that would imply that God is contained by time. Yet since God has truly been present at every moment in time, tenses are applicable to God in some sense, but merely with respect to the interactions or dealings between God and creatures. For these reasons, perhaps it could fit with Anselm's view to speak of "God's history," as long as the temporal changes were understood to be merely *ad extra*.

If this is indeed a fair representation of Anselm's understanding of God's relationship to time as he articulates it in the *Monologium*, then it seems likewise fair to suggest that this understanding is not the merely negative, essential yet insufficient, first step that Barth saw in the *Proslogium*. The expression of a positive relationship between eternity and time, for which Barth was concerned, is present in Anselm's position.

Thomas Aquinas

Thomas Aquinas (1226–1274) located his discussion of divine eternity in the first part of his *Summa Theologiae*,[132] immediately after his discussion of God's unchangeableness. Such a decision on Thomas's part suggests the contours of his discussion of eternity. Thomas's understanding of eternity, we shall see, shares a great deal with the figures we have already examined, and yet has its own particular emphases. These contours or emphases are greatly influenced by the prominence of the concept of God's unchangeableness, just as Anselm's doctrine was greatly influenced

---

132. References to the *Summa* use the Blackfriars edition: St. Thomas Aquinas, *Summa Theologiae*, ed. Timothy McDeErmott, OP (London: Blackfriars, in conjunction with Eyre & Spottiswoode, 1964). I deploy the standard method of citing by part, chapter, and paragraph numbers.

by his focus on the concept of divine simplicity. There are of course other points of difference, as well as significant correspondence.

Exposition: Eternity in the *Summa Theologiae*

Thomas begins his discussion by adopting and defending Boëthius's definition of eternity. From that definition Thomas derives two points. First, an eternal being is limitless, that is, it "lacks both beginning and end." Second, "eternity itself exists as an *instantaneous whole* lacking successiveness." We see here the two aspects of eternity that we highlighted for Boëthius: timelessness and duration. However, Thomas's method is very different, proceeding in a different epistemological direction, and based not (as noted above) on divine simplicity but on divine unchangeableness. For Thomas, "Just as we can only come to know simple things by way of composite ones, so we can only come to know eternity by way of time, which is merely the numbering of before and after in change."[133] The *via cognoscendi* is from the complex (that is, consisting of parts) to the simple, and thus from the concept of time to the concept of eternity. This epistemological method has two implications for eternity: first, since the concept of time arises from the awareness of successiveness that is part of change, then the notion of eternity arises from awareness of changelessness; eternity must then lack successiveness. Second, since changeable things begin and end in time, and time measures those things, then an eternal thing, being unchangeable, must lack both a beginning and an end.

For Thomas, eternity belongs only to God;[134] indeed, God *is* God's own eternity, for God's being and existence are identical, unlike all

---

133. *ST* 1a.10.1.
134. Ibid., 1a.10.3.

other beings.[135] Thus eternity is not a "thing" separate from God. It is rather one of the divine perfections. Thus Thomas makes here a point substantially in agreement with Anselm, who developed his doctrine of eternity out of his doctrine of divine simplicity. For Thomas, the point is used to emphasize the distinction between time and eternity. Furthermore, time and eternity are not distinguished by the limitless character of eternity. Such "is an accidental and not an intrinsic difference," because even if time had no beginning and no end, it would not thereby be eternity. Rather, time and eternity are distinguished in this way: "Eternity is an instantaneous whole whilst time is not." Yet eternity is a form of measurement, like time, with "eternity measuring abiding existence and time measuring change." Indeed, "just as eternity is properly the measure of existence as such, so time is properly the measure of change."[136] Yet the idea of eternity being a form of measurement should not be pushed so far as to conflict with the point that eternity belongs to God and is identical with the being of God. Rather, "the notion of measurement arises only in our way of conceiving the situation."[137]

Barth and Thomas

Barth expressed quite direct objections to Thomas's method of defining eternity. The core of his difficulty seemed to have concerned Thomas's epistemological route for understanding eternity. For Thomas, we understand eternity by first understanding time, just as we understand the simple by means of the complex. In Barth's view, such an approach, proceeding apparently from the negation of the concept of time, is an inversion of the proper order of theological

---

135. Ibid., 1a.10.2.
136. Ibid., 1a.10.4.
137. Ibid., 1a.10.2.

knowledge. For "we know eternity primarily and properly, not by the negation of the concept of time, but by the knowledge of God as the *possessor interminabilis vitae*."[138]

The result of such a reversal, as Barth saw it, was to force the concept of eternity into such dependence on the concept of time that eternity could not exist without time. "The customary treatment of the *Ewigkeitsbegriff* in the theological tradition suffers from the fatal illusion that there might well be no eternity if there were no time, if eternity thus could not be non-temporality; or at least no knowledge of eternity except through time, that is, other than in the form of the negation of the concept of time."[139] We see here an example of a recurring motif in Barth's doctrine of God: he was very concerned that theology not make it seem as if God's existence were dependent on the existence of the world.

These criticisms have a great deal of force. Thomas's epistemological method is theologically abstract.[140] His concept of eternity is linked to the negation of the concept of time. The result does seem to make eternity dependent on the existence of time.

Yet it would be a mistake for one to leave the matter at that. For Thomas does not understand eternity to be *merely* the negation of time. Indeed, when Thomas says that "eternity is an instantaneous whole whilst time is not," one could just as easily conclude that *time* is merely the negation of *eternity*. Such a conclusion would be just as simplistic, and just as wrong. Time and eternity must be distinguished. But they are not merely the negation of each other. For Thomas, time and eternity are forms of measurement, each of them appropriate to that which they measure: time for things

---

138. *CD* II/1, 611.
139. *KD* II/1, 689; *CD* II/1, 611. Rev. trans.
140. Its abstractness lies in its apparent remoteness from relatively concrete theological loci such as the doctrine of Jesus Christ.

changeable, eternity for things unchangeable. Furthermore, God's "eternity comprehends all phases of time."[141] There is no mere negation here, time and eternity in absolute antithesis to each other. Rather, there is the careful distinguishing of different realities, one that comprehends or contains the other.

We should also not rush on to accept Barth's criticisms of Thomas, because doing so may lead us to fail to see what Barth has done. When Barth criticizes Aquinas for his theological method, he insists that our starting point in knowing time and eternity should be with "the knowledge of God as the *possessor interminabilis vitae*." What is striking here is that Barth uses Boëthius to correct Aquinas, for *interminabilis vitae* is a clear allusion to Boëthius's classic definition of eternity (likewise picked up by Anselm in *Monologium* 24 [83]). My point, simply, is that we must be careful about how we understand Barth's criticism of "the *Ewigkeitsbegriff* in the theological tradition." By using the tradition to correct the tradition, Barth is surely not rejecting that tradition as a whole.

Thomas's own contribution to the tradition may be open to some of Barth's criticisms. I am not convinced that those criticisms are fatal, but a thorough analysis would take me beyond the scope of my topic. However, there are two elements to it that must be noted by way of summary, insofar as they either stand unrejected by Barth and constitute possible points of agreement between Thomas and Barth, or as they provide insights into or approaches to understanding divine eternality that we must highlight for a utility that will become clearer later. First, eternity is an attribute of God's being. Second, and less precisely, eternity is a form of measurement, used to measure unchangeable things, just as time is the form of measurement appropriate for the changeable.

---

141. Latin: Ejus æternitas omnia tempora includit. *ST* 1a.10.2.

Schleiermacher

Our survey of these few figures from the classical Christian tradition has highlighted several recurring motifs, a set of ideas or themes that together constitute what could be called the traditional Christian understanding of divine eternity in the West. With Schleiermacher (1768–1834), we turn our attention to the modern period.[142] Yet it is not the case that in Schleiermacher we see an absolute break with the classical Christian traditional reflection on eternity. Rather, we see an attempt to use that tradition and extend it in a new context.

Such harkening back to traditional concepts of eternity was a practice quite in keeping with the Reformation tradition that Schleiermacher embraced. Traditional theological reflections on eternity were not rejected during the Reformation, but continued to constitute the locus of discussion through the Reformation and post-Reformation periods. We may find evidence for such continuity by looking at Heppe's compendium of doctrinal theology, composed of statements drawn from Reformed theologians of the post-Reformation period. In Heppe's section on divine eternity, the influence of Boëthius and of Thomas Aquinas is quite prominent. Important and recurring are the themes of limitless duration and lack of succession: "'Eternity' is that infinite and interminable duration, which is at once whole without any innovation or succession. . . . It is God's eternity by which He is devoid of time as regards limit and succession. . . . Eternity is actual interminable and simultaneous possession of essence." We also may find here a hint of the Thomistic notion that eternity is an attribute of God's being, thus not something separate from God: "Eternity is God's attribute by which He excludes

---

142. There may be as many definitions of *modern* and *the modern period* as there are writers who use these phrases. I believe that the sense intended here is entirely defensible and useful for the purposes of this work, namely, that the modern period begins with the Enlightenment.

all limitations of duration."[143] Absent, however, is the Boëthian stress on "life."

Exposition: Eternity in *The Christian Faith*

In the case of Schleiermacher, his considerations of eternity seem to have been deeply formed by the tradition. Indeed, Schleiermacher may have seen himself as in part (but only in part) defending that tradition. In one of his handwritten notes to the first part of the *Christian Faith*, after quoting affirmatively Boëthius's well-known definition of eternity, Schleiermacher says, "This correct exposition by Boëthius has often been challenged."[144] As to whether Schleiermacher was sympathetic to the tradition, we may look to one of Schleiermacher's later nineteenth century interpreters and critics, Isaak Dorner,[145] who "consider[ed] Schleiermacher's doctrine of God set forth in the first part of the *Glaubenslehre* to be fundamentally a restatement of the traditional concepts of simplicity and immutability."[146]

Yet Schleiermacher's own approach to the question of eternity, just as for all the other figures, is not a simple restatement of the tradition;[147] indeed, it makes its own theological way. In order to understand Schleiermacher's distinctiveness on this question, however, we need to understand something of Schleiermacher's

---

143. Heppe, *Reformed Dogmatics*, 65.
144. "Diese richtige Erklärung von Boëthius ist häufig angefochten worden." Friedrich Schleiermacher, *Der Christliche Glaube nach den Grundsätzen der Evangelischen Kirche im Zusammenhange Dargestellt*, 7th ed., ed. by Martin Redeker (Berlin: Walter de Gruyter, 1960), 1:268, fn. b.
145. Isaak August Dorner, *Divine Immutability: A Critical Reconsideration* (Minneapolis: Fortress Press, 1994).
146. Robert R. Williams, "Introduction," 13. In Dorner, *Divine Immutability*.
147. About Isaakc Dorner's treatment of Schleiermacher, Williams rightly says, "Unfortunately, Dorner spends more space criticizing Schleiermacher's putative traditionalism than giving him credit for his breakthrough." "Introduction," 13.

unique way of dealing with the divine attributes, a way self-consciously distinct from standard approaches. At the very beginning of his discussion of the attributes, Schleiermacher insists that the distinctions between the attributes do not designate actual distinctions within the being of God.[148] They have, as it were, "only subjective significance."[149] To say otherwise is to verge on speculation, to forget the roots of Christian dogmatics "in their ultimate religious basis."[150] For Schleiermacher, the attributes do not refer to distinctions within God, nor is one attribute completely disconnected from another. If each attribute is supposed to give knowledge of God not given by any of the others, then we end up with a composite knowledge of God, and if the knowledge is composite, then so is the object. But God is not composite, for the feeling of absolute dependence does not correspond to a composite object; it points to a simple object.[151]

For Schleiermacher, it was important that "we keep ourselves altogether within the limits of purely dogmatic procedure, both with regard to the content of individual definitions and also as to method" by not "making any speculative demands" and by not using "speculative aids."[152] Indeed, Schleiermacher frequently speaks against the "speculative formulas" and procedures of various theologians.[153] Again and again, Schleiermacher is concerned to stay within the proper limits of dogmatic theology.

But what does Schleiermacher mean by "the limits of purely dogmatic procedure"? For the answer to this question, we must

---

148. *The Christian Faith*, ed. H. R. Mackintosh and J. S. Stewart (Edinburgh: T. & T. Clark, 1986), 194. (Hereafter Chr. F.) Also, "The individual attributes in their differences correspond to nothing real in God" (201, emph. add.).
149. Williams, "Introduction," 13.
150. *Chr. F*, 195.
151. Ibid., 195–96.
152. Ibid., 195.
153. E.g., ibid., 219.

first consider what Schleiermacher meant by "Christian doctrine." According to Schleiermacher, "Christian doctrines are accounts of the Christian religious affections set forth in speech."[154] They are not abstract considerations of the nature of reality, but they spring from the piety of Christians; more specifically, from the experience of redemption offered by the Redeemer, Jesus Christ.[155] Furthermore, Christian doctrines are intimately connected with Christian preaching, which itself has as its content "the state of blessedness which is to be effected through the means ordained by Christ."[156] That preaching, however, did not remain a unitary thing as the church developed, but is "split into three different types of speech, which provide as many different forms of doctrine: the poetic, the rhetorical, and . . . the descriptively didactic."[157]

It is that third type of speech, the descriptively didactic, that characterizes Christian dogmatic propositions.[158] This kind of language aims at specificity, exactness. The first two forms of speech are prone to contradiction, which can be corrected only by reference back to "the original utterances of Christ" and by making the descriptively didactic expression as definite as possible, which consists in part in eliminating rhetorical or poetic elements.[159] Such an undertaking marks dogmatics as a scientific discipline, of a sort. Yet even though it may bear some similarity with regard to form, the dogmatic task is nonetheless to be distinguished from science, or logic, or what Schleiermacher calls "speculative activity," with regard to content.[160] For the dogmatic utterances arise from the religious impulse, but the speculative have as their task "the contemplation of

---

154. Ibid., 76.
155. Ibid., 78.
156. Ibid.
157. Ibid.
158. Ibid., (§16).
159. Ibid., 80–81.
160. Ibid., 81.

existence," and arise from logical considerations or from the work of natural science.[161]

It is within such an understanding of Christian dogmatics and doctrine that Schleiermacher speaks against the speculative character of certain methods of developing the divine attributes. Following "proper dogmatic procedure," Schleiermacher will eschew speculation. That is, the attributes must relate to the Christian religious consciousness. Thus in connection with his exposition of the attributes that relate to the Christian consciousness of redemption, Schleiermacher says that "our Christian consciousness, however expanded, cannot transcend that which stands in relation to us; and all the divine ordering of the world within this sphere, if we would truly appropriate it, we can only interpret by reference to the revelation of God in Christ and the Holy Spirit."[162]

Schleiermacher's very procedure stems from his concern to ward off speculation. For that reason Schleiermacher insists that one must develop the attributes by always relating them to the facts of Christian self-consciousness. Here he departs from the traditional method of developing the attributes. That standard procedure first develops rules for arriving at a proper conception of the divine attributes, and then gives rubrics for categorizing the attributes. That systematizing approach might give the impression that one can fully comprehend God's mystery simply by knowing the attributes. Schleiermacher's procedure, on the other hand, asks about the attributes in connection with "different moments of the religious self-consciousness."[163] For that reason he discusses not all the attributes at once, but in three different places throughout his *Glaubenslehre*, first of all in connection with God's general relationship to the world, and then as those

---

161. Ibid., 81–82.
162. Ibid., 734.
163. Ibid., 196–97.

attributes relate to a consciousness of sin, and finally as those attributes are connected with the Christian consciousness of redemption.

For that reason, Schleiermacher's method for developing the attributes differs from traditional expositions in his almost exclusive use of the *via causalitatis*, and in his significant doubt about the value of the *via negationis* and the *via eminentiae*. That is, Schleiermacher develops the attributes by means of their connection with the divine cause, because "causality stands in closest connexion with the feeling of absolute dependence itself."[164] Only by relating an attribute to the divine causality can the theologian make sure that one is not being speculative about an attribute: "All the divine attributes to be dealt with in Christian Dogmatics must somehow go back to the divine causality, since they are only meant to explain the feeling of absolute dependence."[165]

Evaluation

We are now in a better position to understand Schleiermacher's exposition of God's eternity. For Schleiermacher, his construal of eternity at first appears to be entirely negative. Indeed, for Schleiermacher, eternity is "the absolutely timeless causality of God, which conditions not only all that is temporal, but time itself as well."[166] Scripture may speak poetically about God's eternity being "an existence before time," but such poetic expressions are inadequate for the didactic task of dogmatics. For this reason, then, "the divine causality, since time itself is conditioned by it, must so much the more be thought of as utterly timeless."[167]

---

164. Ibid., 197.
165. Ibid., 198.
166. Ibid., 203.
167. Ibid., 204.

That negativity is seen also in how Schleiermacher insists[168] that God's eternity is not affected by the possibility that time might be infinite. "The eternity of God remains none the less unique, since the antithesis between the temporal and the eternal is not in the least diminished by the infinite duration of time."[169] Indeed, Schleiermacher insists that eternity is not at all to be defined as endless time, for it makes God's Being "intrinsically temporal" and measurable. "We must therefore reject as inadequate," says Schleiermacher, "all those explanations which abrogate for God only the limits of time and not time itself, and would form eternity from time by the removal of limits, while in fact these are opposites."[170]

It is clear that many would judge this aspect of Schleiermacher's understanding of eternity to be inadequate for the theological task.[171] In the context of this project, we may point out that Barth also objected to any understanding of God's eternity that saw it as primarily timelessness. "It is a poor and short-sighted view to understand God's eternity only from the standpoint that it is the negation of time,"[172] says Barth, and although Schleiermacher is not expressly the object of Barth's criticism in this passage, it is certain that Barth would object to Schleiermacher's statement that "divine causality . . . must . . . be thought of as utterly timeless."

Yet I would suggest that, on a more careful reading, Schleiermacher's discussion of divine eternity is not purely negative. For Schleiermacher insists that eternity must be understood at every

---

168. Here he is drawing on Augustine and John of Damascus.
169. Ibid., 204–5.
170. Ibid., 205.
171. See Dorner, *Divine Immutability*, esp. 119–30; cf. also nn147 and 148, above; Pike, *God and Timelessness: Studies in Ethics and the Philosophy of Religion* (London: Routledge & K. Paul, 1970), 167–90. Pike's study of Schleiermacher in the pages here referenced is, in my judgment, a subtle misreading of what Schleiermacher has to say about the divine attributes. Cf. Karl- Hinrich Manzke, *Ewigkeit und Zeitlichkeit: Aspekte für eine theologische Deutung der Zeit* (Göttingen: Vandenhoeck und Ruprecht, 1992), 50–51.
172. *CD* II/1, 610.

point with omnipotence in view, for to do otherwise would make eternity "a so-called 'inactive' attribute." When one separates eternity and omnipotence, one ends up with an abstract representation of God, that is, a "representation of God apart from the manifestations of His power, an idea quite out of harmony with the religious consciousness and so quite empty for us."[173] That is, without thus understanding these attributes in their connection with each other, one's conception of God becomes abstracted from how God is really known.

The importance of this point should not be overlooked. For when Schleiermacher insists that we must understand eternity with omnipotence in view, he is very close to Barth's actualism (his insistence that God's being is a being in act) and to his particularism (his insistence that we know God through God's works).[174] To "represent[ ] . . . God apart from the manifestations of His power" would be to consider God in abstraction from God's act, and to assume that God can be known apart from how God has acted. In such a procedure Schleiermacher has no interest, for it would be entirely speculative. On this point, there is clearly some correspondence between the theological ideals of Schleiermacher and of Barth.

Beyond this correspondence, Schleiermacher's linking of eternity and omnipotence implies that his understanding of divine eternity is not entirely negative. He surely insists on a clear distinction between time and eternity. But he is also concerned that eternity not be merely an "inactive attribute." Eternity, for Schleiermacher, is to be understood in connection with the way in which God acts, God's ever-present causality. So it would seem, by implication, that even

---

173. *Chr. F.*, 203–4.
174. For the terms *actualism* and *particularism*, and the light they shed on Barth work, I am of course indebted to George Hunsinger's *How to Read Karl Barth: The Shape of His Theology* (New York: Oxford University Press, 1991), particularly 30–33.

though time and eternity are radically different, Schleiermacher's view of eternity suggests the idea that eternity is not alien to time, but rather is present to and yet undetermined by time. As we discussed above, such seems to be the view of Anselm. Again, it would probably be deemed by Barth as acceptable, insofar as it goes. At the very least, however, we may say that Barth might agree with Schleiermacher's view as a necessary first step, yet one that, again, may be insufficient.

Hegel

The next figure that we will consider is Georg Wilhelm Friedrich Hegel (1770–1831). Here, the influence on Barth is not as clear as it was in the case of our other figures. Yet there are important aspects of Hegel's reflections on eternity that are either picked up or negated in Barth's work. Thus in this section, I do not argue that Hegel's opinions had any direct influence Barth's thoughts on time and eternity.[175] Rather, I intend to trace some common themes, and to indicate some limited areas of agreement and difference.

A "Hegeling" Barth?

It would help my presentation, however, if I address briefly Barth's appropriation of Hegel. In his article "Barth und Hegel," Michael Welker addresses the confusion generated by two comments Barth made at different times about his own relationship to Hegel. The first, in 1953, is characteristic of Barth's stress on the freedom of the Christian, but gives the impression of a fairly close and positive relationship to the philosopher:

---

175. For such a discussion, I refer the reader to Michael Welker, "Barth und Hegel: Zur Erkenntnis eines methodischen Verfahrens bei Barth," *Evangelische Theologie* 43 (1983): 307–28.

As Christians we must have the freedom to let the most varied ways of thinking run through our heads. For example, I can entertain elements of Marxism without becoming a Marxist. . . . I myself have a certain weakness for Hegel and am always fond of doing a bit of "Hegeling." As Christians we have the freedom to do this. . . . I do it eclectically.[176]

The second comment Barth made about Hegel is quite different. In a 1964 letter to someone who criticized how he portrayed Hegel in *Protestant Theology in the Nineteenth Century* (1932), Barth said,

Hegel has not claimed much of my time since I wrote about him in 1932. I read somewhere that like a blind hen I found the right corn in him and this amused me. But if I now have to read that I didn't understand him, I must put up with this too. . . . I believe more than ever that as a theologian one should know philosophy but should not in any sense become or be a philosopher.[177]

Welker believes that the latter quote is actually truer to the facts. The *Kirchliche Dogmatik* is full of references to Hegel, and even quotes, but one finds no direct engagement with Hegel's texts. Barth did engage Hegel substantively only once, in 1929, as he was preparing his lectures on nineteenth-century theology.[178] However, "one can cite real affinities between Barth's procedure as he described it and Hegel's method, affinities on which the secondary literature and Barth's self-description can at least intuitively fall back."[179]

---

176. Conversation with pastors and lay people from the Pfalz, September 1953. Cited in Eberhard Busch, *Karl Barth: His Life from Letters and Autobiographical Texts*, trans. John Bowden (London: SCM Press, 1976), 387; also Welker, "Barth und Hegel," 307.
177. Barth, *Letters, 1961–1968*, ed. Jüurgen Fangmeier and Hinrich Stoevesandt, trans. Geoffrey W. Bromiley (Grand Rapids: Eerdmans, 1981), 149. Cited by Welker, "Barth und Hegel," 308.
178. Welker, "Barth und Hegel," 309.
179. "Sich tatsächlich Verwandtschaften zwischen Barths dargestelltem Vorgehen und Hegels Verfahren angeben lassen, auf die die Sekundärliteratur und Barths Selbstdarstellung zumindest intuitiv zurückgreifen konnten." Ibid., 324.

Salient Features of Hegel's Understanding of Space, Time, and Eternity

In the rest of this section, I will merely highlight some themes found in Hegel that have some bearing on Barth's own understanding of divine eternity. My concern with Hegel is much the same as with all the other figures in this chapter: to understand his contribution to the concept of eternity, so that we may deepen this context in which we understand Barth's particular contribution.

Hegel's reflections on eternity are found alongside his reflections on time and space, in his lectures on the philosophy of nature. Here he suggests that space and time are not absolutely distinguished, but rather are bound up with each other, and together form a complex we call *space-time*. That these two are so connected means that our experience of time is not merely subjective, but also a feature of spatial reality: "The truth of space is time, so that space becomes time; our transition to time is not subjective, space itself makes the transition. Space and time are generally taken to be poles apart: space is there, and then we *also* have time. Philosophy calls this 'also' into question."[180]

Furthermore, Hegel understands time to be what makes change possible.

> It is said that everything *arises* and *passes away* in time, and that if one abstracts from *everything*, that is to say from the content of time and space, then empty time and empty space will be left, i.e. time and space are posited as abstractions of externality, and represented as if they were for themselves. But everything does not appear and pass in time; time itself is this *becoming*, arising, and passing away, it is the *abstraction* which has being, the *Cronos* which engenders all and destroys that to which it gave birth.[181]

---

180. *Hegel's Philosophy of Nature*; ed. and trans. M. J. Petry, vol. 1 (New York: Humanities Press, 1970), 229.
181. Ibid.

In other words, Hegel understands time to be an attribute of existence, that which characterizes finite, changing beings. Time is not something completely separable from the temporal beings that are determined by time. "Time does not resemble a container in which everything is as it were borne away and swallowed up in the flow of a stream. Time is merely this abstraction of destroying. Things are in time because they are finite; they do not pass away because they are in time, but are themselves that which is temporal. Temporality is their objective determination."[182] Thus finitude and change are precisely what it means to be temporal, and "time" is a conceptual abstraction from these characteristics. Temporality is the mode in which temporal beings exist.

It is on this basis that Hegel points out the ambiguous status that time has for the temporal being, a point we have seen in Augustine.[183] Temporality "is therefore the process of actual things which constitutes time, and if it can be said that time is omnipotent, it must be added that it is completely impotent. The present makes a tremendous demand, yet as the individual present it is nothing, for even as I pronounce it, its all-excluding pretentiousness dwindles, dissolves, and falls into dust."[184] Yet immediately he departs from this quasi-Augustinian point: "It is the universality of these present moments which *lasts*, and the sublatedness of this process of things which does not."[185] With such a departure, Hegel suggests the connection between eternity and time, a connection that is found in the very concepts that constitute reality and which is philosophy's job to make clear. Eternity is not to be found in the present, which is evanescent, but in the abidingness of all of them taken as a whole,

---

182. Ibid., 231.
183. However, judging from the context, Hegel probably was recalling Parmenides and Plato rather than Augustine.
184. *Philosophy of Nature*, 231.
185. *Philosophy of Nature*, 231.

in their "universality," abstracted from their individuality.[186] Eternity is not merely the negative "abstraction of time, and as if it existed outside time"; nor is it to be understood as "coming after time, for by placing eternity in the future, one turns it into a moment of time."[187] Nor is eternity the same as everlastingness or sempiternity, which stress limitless durationality. "Absolute timelessness is *eternity*, which is devoid of natural time, and is therefore to be distinguished from duration."

Eternity, for Hegel, is what time is only fleetingly: "In its Notion [*Begriff*], time itself is eternal however, for its Notion is neither the present nor any other time, but time as such. Its Notion is, like all Notion, eternal, and thus also constitutes the absolute present." Time and eternity are distinguished, however, by the absence of passingness in eternity. "Eternity will not be, nor has it been, it is. Duration is therefore to be distinguished from eternity, in that it is merely a relative sublation of time; eternity is however infinite, that is to say, not relative, but intro-reflected duration."[188]

Although it may not be immediately apparent, such statements do have a bearing on Karl Barth's understanding of eternity. As we have had occasion to note several times in this chapter, Barth insists that the theological concept of God's eternity is not merely the negation of the concept of time, even though God's eternity is not itself time in our normal sense of the word. That is somewhat similar to Hegel's assertions that eternity is to be distinguished from time, although it is not merely the negative abstraction of time.

Yet for Hegel, eternity is linked with the Notion, with the Idea, with spirit. It is a principle of reality, and one that human beings may grasp unaided by revelation, simply by reflecting on reality with

---

186. This passage thus also attempts to makes sense both of our experience of time's passage and of our experience of time's abiding nature.
187. *Philosophy of Nature*, 231.
188. Ibid., 231–32.

clarity and self-discipline. Thus it is clear that, in the end, Hegel and Barth are not really talking about the same thing at all. For Barth understands eternity to be a perfection of God's being and not a principle of reality. Furthermore, Barth insists that eternity is not perceivable by the unaided human intellect.

Summary

In this chapter, I have attempted to undertake three tasks. First, I have sought to describe the understandings of eternity, and occasionally, of time, held by several figures. More than any others, these theologians and philosophers, I believe, influenced Karl Barth's own understanding of eternity. I have taken considerable care in describing each position in context, so that the import and strength of them might become clear. Together, most of these figures constitute a "tradition" of reflection on time and eternity. Moreover, this "tradition" is frequently derided in contemporary theological and philosophical reflection on the nature of eternity and time. My approach has implied a challenge to such derision. The concepts and arguments we see in these figures, in their similarities and in their differences, provide a necessary background for any adequate theological account of God's relationship to time. Their suggestions should be taken seriously, as it is unwise rashly to dismiss them.

Second, I have tried to describe these figures in such a way that some initial comparisons might be made, even at this early stage, between their views and Barth's own. In particular, I have attempted to highlight, not only differences, but also significant areas of agreement between Barth and his forebears. Such areas are important, for they suggest that Barth held a greater appreciation for this traditional reflection on eternity than readers typically recognize. I have attempted to set Barth's criticisms in context, thereby clarifying the nature of the disagreement, and likewise leaving open the possibility of significant agreement. A disturbing implication of some of these comparisons is that Barth seems to misunderstand those whom he criticized and overlook points of agreement that could help advance his primary theological concern. Certainly, such examples are not rare in theology or any other discipline. Regardless, in suggesting these comparisons I hope to have anticipated certain aspects of Barth's thought that will become clearer in the later chapters. For the most part, however, I believe that I have laid the necessary groundwork for later discussions in these pages.

Third, I have sought to develop with the reader a shared vocabulary and set of concepts that will continue to prove essential throughout this work. In the figures examined, we have encountered several terms and themes, many of them recurring. Successful advancement of my argument depends, in part, on my having developed at this stage some description of the meaning and significance of certain ideas. After all, because Barth was not only a critic of that tradition but also a part of it, Barth's own understanding of eternity makes use of many of the terms and concepts we have seen in this chapter.

3

Aside

Reflections on Eternity after Barth

As I argued in the previous chapter, our ability to understand Barth appreciatively and constructively is enhanced by considering the so-called classic figures that influenced him. Barth's theological reflections on time and eternity clearly show deep interaction with concepts and positions from the tradition. Attention to those aspects with which Barth was in conversation will benefit one's understanding of Barth's own position.

Such benefit may be compounded by considering as well more recent theological and philosophical reflections on time and eternity. Some of these recent approaches can help us see easily overlooked aspects of Barth's thought, while others might give us a new way of discerning and articulating Barth's intention. For that reason, in this section I will extend the conceptual survey to figures that have come on the scene since Barth. In justification of this, I suggest that the conceptual context in which we understand Barth includes not only those figures that probably influenced Barth but also any who enhance our understanding of Barth's work and its implications, including those who came after. Furthermore, those recent figures may provide other ways of expressing God's relationship to time that, although perhaps not open to Barth, would nonetheless fit with his fundamental orientation.

Orientation

As I said in the introduction, the idea of God's eternity has been much discussed in recent years. That discussion has revolved around the question of whether it does, in fact, make sense to speak of God's eternity as timelessness, or whether it is better to say that God exists everlastingly through time. Indeed, for the last several decades the "majority opinion" has been that the traditional definition of eternity does not make sense, and that God's eternity is either better defined as perdurance in and through time, what Boëthius and other classical authors called *sempiternity*,[1] or discarded as a concept altogether. There are several examples of this latter position. I take Robert Jenson to be one, because of how unhelpful and misleading he believes the concept of *eternity* to have been to Christian theology.[2] A very different exemplar would be Charles Hartshorne, whose restriction of eternality to an abstract pole of God's nature (as opposed to God's "concrescence")[3] can be viewed as a way of so limiting and

---

1. I would count the following as examples: Martha Kneale, "Eternity and Sempiternity," *Proceedings of the Aristotelian Society* 69 (1969): 223–38; Nelson Pike, *God and Evil: Readings on the Theological Problem of Evil* (Englewood Cliffs, NJ: Prentice-Hall, 1964); Alan G. Padgett, *God, Eternity, and the Nature of Time* (New York: St. Martin's Press, 1992).
2. Robert W. Jenson, *Unbaptized God: The Basic Flaw in Ecumenical Theology* (Minneapolis: Fortress Press, 1992), particularly chaps. 8 and 10; Jenson, "Does God Have Time? The Doctrine of the Trinity and the Concept of Time in the Physical Sciences," *CTNS Bulletin* 11 (1991): 1–6.
3. Hartshorne and Reese, *Philosophers Speak of God* (Chicago: University of Chicago Press, 1953), 15.

redefining the concept of eternity as to amount to discarding the traditional concept entirely.

A few philosophers, however, have taken a second look at the traditional doctrine of eternity. They argue that the traditional doctrine is not fatally flawed or incoherent, as its detractors allege. Moreover, they argue that any problems it does have are best handled by correcting and building on the tradition, rather than by rejecting it. Eleonore Stump and Norman Kretzmann were among the first to take that second look. In their important 1981 article, they argued that the classical doctrine has been badly misunderstood or misrepresented by its critics.

> Eternality—the condition of having eternity as one's mode of existence—is misunderstood most often in either of two ways. Sometimes it is confused with limitless duration in time—sempiternality—and sometimes it is construed simply as atemporality, eternity being understood in that case as roughly analogous to an isolated, static instant.[4]

The contribution of Stump and Kretzmann, as well as some others, has been to show how "the picture of eternity as a frozen instant is a radical distortion of the classic concept." Along with Brian Leftow in particular,[5] they have offered a correction of this distortion and demonstrated some of the philosophical and theological ramifications of a corrected understanding of timeless eternity. I find these contributions to be compelling. Furthermore, they shed light on the traditional doctrine of eternity as well as on Barth's own position.

We have, then, a debate between those who, on the one hand, would defend or build on the classical understanding of God's eternity, and, on the other hand, those who in different ways reject, or modify to the point of rejection, this classical understanding.

---

4. Eleonore Stump and Norman Kretzmann, "Eternity," *Journal of Philosophy* 78 (1981): 430.
5. Leftow, *Time and Eternity* (Ithaca, NY: Cornell University Press, 1991).

I take the modern debate to be important for this study. In the subsequent pages I will attempt to describe in greater detail the various positions, with an eye toward advancing my argument about how best to interpret Barth and how we ought to think theologically about eternity.

Exposition

In describing the contemporary discussion, I believe it is helpful at the outset to consider what we should call these positions. Too often, they are described in ways that introduce confusion into the discussion, though this is understandable, as the topic is very complicated and subject to misunderstanding. Still, it would be good to consider the terms we use with regard to their appropriateness and utility. A more serious problem arises when the terms chosen to describe the question appear to be selected for rhetorical flourish, and serve to cast aspersions upon one side of the issue.

That is certainly the case with a common approach, which describes the positions as answers to the question, "Is God within or outside of time?" I find such a question, as well as the understanding presupposed in the question, inadequate for several reasons. To name only one, it uses spatial images and metaphors for understanding the relationship between time and eternity, and uses them in a careless fashion, heedless of the problems inherent in those metaphors or the category mistakes their use often occasions. As Stump and Kretzmann put it, "Spatial metaphors for eternity or time are troublesome even when they are helpful."[6]

Indeed, it is quite common to use comparative phrases that construe the relationship between God and time as if the relationship

---

6. Eleonore Stump and Norman Kretzmann, "Atemporal Duration: A Reply to Fitzgerald," *Journal of Philosophy* 84 (1987): 219.

was a spatial one. For example, the question, "Is God within or outside of time?" uses spatial imagery, and the use is so subtle that one may easily overlook it. The problem with the use of spatial imagery in describing the God/time relationship is that it often leads to ambiguities, confusions, and false comparisons. Arguments that speak of God "in," "within," or "outside of" time too easily have led to assertions that betray an ignorance of the significantly analogical use of these spatial terms. For example, Robert Jenson insists that "Catholics and Protestants alike think of time as outside God, a supposition that is plainly false. Time does not occur outside personal reality, so that if time is outside God then he is not its creator. Since the gospel affirms a Creator, we ought to know what person it is in whom time is located."[7]

In a sense, I agree with part of what Jenson says. It *is* "plainly false" that time is "outside God," but not for the reasons Jenson seems to have. It is false because time is not a spatial object that is spatially located within or outside of beings. However, the multiple spatial metaphors occurring in the above brief quote (Does "outside" mean "distinct from," or" apart from"? Does "in" imply possession, or identity, or actual "physical" location?) drive toward ambiguity rather than clarity.

Much more helpful is George Hunsinger's approach. He explains the difference between the two primary options as one that corresponds to two different ways of understanding what constitutes "the present." Typically the two choices have been understanding the present either as that which *is*, the elemental point that is "now," or as that which *persists*, the flowing of moments from one to the next.[8] Taking these ideas about the present as a conceptual basis for

---

7. Jenson, *Unbaptized God*, 118.
8. Hunsinger, "*Mysterium Trinitatis*: Karl Barth's Conception of Eternity," in *Disruptive Grace: Studies in the Theology of Karl Barth* (Grand Rapids: Eerdmans, 2000), 186–87.

thinking about eternity, one typically would adopt an understanding of eternity that corresponds to one of those views of the present. "One view [of eternity] resembles the abiding present of the unitary consciousness (*nunc stans*), while the other aligns itself with the flowing present of successive instants (*nunc fluens*). Until modern times, the former view has been most familiar in Christian theology."[9] The second view has come into its own in the modern era, particularly through theologians influenced by Hegel and then, alternatively, by Whitehead, a view Hunsinger calls the "processional."[10]

Hunsinger's way of describing the differences between the major schools of thought on eternity is quite helpful. Yet in my view it does have some limits, mainly in its apparent dependence on spatial metaphors (e.g., point, line, sphere) for understanding the relationship between time and eternity, which, as I have said, tend to be problematic. I would also like to have matters described so it was clearer that the eternity of which we speak is not a "thing" other than God but is itself an aspect of the being of God. Moreover, this way of describing the two main positions seems to allude to the argument over tensed and tenseless theories of time, and seems to suggest that an atemporal (*nunc stans*) understanding of eternity is dependent on a tenseless theory of time. As we will discuss later in this chapter, although some theories of divine timeless eternality may depend on a tenseless theory of time, not all do.

How then shall we describe the two typical approaches or schools in the debate? I prefer to speak of the "temporalist" and the "atemporalist" approaches. At the risk of being overly simplistic, let me suggest that the difference may be describes like so: the temporalist position holds that God is in some important respect

---

9. Ibid., 187.
10. Ibid., 188.

temporal, while the atemporalist position affirms that God, unlike us creatures, is not temporal. I make no claim that these terms are perfect; for my purposes here, however, they have significant benefits.

The heart of the benefit is in how instructive or useful the terminology is. I believe that my way of casting the issue, as a choice between temporalist and atemporalist approaches, is instructive for four reasons. First, it eschews spatial imagery. Second, to describe the issue as a debate between temporalist and atemporalist approaches does not prejudice the case against the atemporalist by implicitly associating that position with deism. Such "guilt by association" is likely when one (mistakenly) describes atemporalism as affirming that God exists "outside of" time, which seems to remove God from all interaction with the created order.[11] My third reason for describing the issue in this way has to do with what I wish to affirm about the being of God. To speak of temporalist and atemporalist positions makes it easier to recognize that the question of God's relationship to time is a question about the being of God, that is, about the modality of God's existence. Fourth, the temporalist/atemporalist paradigm is sufficiently broad, for the "temporality" that is affirmed or denied of God remains to be defined. For example, one could define temporality as a static concept that would apply the same to every being that possessed it, whether divine or creaturely. Or one might define temporality in such a way that it would mean one thing when exemplified by human beings, and a very different thing when exemplified by God. Of course, such multiple meanings must at the very least be acknowledged from the start, and explained, if the theory is not to be merely contradictory.

---

11. I intend to show that an atemporalist concept of God need not entail that God is alienated from time, as Jenson insists.

Such breadth leads to an observation that is fairly obvious. The temporalist and the atemporalist approaches to the question of God and time are by no means monolithic. It is inaccurate to call them "schools." For example, on the temporalist side of the divide, the theological differences between Robert Jenson and Charles Hartshorne are perhaps as great as they could be. Jenson's theological concerns, marked by an insistence on retrieving the core of the Christian theological tradition from pagan philosophical encrustations, are radically different from the philosophically developed natural theology that animates Hartshorne's work.[12] In short, within each approach (the temporalist and the atemporalist) there are a variety of judgments in how best to construe God's relationship to time. There are also different gains and different problems that tend to surface within each of the two broad approaches.

Temporalism

The temporalist approach is a rather recent option within the history of ideas, although one might find some suggestions of the approach in the work of John Duns Scotus.[13] It argues that if God exists, then God exists in time, at every point in time, without ever ceasing to exist. That is the basic position of the temporalist, but the difference is in the details. One of those differences has to do with the modality of time, that is, whether time is necessary or contingent, and in what respects. Most temporalists want to say that time is contingent, not necessary, and thus finite, and that God existed "before" time, and "then" created time. Thus as long as time exists, God is temporal, and

---

12. Hunsinger helpfully places Jenson in the Hegelian stream of modern processionalism. Hunsinger doesn't mention Hartshorne, but surely he is in the Whiteheadian school. Hunsinger, "*Mysterium Trinitatis*," 188.
13. See Leftow, *Time and Eternity*, 228, 230.

thus by implication contingently so. Others, however, in particular Charles Hartshorne, seem to suggest that time is not contingent but necessary, just as God's existence is not contingent but necessary; thus God, as temporal, is necessarily temporal. There has always been time, as there has always been God. Still others (a minority) would argue that God is indeed contingent and not necessary, similar to time. Consequently, God exists in time, at every moment in time, but might cease to exist just as time might cease to exist.

Accompanying the temporalist position are what we may call several core objections to the idea that God is timeless. First of all, there is the suspicion that the doctrine of divine timeless eternality[14] is a Greek import into the Christian doctrinal tradition, and that this pedigree insists on a specious denigration of change. Such an argument seems often to degenerate into what I call a "Harnackian" approach to the problem,[15] so that *any* influence of so-called Greek thought is believed to count as evidence of "pure" Christianity's corruption. One sees this approach in the work of many theologians. Cullmann[16] and Jenson are obvious exemplars. I believe that this argument, about the supposedly corrupting influence of "Greek thought" on "pure Christianity," is unsustainable historically and logically. A direct and complete answer to this argument, however, is beyond the scope of this book.[17] Be that as it may, its problems do

---

14. The term *divine timeless eternality* is suggested and developed by Brian Leftow. In this subsection, I will usually use the term to refer to the basic affirmation that God's eternity is God's atemporal existence, and not to Leftow's (or anyone else's) specific, fully developed explanation of divine timeless eternality. It will be clear when I am developing the term into a position that is more than a placeholder for a generic position rejected or defended by temporalists or atemporalists.
15. I call it this because of Harnack's treatment of much Christian doctrine after the earliest years of Christianity as a corruption by Greek thought patterns. See, e.g., Adolph Harnack, *What Is Christianity?* (Gloucester, MA: Peter Smith, 1978).
16. Oscar Cullmann, *Christ and Time: The Primitive Christian Conception of Time and History* (London: SCM Press, 1962).
17. An excellent treatment of these issues may be found in Paul Helm, *Eternal God: A Study of God without Time* (Oxford: Oxford University Press, 1988), particularly chapter 1.

not invalidate the other, more basic, argument that classical notions of time and eternity in fact denigrate temporal and physical "change"; such an argument must be answered on its own merits.

A second core objection found in temporalist positions is that any doctrine of divine timeless eternality raises serious problems with regard to several key doctrines of Christianity, such as the incarnation, the efficacy of prayer, or the affirmation that God is personal. If an ancillary doctrine, it is argued, stands in contrast with other, more fundamental doctrines, then that ancillary doctrine, in this case divine timeless eternality, should be discarded. Thus Nicholas Wolterstorff claims, "God the Redeemer cannot be a God eternal. This is so because God the Redeemer is a God who changes."[18]

Third, temporalist arguments typically assert that any doctrine of divine timeless eternality threatens the freedom of the will.[19] If everything is present to God, then how can free beings act with a will of their own, one that is not predetermined toward an end specified by God's knowledge of all that is? A future act of any freely acting agent (so the temporalist argues) must be as indeterminate or unknown to God in the present as to any other observer.

A fourth and final core objection in temporalism is that divine timeless eternality denies the reality of time as we experience it, that is, as a process in which beings and events are real at particular times, and not until then; time is a process where past events are no longer

---

18. Wolterstorff, "God Everlasting," in *God and the Good*, ed. Clifton J. Orlebeke and Lewis M. Smedes (Grand Rapids: Eerdmans, 1975), 182, cited in Stump and Kretzmann, "Eternity," 429. Of Wolterstorff's assertion and the article of which it is a part, Stump and Kretzmann say, directly, "we think [Prof. Wolterstorff] is mistaken in his assessment of the logical relationship between the doctrine of divine eternality and other doctrines of orthodox Christianity, including the doctrine of redemption, even in their biblical formulations."
19. This is really a quite common objection, found in much of the temporalist literature we have already cited. See, e.g., Anthony Kenny, "Divine Foreknowledge and Human Freedom," in *Aquinas: A Collection of Critical Essays*, ed. Anthony Kenny (Garden City, NY: Doubleday-Anchor, 1969), 255–70.

and future events are not yet.[20] How can one affirm that, for God, all events that have ever existed and will ever exist are "present," without denying the real coming into and departing from being that these events have?

There are other arguments that one affirming a temporalist position may use, but I take these to be the more common ones, indeed, the ones that constitute the core. From these objections, it becomes apparent that the bulk of the temporalist position may be construed as an argument about the *coherence* of the doctrine of divine timeless eternality. This is to say that the arguments above focus on how well divine timeless eternality coheres with other doctrines, ideas, or features of life that are significant to hold and that surely count as more important than divine timeless eternality.

By raising the question of coherence, the advocate of the temporalist position thus makes an affirmative contribution: she or he ask about the connections between the doctrine of divine timeless eternality and other religious doctrines, such as prayer or the personal nature of God, and also general doctrines, such as free will. The temporalist position also appears to be able to make more sense of the doctrine of the incarnation, for, it seems, in becoming incarnate, God has taken on something new, and presumably this makes a difference not only to us but also to God.[21]

In short, arguments about coherence are a major feature of the temporalist position, and have been a driving force for its development.

---

20. This would be characteristic of Charles Hartshorne's position, as well as that of Alan Padgett.
21. I would question, however, whether this reflects a mistaken understanding of the incarnation. Exploring that question would take us far afield. However, no doubt it would lead us into a discussion of Barth's Christology and his use of the anhypostasis/enhypostasis doctrine.

Modality and Temporality

These advantages come at a price, however. For by arguing that God is temporal, the proponent of the temporalist position introduces new problems. One such problem concerns the nature of God. Until recent times, much of the Christian theological tradition has affirmed the doctrine of divine simplicity, that is, that God's being is "simple," whose "attributes" are not "parts" of a composite or compound divine nature but are expressions of that single, simple nature.[22] The temporalist position, as it is typically expressed by most of its recent advocates, appears incompatible with the doctrine of divine simplicity. If God is temporal, then God has temporal parts, such as past, present, and future, or earlier and later. Granted, most temporalists are willing to live with a weakened or discarded doctrine of divine simplicity. Yet I am troubled that many who discard it seem to do so implicitly, without recognizing what they are doing.

A second problem involves a type of logical inconsistency. Here, we are driven to a consideration of the *modality* of temporality and of timelessness, that is, whether these are necessary or contingent. In short, the relevant question is, does it make sense to assert that a being may be timeless, then, at the first moment of time, become temporal? Can a being really be only contingently temporal? Can the mode of existence we call "temporality" be transitive?

In support of this, I offer a two-step argument. The first step is to suggest that eternality and temporality are "modes of existence." Some authors seem to ignore the very idea of temporal modality, while others appear to reject it. Both assume that temporality is

---

22. Although a product of the Reformed tradition in the Low Countries and not a philosophical document, the Belgic Confession expresses this doctrine admirably: "We all believe in our hearts and confess with our mouths that there is a single and simple spiritual being, whom we call God—eternal, incomprehensible, invisible, unchangeable, infinite, almighty; completely wise, just, and good, and the overflowing source of all good" (article 1).

the only mode of existence that real existing beings (as opposed to numbers and concepts) may possess. At this point, let's simply mention one conclusion Stump and Kretzmann draw from Boëthius's understanding of eternity: that the classical concept of eternity proposes "two separate modes of real existence. Eternity is a mode of existence that is, on Boëthius's view, neither reducible to time nor incompatible with the reality of time."[23]

The next step is to inquire into the modal status of this mode of existence we call temporality, that is, to ask whether it is necessary or contingent. We must note here that to ask whether *temporality* is necessary or contingent is not to ask whether *time itself* is necessary or contingent. The question of the modal status of temporality is also to be distinguished from the question of whether *temporal events* are necessary or contingent. These are all different, albeit related, questions of modality.

To spell this out in clearer detail, let us consider the different meanings possible for the affirmation *Time is contingent* (or, *It is possible for time not to exist*) (*1*). Here "time" may have different possible meanings, signifying either "the dimension of time" or "an event in time." The first possible meaning (which we'll designate as *1a*) is "the 'dimension' of time exists (even as a fundamental and determinative feature of temporal existence) but could possibly cease to exist." The second possible meaning of *Time is contingent* is (*1b*) "for any event that exists temporally, it might possibly not exist, and need not have existed." The negation of each of these (implied by the affirmation *Time is necessary*, or, *It is not possible for time not to exist*) would be (~ *1a*) "the 'dimension' of time exists and must always exist" and (~ *1b*) "for any event that exists temporally, it must necessarily exist, and could not possibly have not existed."[24]

---

23. Stump and Kretzmann, "Eternity," 434.

Yet both of these understandings of the affirmation *Time is contingent* (*1a* and *1b*) are to be distinguished from another affirmation, one that takes *temporality*, rather than time, as the subject. This yields (*2*): "Temporality, as a mode of existence, is contingent for beings that exist in that mode."[25] This distinction is important because temporality is a characteristic of a being, rather than the being itself, and thus the modality of a being possessing or not possessing that characteristic cannot be expressed the same way as *1a* or *1b*. Consequently, affirmation *2* would hold that temporal beings could possibly be not temporal; that is, they could exist as something other than temporal, namely, atemporal.[26]

So we now have three different affirmations regarding modality and time: *1a*: time as a dimension of reality might possibly not exist; *1b*: a temporal event might possibly not exist; and *2*: a being that exists temporally might possibly continue to exist but not temporally. I suggest that some temporalists seem to conflate these three possibilities. Some confuse the contingency of temporal events with the question of the contingency or necessity of the dimension of time itself, namely, of *1a* with *1b*. Others confuse the contingency of either of these, *1a* or *1b*, with *2*, the question of the modality of temporality.

An example of this latter confusion might be found in Alan Padgett's work. He argues for an understanding of God's relation to time that sees God as "relatively timeless," as opposed to "absolutely timeless" or "temporal." A doctrine of relative timelessness would hold God to exist in time, but not in any specific system of "Measured

---

24. Put this way, it is clear that the first form of "time is necessary" is worth consideration (indeed, it appears to be affirmed by several contemporary philosophers and cosmologists), while the second is absurd.
25. Its negation would be "temporality, as a mode of existence, is necessary for those that exist in that mode."
26. Its negation instead would insist that temporal beings may exist temporally, and only temporally, as long as they exist at all, and that atemporal beings are necessarily atemporal, and may not become temporal.

Time." "In this case, something will be 'timeless' if it does not exist within any Measured Time."[27] In short, he seems to take both the dimension of time and temporal events as contingent.[28] Yet he insists that God may be atemporal "before" time exists and temporal "during" time. He thus, in effect, understands temporality (a mode of being) also to be contingent.

The problem lies in the modality of the modes of existence. Does it make sense to say that a temporal entity may possibly be atemporal? Is affirmation 2 above logically sustainable? Temporality is the experience of existing temporally, that is, of having one's existence as a series of temporally ordered events. As Ian Crombie puts it, "A temporally enduring substance is . . . one whose existence consists of phases any one of which necessarily has some temporal relation with any other; the one phase must be wholly earlier than, wholly later than, wholly contemporary with, or partially overlapping the other."[29] It would seem, then, that assertions that a being could be contingently temporal, that is, it could possibly be not temporal, do not logically hold.

Recall that the being whose possible temporal contingency is proposed is God. And it is concerning God that the logical inconsistency of contingent temporality really starts to show its flaws. Recall what Crombie said about "a temporally enduring substance." It must have its existence in successive phases. Consequently, such a succession of phases "must hold of God's existence, if this is temporal."[30] That is, if God is temporal, then there must be phases in God's life that are earlier than other phases in God's life and later than others. With finite creatures, one temporal phase grows out of earlier

---

27. Padgett, *God, Eternity, and the Nature of Time*, 19.
28. Affirming *1a* and *1b*.
29. Ian M. Crombie, "Eternity and Omnitemporality," in *The Rationality of Religious Belief*, ed. William J. Abraham and S. W. Holtzer (Oxford: Oxford University Press, 1987), 181.
30. Ibid.

ones.[31] In short, to be temporal is to have part of one's life earlier than another part. Following Leftow, we may say that, similarly, to be atemporal is to have *all* of one's life *as a whole*, and not in parts. How could these two modes of existence, temporality and atemporality, possibly be combined? Leftow puts the matter as follows:

> Nothing can be contingently temporal. So if God is temporal, God is necessarily temporal. If God is necessarily temporal, time is an absolutely necessary precondition of God's own existence. Thus if God exists necessarily . . . , so does time, for [God] cannot exist unless it does. But time exists contingently. Hence either God exists contingently or God is timeless. Hence again, as God exists necessarily, God is timeless.[32]

Padgett seems to affirm not only the contingency of time and of temporal events, but also the contingency of temporality. That is the clear implication of Padgett's position, even though he does not explicitly consider the modality of a being's temporality. However, as we have seen, it is difficult to see what sense can be made of the implication that temporality is a contingent mode of being.

From Padgett we may distinguish Charles Hartshorne, who appears to understand the dimension of time to be necessary (~ *1a*), and likewise takes temporality to be a necessary mode of existence for temporal beings. Yet it may be that Hartshorne also does not adequately distinguish the modal status of time from the modal status of temporality: they are so linked together, for him, that all beings, including God (or rather, as we shall see, *especially* God), must be temporal. For Hartshorne, in order for anything at all to exist concretely, it must exist temporally. And so time becomes a necessary precondition of all existence, including God's. Furthermore, Hartshorne seems to hold that existence of some sort is necessary, entailing that something must exist, and that absolute nonexistence

---

31. Ibid.
32. Leftow, *Time and Eternity*, 273.

is impossible. This would then entail that time is necessary, even as existence is necessary.

In fact, Hartshorne likewise affirms the necessity of God's existence. This is clear from his several writings on the ontological argument.[33] Yet it is important to make clear that Hartshorne did not affirm a classical understanding of the nature of God, and thus of God's necessity. Rather, he promoted a *dipolar* understanding of God's being, according to which that being was to be conceived as having two poles: the abstract and the concrete.[34] It was the former pole, God's abstract nature, that Hartshorne asserted is necessary, while God's "concrescence" is to be understood as supremely contingent, which, for Hartshorne, allows God to be supremely relational.

With regard to the modality of time and of temporality, then, Hartshorne affirms the contingency of temporal events (*1b*) but sees time itself as necessary (~ *1a*). He understands time as necessary only with regard to God's abstract nature, but as contingent with regard to God's concrete nature. It is only in relation to this dipolar understanding of the divine nature that talk about temporality and atemporality would make sense from a Hartshornian perspective. In short, atemporality would refer to God's abstract, absolute nature only, while temporality would characterize God's concrete, relative

---

33. Among them see Charles Hartshorne, "The Formal Validity and the Real Significance of the Ontological Argument," in *The Philosophical Review*, vol. 53, 3 (1944): 225–45; "The Logic of the Ontological Argument," *Journal of Philosophy* 58, no. 17 (1961): 471–73; "What Did Anselm Discover?" *Union Seminary Quarterly Review* 17, no. 3 (1962): 213–22; "Ten Ontological or Modal Proofs for God's Existence," in *The Logic of Perfection and Other Essays in Neoclassical Metaphysics* (LaSalle, IL: Open Court, 1962), 28–117; "Introduction," in *Saint Anselm: Basic Writings—Proslogium, Monologium, Gaunilon's On Behalf of the Fool, Cur Deus Homo*, 2nd ed. (LaSalle, IL: Open Court, 1962), 1–19; "Rationale of the Ontological Proof," *Theology Today* 20, no. 2 (1963): 278–83; *Anselm's Discovery: A Re-Examination of the Ontological Proof for God's Existence* (LaSalle, IL: Open Court, 1965); "Kant's Refutation Still Not Convincing: A Reply," *Monist* 52, no. 2 (1968): 312–16; and "John Hick on Logical and Ontological Necessity," *Religious Studies* 13, no. 2 (1977): 155–65.
34. See, e.g., Hartshorne and Reese, *Philosophers Speak of God*, 1–15.

nature. However, because time (both as necessary dimension and as contingent discrete events) likewise seems to be understood both as dipolar and as determinative of all concretely existing things (including God), then it is reasonable to wonder whether, for Hartshorne, there is finally any real philosophical difference between God and time.

Atemporalism

As I suggested earlier, some philosophers have taken a new look at the traditional concept of God's eternity, believing that it has been misunderstood and that its faults are correctable. The primary examples of this approach are Eleonore Stump and Norman Kretzmann in their collaborative work, and Brian Leftow. We've seen some features of this approach earlier, but here we present their positions in greater detail. There are differences between them, as we shall see. At this stage, let me note some basic commonalities between them. Both Stump/Kretzmann and Leftow affirm the following about divine timeless eternity:

1. That God's existence is more accurately conceived of as timeless rather than as temporal.
2. That God's timelessness, however, is to be understood in Boëthian fashion, as entailing life, and not in Platonic fashion, implying a frozen instant. Thus divine timeless eternality does not imperil the deeply held religious conviction that God is a living being, but may, paradoxically, enhance that conviction.
3. That eternality is better thought of as a mode of existence, rather than as a being's location *in* or *out* of time.
4. That spatial metaphors for speaking of time and God's relationship to time are precisely that, metaphors, and should be recognized and treated as such;

We will consider each of these contributions to the discussion in turn. My task will not be to give a full description of their positions, but rather to sketch the main points of their arguments insofar as those are important for understanding the possibility of a modern philosophical retrieval of the traditional concept of eternity as God's nontemporal existence.

It may have been Stump and Kretzmann's two articles in the *Journal of Philosophy*, "Eternity"[35] and "Atemporal Duration,"[36] that first gave coherent objection to the broad temporalist position that had, by then, become the norm in both philosophical and doctrinal theology. Their approach was to offer an interpretation of Boëthius's definition of eternity, and to use a feature of relativity theory for resolving some of the apparent incoherence in Boëthius's doctrine of eternity.

We have already considered Boëthius's definition in some detail, and in that exploration Stump and Kretzmann's work was very helpful. By way of reminder, Boëthius defined eternity as "the whole, simultaneous and perfect possession of boundless life." Stump and Kretzmann interpret this definition as proposing that time and eternity are "two modes of real existence." That latter mode, eternity, is distinct in that it "is a mode of existence that is . . . neither reducible to time nor incompatible with the reality of time."[37]

They acknowledge that Boëthius's definition is open to a charge of incoherence, because of its combination of the concept of *atemporality* with that of *duration* and *life*. They intend to resolve that incoherence by explicating the concepts of *the present* and *simultaneity*. After all, any life has presentness and simultaneity. But, they insist, the classical understanding of eternity recognizes two forms of the present, not

---

35. Stump and Kretzmann, "Eternity."
36. Stump and Kretzmann, "Atemporal Duration."
37. Stump and Kretzmann, "Eternity," 434.

just one: the *temporal present* and the *eternal present*. "The temporal present is a durationless instant, a present that cannot be extended conceptually without falling apart entirely into past and future intervals. The eternal present, on the other hand, is by definition an infinitely extended, pastless, futureless duration."[38]

Given that distinction between types of the present, Stump and Kretzmann propose a distinction between two kinds of simultaneity: *T-simultaneity* (two or more events occurring at one and the same temporal present) and *E-simultaneity* (two or more events occurring at one and the same *eternal* present). Their next step is to combine the two, so that coherent sense can be made of an affirmation that distinct, nonsimultaneous temporal events can nonetheless be present to God in God's one eternal present. "What we want now is a species of simultaneity—call it *ET-simultaneity* . . . —that can obtain between what is eternal and what is temporal."[39]

The problem is that there is no one mode of existence for which, if we were to refer to it, we could fill in the blank in the phrase *Existence or occurrence at one and the same [x]*. To overcome this obstacle, Stump and Kretzmann draw on relativity theory for conceptual assistance, which suggests that even temporal simultaneity is not as simple as it at first appears. "Events occurring at different places which are simultaneous in one frame of reference will not be simultaneous in another frame of reference which is moving with respect to the first. This is known as *the relativity of simultaneity*."[40]

Temporal simultaneity, then, must be understood in a relativistic manner: "RT-simultaneity = existence or occurrence at the same time

---

38. Ibid., 435. Similarly, George Hunsinger says about this view of eternity that it holds that "God's eternal now is in one sense more like a mathematical point than a straight line, since it cannot be divided into parts; yet it also seems analogous to a circle or a sphere, since it encompasses all temporal moments simultaneously within itself." Hunsinger, "*Mysterium Trinitatis*," 187.
39. Stump and Kretzmann, "Eternity," 436.
40. Ibid., 437.

within the reference frame of a given observer."[41] When two events are said to be simultaneous in time, then the time frame in which those events are observed must be specified. The events "occur at the same time in the reference frame of one observer and do not occur at the same time in the reference frame of a different observer."[42] It is for this reason that questions about whether two events "are *really* simultaneous" truly are "incoherent." "The question is asked about what is assumed to be a feature of reality, although in fact there is no such feature of reality; such a question is on a par with 'Is Uris Library *really* to the left of Morrill Hall?' There is no absolute state of being temporally simultaneous with, any more than there is an absolute state of being to the left of."[43]

If T-simultaneity is not as simple as commonly defined, and RT-simultaneity is fairly complex, ET-simultaneity is then likewise difficult to define. An adequate definition must take into account two reference frames, and two observers whose modes of existence are not reducible to that belonging to the other. Stump and Kretzmann, then, offer this as their definition of ET-simultaneity:

(*ET*) For every x and for every y, x and y are ET-simultaneous iff

(i) either x is eternal and y is temporal, or vice versa; and (ii) for some observer, A, in the unique eternal reference frame, x and y are both present—i.e., either x is eternally present and y is observed as temporally present, or vice versa; and (iii) for some observer, B, in one of the infinitely many temporal reference frames, x and y are both present—i.e., either x is observed as eternally present and y is temporally present, or vice versa.[44]

---

41. Ibid., 438.
42. Ibid.
43. Ibid.
44. Ibid., 439. Note that in logic, *iff* is shorthand for "if and only if."

It might be helpful for me to give this a less formal expression. For this prosaic articulation of ET-simultaneity, we start with the affirmation that God is eternal and the unremarkable and obvious assertion that I am temporal. In order for God and me to be ET-simultaneous, two other things must be true. First, from God's point of view, God would be eternally present and God would see me as being temporally present. Second, from my point of view, I would observe God as eternally present and myself as temporally present. We each see the other as "present," but in different respects, from different perspectives and time frames.

The importance of this definition is that two events that are ET-simultaneous retain their integrity as respectively eternal and temporal events. The events are not simply simultaneous with each other. They are *ET*-simultaneous; that is, they are simultaneous within the distinct reference frames of eternal and temporal beings. "On our definition, if x and y are ET-simultaneous, then x is neither earlier nor later than, neither past nor future with respect to, y . . . . Further, if x and y are ET-simultaneous, x and y are not temporally simultaneous; since either x or y must be eternal, it cannot be the case that x and y both exist *at one and the same time* within a given observer's reference frame."[45]

Their definition, and, more importantly the concept of eternity that lies behind it and which it supports, has this significant implication: "There is one objective reality that contains two modes of real existence in which two different sorts of duration are measured by two irreducibly different sorts of measure: time and eternity."[46] Eternity, as that frame of reference, is characterized by a kind of duration that is not given to the imperfections of "normal" duration. "Genuine duration is fully realized duration. . . . Atemporal duration

---

45. Ibid.
46. Ibid., 443.

is duration none of which is not—none of which is absent (and hence future) or flowed away (and hence past). Eternity, not time, is the mode of existence that admits of fully realized duration."[47]

This concludes our survey of Stump and Kretzmann. Another recent proponent of a revamped philosophical defense of the God's timeless eternality is Brian Leftow. In his book *Time and Eternity* he presents a large scale argument for the view that God is timeless: that is, that God exists, but exists at no time, or rather, "outside" of time.

Central to Leftow's understanding of divine timeless eternality is a distinction between time and eternity, on the one hand, and temporality and eternality, on the other. Leftow holds that time and eternity are measures or frames of reference, while temporality and eternality are exclusive modes of being. As we have seen earlier, temporality is existing in successive parts, while eternality is having one's life all at once. Leftow argues that God necessarily must be timeless. Furthermore, temporal beings exist in time, but not only in time: they exist also in eternity.[48] That does not make them eternal; rather, temporal beings are measured at a certain time in the temporal reference frame (say, at 12:28 p.m., February 4, 1994), but are also measured at a certain "time" in the eternal reference frame, namely at the one simultaneous "time" that there is in eternity. According to the special theory of relativity, two events may be simultaneous in one reference frame and not simultaneous in another. So, Leftow argues, temporal events are simultaneous in eternity, but this does not mean that they are simultaneous in time, for to exist in eternity is not to

---

47. Ibid., 445.
48. Cf. Leftow, *Time and Eternity*, chap. 10, "A Theory of Time and Eternity." "Relative to God, the whole span of temporal events is actually there all at once. Thus in God's frame of reference, the correct judgment of local simultaneity is that all events are simultaneous. But all events are simultaneous in no temporal reference frame. Therefore the reference frame God shares with all events is atemporal," ibid., 228. Also see 230: "The Anselmian theory denies the Scotist argument's nub, the claim that events occur only at the temporal location of their occurrence. It holds instead that events also occur at the 'time' of eternity."

exist *simpliciter*, but a temporal event must also come to exist at its appropriate moment in time.[49]

As an example of how Leftow's conception of time can be deployed, we might consider the common charge that the atemporalist approach leads to absurdities about the relationship between temporal events and eternity. One entertaining example is this: My typing is simultaneous with eternity. The burning of Rome is simultaneous with eternity. Thus as I type, Nero fiddles away.[50] Such a *reductio ad absurdum* may be a decisive blow to some forms of divine timeless eternity. However, I don't believe it is to all forms. Leftow's position suggests that the "fiddling Nero" *reductio* conflates the time and eternity reference frames. Again, Leftow holds that even though an event may exist in the eternal reference frame and is simultaneous with other events within that eternal frame of reference, nonetheless that event, if it exists in time, is simultaneous, within the temporal reference frame, not with all other events but only with some.

In the final stage of Leftow's book he attempts to answer the various objections that have often been lodged against any doctrine of divine timeless eternality. The arguments that he considers are what I will call here "large-scale" objections against divine timeless eternality; there are also numerous general objections that Leftow does not expressly argue against here, but which he has argued against (implicitly or explicitly) throughout the book. I will first consider here the large-scale objections, after which I will consider Leftow's handling of two general objections.

---

49. "[William Lane] Craig, [Delmas] Lewis, and the others [viz., Bowman Clarke and Richard Creel] seem to suppose that if an event occurs in eternity, then it occurs simpliciter and so does not remain to be brought into existence with the passage of time. I think this conditional is false." Leftow, *Time and Eternity*, 231.
50. Kenny, "Divine Foreknowledge and Human Freedom," 264. Cited also in Stump and Kretzmann, "Eternity," 447.

Divine Foreknowledge and Human Freedom

Opponents of divine timeless eternality often raise the problem of divine foreknowledge and human freedom. This is perhaps the most common objection to divine timeless eternality: it argues that if God is eternal, then God knows everything that ever will happen. According to the objection, this makes all creaturely action necessary rather than contingent, and thus eliminates free will. Leftow's response takes two different tacks in response.

First, Leftow suggests a quasi-Molinist[51] approach to the problem of God's knowledge of future creaturely events. According to such an approach, God has knowledge of the constitution of all free creatures, and an understanding of all possible circumstances in which these creatures may find themselves. God knows what free creatures will do, yet these creatures are still free; this is because the free creatures act according to their characters and dispositions, all of which are free. Crucial to this position is Leftow's suggestion that libertarian freedom does not consist of wildly random responses, but is constituted by the characters and dispositions of the free agents who engage in that freedom. The quasi-Molinist position thus holds that humans are free agents, because God's knowledge does not determine the acts of free agents.

Leftow considers this quasi-Molinist approach, then, to be an adequate answer to objections about divine timeless eternality. But he finds it lacking to the extent that it seems to establish a causal relationship between creaturely acts and divine knowledge, thus threatening the doctrine of divine simplicity. It's at this stage that Leftow incorporates his understanding of eternity. As we have seen,

---

51. After the sixteenth-century scholastic philosopher Luis de Molina.

according to Leftow temporal beings and events exist not only in time but also in eternity. Time and eternity are different "measures" of a being or event. In that case, since divine timeless eternity is not a *fore*-knowledge at all, inasmuch as divine knowledge and free creaturely activity are simultaneous in the eternal frame of reference, then divine timeless eternity is not a threat to creaturely freedom. If creaturely freedom is problematic, it is so for reasons not peculiar to divine timeless eternity.

A Personal God

Opponents of divine timeless eternity often object that a timeless God cannot be personal. Leftow's response approaches this problem by considering what constitutes something being personal. He takes it that the objectors have in mind the ability to have purposes, intentions, and deliberations. He concludes that there are no good arguments against a timeless being possessing these attributes of personality, none, that is, that do not already assume that no being but a temporal being can have them. Furthermore, Leftow believes that any argument about divine personality needs to be quite clear about the method of analogical predication with which one is working. He believes that he is thus clear, and that he can articulate a view of divine purposes, intentions, and deliberations that is meaningful and yet preserves the distinction between eternality and temporality as distinct modes of being.

God's Knowledge

Opponents of divine timeless eternity often object that a timeless God can have no knowledge of temporal indexicals, or of the passage of time. Leftow believes that God can have such knowledge, although it will be timeless knowledge of them. If God views the extension of time all at once, then God can view at what point in the temporal extension something occurs, although God will so view that point timelessly.

God's Ability to Act

Opponents of divine timeless eternality often object that a timeless God cannot act in time. This is Nelson Pike's argument. Leftow responds by rejecting Pike's assumption that the cause of a temporal effect must be located in time. Even more integrally to Leftow's view of eternity, he argues against those who assume that if something occurs in eternity, then it occurs *simpliciter*. For Leftow, something that occurs in eternity remains to exist in time, and it will occur at a specific time.

In addition to the above objections, to which Leftow devotes entire chapters, there are two other objections to which Leftow responds throughout the book. Foremost of these general objections is the idea that any argument for divine timeless eternality depends upon a tenseless theory of time. Leftow describes these theories of time as follows:

> We have two distinct ways of speaking about temporal facts. One way involves the system of verb tenses, which relates events, processes, etc., to the times of sentences' utterance. Present-tensed propositions have a variety of uses, but in one central sort of use, a present-tensed claim that P ("the baby is crying") entails that P will take place after the claim that P is made. Such tensed utterances thus can cease to be true; "he will learn to read" ceases to be true when this process is no longer in the future. Tenseless utterances, on the other hand, cannot cease to be true.
> Tensed theories of time take tensed speech about time, and its associated ceasings to be true, as revealing time's inmost nature.

> Tenseless theories of time accord tenseless speech about time this role. This leads the theories to disagree at several points. Tensed theories hold that tensed propositions change truth-value because the events of which they speak come and cease to exists. According to tensed theories, there is a great difference between present and future events: present events exist, and future events do not. According to tenseless theories, both present and future events exist: present events exist now, and future events also exist, but at a later location in time.[52]

Throughout his book, then, Leftow seeks to show that a theory of divine timeless eternity does not require a tenseless theory of time, as several philosophers argue. Such an argument in fact figures prominently in Alan Padgett's *God, Eternity, and the Nature of Time*. Although Padgett's book was not available when Leftow wrote his, I take it that he would consider Padgett to represent this view. Throughout *Time and Eternity*, Leftow argues in a way that, on the whole, makes irrelevant one's view about time. Again and again, he will construct an argument using a tenseless theory of time, and then reformulate it using a tensed theory of time. I consider the book as a whole, then, to offer an implicit argument against the contention that any theory of divine timeless eternity must rely on a tenseless theory of time.

The other general objection Leftow considers throughout his book is the view that any view of divine timeless eternity will conflict with certain essential doctrines of the Christian faith. Leftow does not respond as Stump and Kretzmann do, that is, by saying that divine timeless eternity has as much right to be considered essential to Christianity as many other doctrines. Rather, Leftow acknowledges that divine timeless eternity is not as important. Instead, he argues that if divine timeless eternity can be shown not to conflict with other doctrines, then that is *prima facie* evidence that it ought not to

---

52. Leftow, *Time and Eternity*, 17.

be rejected immediately. From there he goes on to consider specific doctrines with which, it is alleged, divine timeless eternality conflicts. These doctrines include the incarnation and creation. His defense of the compatibility of his divine timeless eternality with the Christian doctrine of creation is to turn the tables, and show how temporalism is incompatible with the doctrine of creation.

We are now in a position to consider one last feature of Leftow's contribution, his concept of the "Zero Thesis," which he uses as a conceptual bridge to his understanding of divine timeless eternality.[53] The Zero Thesis takes as its point of departure the traditional theistic affirmation that God is not spatial. Since God is not spatial, God cannot be spatially located. Furthermore, building on the concept of divine simplicity, Leftow notes that as God cannot have parts, so also God cannot have spatial parts. For this reason, "the distance between God and every spatial creature is zero."[54]

That, in brief, is the Zero Thesis: a postulation that the spatial distance between God and any other creature is zero. It should not be surprising that such an idea is not entirely new with Leftow. Rather, it is a conclusion reasonably drawn from other common affirmations in philosophical theology, and we would likely find something like it elsewhere. Although Leftow himself does not cite him, we see something like his Zero Thesis in the work of Jonathan Edwards. In his *Miscellanies* we find this interesting entry:

> That is a gross and an unprofitable idea we have of God, as being something large and great as bodies are, and infinitely extended throughout the immense space. For God is neither little nor great with that sort of greatness, even as the soul of man; it is not at all extended, no more than an idea, and is not present anywhere as bodies are present, as we have shown elsewhere. So 'tis with respect to the increated Spirit. The greatness of a soul consists not in any extension,

---

53. Leftow, *Time and Eternity*, 222–28.
54. Ibid., 222.

but [in] its comprehensiveness of idea and extendedness of operation. So the infiniteness of God consists in his perfect comprehension of all things and the extendedness of his operation equally to all places.[55]

So, Edwards affirms that God is not present to some or other places as a body would be, because God has no "body," neither large nor small. Rather,

> God is present nowhere any otherwise than the soul is in the body or the brain, and he is present everywhere as the soul is in the body. We ought to conceive of God as being omnipotence, perfect knowledge and perfect love; and not extended any otherwise than as power, knowledge and love are extended; and not as if it was a sort of unknown thing that we call substance, that is extended.[56]

Edwards's use of the word *present* in the above passage is suggestive, for it is a word that, although there used in a context denoting spatiality, it is most at home in a temporal context. We see such multivalency suggested in, of all places, a statement by Schubert Ogden, as he offers an interpretation of Charles Hartshorne: "God is not located in a particular space and time, but rather is omnipresent and eternal, in the sense that he is directly present to all spaces and times and they to him."[57]

Such a suggestion is what Leftow develops with his Zero Thesis, in a section called "From God's Spacelessness to Creatures' Timelessness."[58] The Zero Thesis is simply stated: "The distance between God and every spatial creature is zero."[59] The distance between one spatial creature and another may change (indeed, it often does), and it is always greater than zero. We call that change

---

55. Jonathan Edwards, *The "Miscellanies" (Entry Nos. a–z, aa–zz, 1–500)*, ed. Thomas A. Schaffer (New Haven: Yale University Press, 1994), 334–35.
56. Ibid.
57. Shubert M. Ogden, *The Reality of God and Other Essays* (New York: Harper & Row, 1966), 175–76.
58. Leftow, *Time and Eternity*, 222–28.
59. Ibid., 222.

motion. But between God and every spatial creatures, there is no motion, as there is no distance. This is a "startling consequence" of the Zero Thesis: "If God is spaceless, there is no motion relative to God. This does not, however, deny the reality of motion *tout court*."[60] Nor does it deny the belief in God's omnipresence.

From this it is an easy step to affirming that the *temporal* distance between God and every creature in time is zero. Leftow takes his Zero Thesis and combines it with the postulate of modern physics that "only spatial things are temporal,"[61] and comes up with a plausible conceptual tool for understanding the notion of divine timeless eternality. "Relative to God, the whole span of temporal events is actually there all at once. Thus in God's frame of reference, the correct judgment of local simultaneity is that all events are simultaneous. But all events are simultaneous in no temporal reference frame. Therefore the reference frame God shares with all events is atemporal."[62]

In short, Leftow's doctrine of eternity, as well as his use of the Zero Thesis, may be seen in the fine statement at the conclusion to his book: "The God who creates time can also act within it and is closer to spatial and temporal creatures than any spatial or temporal creature can be. Yet paradoxically, [God] is with all times 'at once,' and so (speaking loosely) both our past and our future are now and ever before [God]."[63]

---

60. Ibid., 226.
61. Ibid., 227. We also saw this theme in Hegel.
62. Ibid., 228.
63. Ibid., 361.

Summary

In chapter 2, we surveyed a tradition of reflection on time and eternity. This tradition held that God existed timelessly, and asserted that eternity is to be thought of as timelessness. Karl Barth was in conversation with this tradition, and in it he found parts to approve and parts to correct. Overall, however, it is clear that he was formed by that tradition, and saw himself as standing within it. That was the burden of chapter 2: to demonstrate not only his criticism of the tradition, but also his dependence upon and agreement with it.

As I said in that chapter, this tradition of theological and philosophical reflection on eternity and time has come under severe criticism since Barth. Some of its harshest critics see themselves as students of Barth, and understand their criticisms as an appropriate extension of his work. If only for that reason, we should examine these recent criticisms of divine timeless eternality. Moreover, we should not simply assume the truth of this criticism, nor should we uncritically accept the suggestion that it does, in fact, continue some trajectory in Barth. The work of this chapter, then, has been to describe both this new philosophical criticism and those positions that reject the criticism and defend (or reinterpret) the traditional understanding of divine eternality as timeless.

In the course of this work, I have sought to show how atemporalism, as a theory of divine timeless eternality, may avoid charges of incoherence. Moreover, I have attempted to demonstrate incoherence in some forms of temporalism. Certainly, a thorough defense of atemporalism, or a complete critique of temporalism, would be far broader than the limits set by this book. Even so, what I have done should be sufficient to suggest that the overwhelming hegemony of the temporalist position may not be entirely well founded.

ASIDE

For the purposes of this book, we must acknowledge that the coherence of atemporalism here defended and the incoherence of temporalism here suggested relate to issues of concern to Karl Barth. I have in mind, of course, Barth's emphasis on the freedom of God, and his insistence that God not be understood as a frozen Platonic ideal but, recalling Boëthius, as that being who supremely possesses life. I believe that the defense of atemporalism shown above, particularly in the work of Brian Leftow, goes a long way toward satisfying Barth's concerns about how doctrines of timeless eternity sometimes develop in the hands of some theologians and philosophers. Indeed, it strikes me that the instances of incoherence I find in temporalism would likewise concern Barth. Temporalism, as I have understood it, seems to raise greater questions about God's freedom than pre–Stump/Kretzmann atemporalism, especially when we follow the logical implications of Hartshorne's position.

In short, I believe that the atemporalist position is historically, logically, and theologically superior to the temporalist position. Furthermore, it provides a better vantage point from which to understand and assess Barth's understanding of God's eternity. This is not to say that Barth's position is to be understood as strictly atemporalist. Indeed, Barth's understanding of eternity appears to be one that mediates between atemporalism and temporalism. As Hunsinger puts it, "Karl Barth's conception of eternity does not fit neatly into either of these standard views. His conception overlaps elements of each while transcending both. More precisely, although Barth stands mainly in the tradition of Augustine, Boethius, and Anselm, he modifies this tradition in order to appropriate what is valid in Hegel."[64]

---

64. Hunsinger, "*Mysterium Trinitatis*," 188.

Accepting this, I would add that such modification comes about with a clear emphasis on and preference for the atemporalist tradition, whereby Barth seeks to expand that tradition and overcome its faults, rather than to abandon it. Moreover, the motivation for this modification is not some eagerness to incorporate the insights of Hegel, but a desire to be more faithful to the subject of theology, the triune God who loves in freedom. Barth's "primary motivation . . . is not to reconcile these divergent traditions. It is rather to think through the conception of eternity in thoroughly trinitarian terms."[65]

---

65. Ibid., 188–89.

4

The Developmental Context

In the previous two chapters, I proposed and illustrated the conceptual context in which Barth's mature understanding of divine eternality must be placed if it is to be understood adequately. In the course of those chapters, I offered an interpretation of the concepts of time and eternity developed by several classic and modern figures, and suggested how we ought to understand Barth's relationship to them. Throughout, I attempted to demonstrate how our understanding of Barth is enhanced as we grapple with these other figures and with the fundamental issues they address.

With this chapter, I turn to a second interpretive component, another context in which Barth's mature understanding of divine eternality should be viewed. This context is the development that took place in Barth's theology overall and in his ideas of time and eternity in particular. Specifically, I will here sketch the development in Barth's understanding of time and eternity from the second edition of his commentary on Romans[1] until his *Church Dogmatics*.

Barth "Early" and "Late"

Clearly, this development of Barth's concepts of time and eternity is connected with other widely recognized theological changes in Barth's thought during the same period. Regrettably, these theological changes are often reduced to certain unhelpful slogans, chief among them *the early Barth* and *the later Barth*. These catchphrases may be a handy way of referring to different periods in Barth's development. But their usefulness breaks down when they are taken to suggest an absolute break in Barth's development. In short, this is surely a misleading caricature. To be sure, Barth changed, those changes marked by different forms of theological expression or conceptuality that can be taken as characteristic of periods in Barth's work. Yet the uncritical adoption of these stock phrases implies that the differences between the two periods are stark (yielding "two Barths") and that the slogans tidily express these differences. In that case, these shorthand phrases flatten the nuances of the theological differences *and* similarities between these stages of Barth's work.

The roots of such an understanding of Barth's development are easy to find. Under the influence, separately, of Hans Frei[2] and Hans Urs von Balthasar,[3] Barth scholarship of the 60s through the 80s (especially in the United States) commonly spoke of a major break in Barth's development, and of a turn "from dialectic to analogy," a turn signaled by Barth's 1931 Anselm book.[4] This way of describing

---

1. The differences between the first and second editions of Barth's commentary are not significant for my argument. Moreover, it is widely accepted that the second edition represents Barth's enduring contribution. Hereafter I frequently refer to this edition of the *Römerbrief* as *Romans* II.
2. Hans W. Frei, "The Doctrine of Revelation in the Thought of Karl Barth, 1909 to 1922: The Nature of Barth's Break with Liberalism" (PhD diss., Yale University, 1956).
3. Hans Urs von Balthasar, *Karl Barth: Darstellung und Deutung Seiner Theologie* (Köln: Verlag Jakob Hegner, 1951); E.T.: Hans Urs von Balthasar, *The Theology of Karl Barth: Exposition and Interpretation* (San Francisco: Ignatius Press, 1992).
4. Karl Barth, *Fides quaerens intellectum: Anselms Beweis der Existenz Gottes im Zusammenhang seines theologischen Programms* (Zollikon: Evangelischer Verlag, 1958); E.T.: Karl Barth, *Anselm:*

Barth's development has in recent years been challenged from two directions: from investigations of Barth's theological development through the 1920s and 30s, and from fresh readings of the *Church Dogmatics*.

In his 1989 Princeton dissertation and his 1995 book, Bruce McCormack drew on Swiss and German revisionist work,[5] and called into question the whole "from dialectic to analogy" scheme, as well as the common description of Barth as neoorthodox." He concluded that these lead to seriously inadequate understandings of Barth and his development. He insisted that "the lessons learned during Barth's 'dialectical phase' were never simply left behind,"[6] lessons that, I would argue, apply also to Barth's understanding of God and time.

George Hunsinger has argued that many interpreters of Barth's *Church Dogmatics*, including von Balthasar, are led astray from achieving an accurate interpretation of Barth by the search for a single *Denkform* (thought form) that would alone make comprehensible the whole of the *Church Dogmatics*.[7] Moreover, I suggest that, by identifying a single thought form or conceptual basis, one also runs a greater risk of overstating the differences between *Romans* II and the *Church Dogmatics*, because the theological depth of the *Church Dogmatics* is reduced to one abstract idea that can easily be "contrasted" with one chosen from *Romans* II (for example,

---

Fides Quaerens Intellectum—Anselm's Proof of the Existence of God in the Context of his Theological Scheme (London: SCM Press, repr. Pickwick Publications, 1960).

5. Primary among these are Michael Beintker, *Die Dialektik in der "dialektischen Theologie" Karl Barths: Studien zur Entwicklung der Barthschen Theologie und zur Vorgeschichte der "Kirchlichen Dogmatik,"* Beiträge zur evangelischen Theologie (München: C. Kaiser, 1987) and Ingrid Spieckermann, *Gotteserkenntnis: Ein Beitrag zur Grundfrage der neuen Theologie Karl Barths* (München: Chr. Kaiser, 1985).

6. Bruce L. McCormack, "A Scholastic of a Higher Order: The Development of Karl Barth's Theology, 1921–31" (PhD diss., Princeton Theological Seminary, 1989), ii. See also Bruce L. McCormack, *Karl Barth's Critically Realistic Dialectical Theology: Its Genesis and Development, 1909–1936* (New York: Oxford University Press, 1995).

7. See, e.g., Hunsinger, *How to Read Karl Barth: The Shape of His Theology* (New York: Oxford University Press, 1991), 9.

the use of dialectic in *Romans* II over against the use of analogy in the *Church Dogmatics*). Indeed, it is doubtful whether a work of such complexity as the *Church Dogmatics*, and one composed over so many years as it was, can adequately be reduced to one controlling concept. Hunsinger's contribution is to call attention to the problems with the *Denkform* approach, and to propose instead a series of six motifs (actualism, particularism, objectivism, personalism, realism, and rationalism), that in their "interrelations can help to disclose the shape of Barth's theology as a whole."[8]

These two instances of "rethinking" Barth lead me to adopt two principles for interpreting Barth's development. The first, negatively, is to treat with skepticism any assertion of radical differences between the so-called early and late Barth. The second, positively, is to seek out points of doctrinal continuity between the two periods. In this book, of course, the discontinuity to test with skepticism and the continuity to explore critically are with regard to possible changes in Barth's understanding of time and eternity.

To be sure, there are real differences in how Barth spoke of eternity in *Romans* II and how he spoke of eternity in the *Church Dogmatics*, just as there are real differences between the "early" and the "late" Barth. Yet what, precisely, are those differences? And, once we identify those differences, what change do they signify?

To answer those questions, we must look not only at Barth's statements on time and eternity in *Romans* II. We must also look at passages from the *Church Dogmatics* that suggest differences, and read those passages closely to understand what the fundamental differences really are. Furthermore, we may also look at other documents in the years between *Romans* II and the *Church Dogmatics*, particularly his dogmatics lectures from Göttingen in 1924–25.[9] In the course of

---

8. Ibid., 23.

this analysis, we will need to make clear the theological role Barth's relevant statements played. From such an analysis, it will become clear that the differences between the so-called early and late Barth with regard to the topic of time and eternity grew out of theological convictions that remained the same, or became clearer, throughout his career. I will seek to show that changes in expression are not to be seen as radical conceptual revolutions, but as the adoption of theologically more adequate ways of expressing enduring theological convictions. The analysis of those intervening documents will also suggest, however, the genesis of some of the key features of Barth's articulation of God's eternity in the *Church Dogmatics*.

Although one could undertake a thorough investigation of time and eternity in *Romans* II and in all of Barth's work up until the *Church Dogmatics*, this chapter must restrict itself to a more modest goal. I will focus here on these topics: the theological role of the time-eternity dialectic in *Romans* II, and Barth's progressive exploration of christological resources for understanding time and eternity, not only in *Romans* II, but also in works from 1924 to 1930.

Der Römerbrief

Any statement of the differences between the Barth of *Romans* II and the Barth of the *Church Dogmatics* is risky, prone to oversimplification or overstatement. This risk is not diminished if the specific topic is Barth's understanding of time and eternity in each of those works. Nonetheless, it is a risk I will hazard, for not only can some careful

---

9. Karl Barth, *Unterricht in der Christlichen Religion, vol. 1: Prolegomena, 1924*, ed. Hannelotte Reiffen, Karl Barth Gesamtausgabe (Zürich: Theologischer Verlag, 1985); Karl Barth, *Unterricht in der Christlichen Religion vol. 2: Die Lehre von Gott/Die Lehre vom Menschen*, 1924/1925, ed. Hinrich Stoevesandt (Zürich: Theologischer Verlag, 1990); E.T.: Karl Barth, *The Göttingen Dogmatics: Instruction in the Christian Religion*, ed. Hannelotte Reiffen, trans. Geoffrey W. Bromiley, vol. 1 (Grand Rapids: Eerdmans, 1991).

affirmations be made, but such affirmations will also frame our discussion.

Synopsis

Clearly, *time* and *eternity* have heightened theological import in *Romans* II. There Barth used the words to express the distinction between humanity and divinity. Time and eternity thus together demarcate the border separating two radically distinct realms, a border that cannot at all be crossed by human initiative, but may be crossed only by the grace of God. Together these terms are placed in antithesis, the purpose of which is to highlight the crisis of human pretensions to holiness, a crisis brought about by the righteousness of God revealed in Jesus Christ. Thus in *Romans* II *time* and *eternity* express and highlight this primary recurring theological theme: the "crisis."[10] Correlatively, these terms are never used with the precision they would have in a technical discussion of time and eternity *per se*, whether that discussion be theological or philosophical. In *Romans* II, Barth never analyzes time or eternity, nor does he specifically address them as independent realities to be investigated. We do not even find anything like Augustine's famous line from book 11 of *The Confessions*: "What then is time? Provided that no one asks me, I know."[11] In *Romans* II, Barth uses the terms *time* and *eternity* emblematically. Together they represent the broader theological

---

10. McCormack correctly highlights this, and points to the excellent work of Michael Beintker: "It is Beintker's great merit to have shown convincingly that the oft-discussed time-eternity dialectic functions in the theology of Romans II not to set forth a metaphysical dualism (as has often been thought), but rather to serve the purpose of witnessing to the dialectic of judgement and grace in the 'crisis' brought about by revelation. Thus the time-eternity dialectic—so far from setting forth a metaphysic—has its home within the framework of soteriology." McCormack, *Critically Realistic*, 12. See Beintker, *Dialektik*.
11. *Conf.* 11.14.17

problem of human creatureliness vis-a-vis the divine initiative in revelation.

In the *Church Dogmatics*, Barth uses these two terms somewhat differently. Rather than strictly demarcating a diastasis, these terms have a much greater christological and trinitarian focus that drives toward overcoming the diastasis. Separately, *time* and *eternity* describe the respective forms of existence (*Daseinsformen*, as Oblau would call them) appropriate to creatures and Creator, forms that were experienced by Jesus Christ, the "God-man." Together, they correlate with the revelational dialectic of God's presence in our midst (time) and God's being *a se* (eternity). In contrast to their use in *Romans* II, the *Church Dogmatics* deploys these terms in conversation with other theological and philosophical uses. Yet in the *Dogmatics*, just as in *Romans* II, the appearance of *time* and *eternity* is rarely marked by philosophical concern and always for a theological purpose.

Indeed, the theological purpose is precisely what one must discern if the actual differences between *Romans* II and the *Dogmatics* with respect to this topic are to be accurately stated and not overstated. With regard to the change between *Romans* II and the *Dogmatics* in how Barth deploys the terms *time* and *eternity*, let me suggest the following as a formulation. First of all, these terms (in their use together) designate different objects and perform different theological functions in each of the works. Second, whereas in *Romans* II the terms designate an unavoidable problem, the fundamental religious situation of the human being before God, in the *Dogmatics* they also sketch the outline of the solution to that problem forged by the triune God, the overcoming of divine-human alienation by the God-Man.

Having taken the risk by suggesting such a simple formulation, I turn now to an attempt to demonstrate its adequacy and cogency.

Time and Eternity in Opposition

In *Romans* II, time and eternity are from the beginning placed in apparently strict opposition. This is illustrated from the famous statement that occurs in the preface to the second edition: "If I have a 'system', it consists in this, that I keep in mind as firmly as possible what Kierkegaard called *the 'infinite qualitative distinction' between time and eternity*, in its negative and positive significance. 'God is in heaven, and you are on earth.'"[12] The phrase *time and eternity* expresses the radical distinction between Creator and creature. The terms *time* and *eternity*, in their explicit and implicit opposition, point to that substantive theological stance. This stance, having positive and negative significance, is as much an affirmation of God's grace and readiness to reveal as it is of God's hiddenness and human inability to comprehend the divine unaided.[13] But the rhetorical force of the time-eternity dialectic certainly is mainly negative. Of course, that emphasis was intentional, as well as historically situated. Barth stressed the negative in order to work against the dominant theological tendencies of the day, which asserted a positive connection between human experience and the being of God, and assumed that knowledge of the divine was a capacity of the human spirit. Barth's entire theological project in

---

12. My translation, emphasis added, Karl Barth, *Der Römerbrief*, 2nd ed., 1922 (Zürich: Theologischer Verlag, 1989), xx, subsequently cited as *Römerbrief*; E.T.: Karl Barth, *The Epistle to the Romans*, trans. Edwyn C. Hoskyns (London: Oxford University Press, 1976), 10, subsequently cited as *Romans*.
13. That is one reason why the "time-eternity dialectic" is indeed a *dialectic*, and not merely an opposition of two contrasting concepts.

Romans can be understood as rejection of this starting point inherent in the continental Protestant theology he knew.[14]

However, such opposition in *Romans* II is almost entirely implicit rather than explicit. Only rarely do the terms *time* and *eternity* occur together. One looks in vain for the entries *Ewigkeit* or *Zeit* in the index. Perhaps it is significant that we do see the terms placed together, and in opposition, in the preface to the second edition. For it was there that Barth offered a defense of the theological method deployed in the first edition and continued, with modifications, in the second. Besides the famous statement about Kierkegaard cited above, we read in the preface that one of Barth's primary exegetical assumptions is that Paul "really spoke . . . of the permanent crisis of time and eternity," and not of some general principle discoverable by philosophical inquiry.[15] Such a methodological assertion is significant, in ways which we will explore more fully below. An assertion somewhat similar in meaning to the other passages already brought forward is found near the end of the commentary: "The theme of theology is grace, the absolute 'Moment', the greedy dialectic of time and eternity."[16] But those are nearly the only places of note in which the terms *Zeit* and *Ewigkeit* are discussed together. Explicit mention of *time* and *eternity* is hard to locate.

Michael Beintker helpfully suggests that the famous statement about "the infinite qualitative distinction between time and eternity" expresses a *Grundmotiv* (fundamental motif), namely, "the fright in the face of the distance between God and Man." It is this motif that, as Beintker puts it, "finds passionate expression in Barth's exegesis. The relationship of eternity and time is equivalent with the relationship

---

14. *Church Dogmatics*, trans. Geoffrey W. Bromiley, et al (Edinburgh: T. & T. Clark, 1956–69), II/1, 635.
15. *Römerbrief*, xxi; *Romans*, 11.
16. *Romans*, 530.

of God and man or God and world, it is a matter of two dimensions that admit no comparison."[17] Moreover, the partial phrase *infinite qualitative distinction* is not isolated to the preface of *Romans* II, but rather is found in several other phrases Barth uses throughout the commentary. "The assertion about the 'infinite qualitative distinction' weaves through the interpretation in *Romans* II like a red thread. Barth favors the expression 'infinite qualitative distinction of God and Man.' . . . The phrase is used once with 'God and World.' . . . In analogous form Barth can also speak of the 'infinite contrast of Gospel and Church.'"[18]

Thus the terms *time* and *eternity* are used in *Romans* II much like other terms with which they can be understood as cognates, as somehow parallel, or as expressing aspects of broader categories. The contrasts between *time* and *eternity* are deployed to illustrate theological affirmations suggested by the contrasts between other terms. In short, they are used emblematically, to illustrate rather than to define an important theological distinction, one that may also be illustrated by other terms used likewise.

One may see this emblematic usage also in Barth's lectures on John Calvin's theology, delivered at Göttingen in the summer of 1922, the same year as the publication of *Romans* II.[19] Barth's fondness for dialectical contrasts, characteristic of *Romans* II, does not suddenly disappear when he lectured on Calvin, but is just as present there as in *Romans* II. In those lectures, Barth uses *time* and *eternity*, along with

---

17. Beintker, *Dialektik*, 32.
18. "Die Behauptung des 'unendlichen qualitativen Unterschieds' durchzieht die Auslegung in Römer II wie ein roter Faden. Barth bevorzugt die Wendung 'unendlicher qualitativer Unterschied von Gott und Mensch.' . . . Singulär ist der Gebrauch der Wendung im Blick auf 'Gott und Welt.' . . . In analoger Form kann Barth auch vom 'unendlichen Gegensatz von Evangelium und Kirche' sprechen." Ibid., 33.
19. Karl Barth, *Die Theologie Calvins 1922*, ed. Hans Scholl (Zürich: Theologischer Verlag, 1993); E.T.: Karl Barth, *The Theology of John Calvin*, trans. Geoffrey W. Bromiley (Grand Rapids: Eerdmans, 1995).

other expressions, in a manner similar to that found in *Romans* II, to articulate a contrast between this world and the world to come. Here, time and eternity are yet another way of depicting the contrast, the problem, and the deep grace-filled connection between "this" world and "that" world, between God and humanity, between now and then.

In the Calvin lectures, as in *Romans* II, the terms *time* and *eternity* are called on to express, in broad, conceptually suggestive rather than precise ways, matters of deep theological import. Barth seems to enjoy piling together phrases to suggest fundamental yet far-reaching theological themes. This is seen, for example, when he says of "the Catholic doctrine of the appropriation of grace" that it remarkably considers all these elements: "Nature and grace, humanity and God, freedom and dependence, a justifiable sense of self and humility before God, doing and receiving, meriting and being given, time and eternity."[20] In similar fashion:

> Synthesis is something completely original, creative, preceding all particular deliberation, itself not the deliberating but that which is deliberated on in all deliberations. Synthesis is the ability and the will for comprehending antitheses in their connection, equivalently, no matter whether one has in mind spirit and nature, inner and outer, eternity and time, faith and ethics, revelation and history, intuitive and discursive thinking, or however one defines it.[21]

Fundamentally, then, what is expressed by the terms *time* and *eternity* in these passages of the Calvin lectures is the contrast and connection between life as we commonly experience it and the reality that lies

---

20. Barth, *Theology of Calvin*, 33; *Die Theologie Calvins 1922*, 43.
21. Rev. trans. "Synthese ist etwas ganz Ursprüngliches, Schöpferisches, aller Einzelüberlegung Vorausgehendes, selber keine Überlegung, sondern das Überlegte in allen Überlegungen. Synthese ist die Fähigkeit und der Wille zur *Zusammenschau* der Gegensätze, gleichviel, ob man dabei an Geist und Natur, Inneres und Äußeres, Ewigkeit und Zeit, Glaube und Ethos, Offenbarung und Geschichte, intuitives und diskursives Denken oder wie man es immer definiere, denken möge." *Die Theologie Calvins*, 212; *Theology of Calvin*, 159f.

beyond, for which we hope, and which God in Christ grants to us.[22] With Barth's suggestion of "the decided orientation to the next world that governs all Calvin's life and work," Barth asserts that "no reformer was more strongly shaped than he was by the antithesis of time and eternity."[23] By this and the subsequent discussion, Barth demonstrates that *time* and *eternity* are a means of discussing the connection between ethics and doctrine, or ethics and eschatology, between the practical world of affairs and the promised life to come, which for Calvin and Barth were each and all comprehended by the gospel.

The similarities in expression and rhetorical style between *Romans* II and the Calvin lectures are clear. We see in Barth's *Romans* not only the same looseness and expressiveness with these terms, but also the same fundamental theological content: the expression of a dialectical connection between *diesseitige* and *jenseitige* perspectives, the world and God, law and gospel, ethics and eschatology. Of particular concern for Barth in his commentary on Romans is the connection between ethics and the gospel, and this we see also in the Calvin lectures.

The point to be emphasized at this stage is this: the opposition of time and eternity in *Romans* II must not be understood literally, but *functionally*, that is, with regard to the theological themes underlying the various contrasting phrases, and thus concerning those contrasting dimensions (however expressed) and their theological significance. It is in those themes that we can more clearly see not only the differences between the Barth of *Romans* II and the Barth of the *Church Dogmatics*, but also their deep similarities.

---

22. Cf. Barth, *Theology of Calvin*, 73–74. *Die Theologie Calvins 1922*, 98–99.
23. Barth, *Theology of Calvin*, 125; *Die Theologie Calvins 1922*, 168.

Let us now explore some of the passages where the implicit opposition of time and eternity in *Romans* II may reasonably be thought to be present. There are several discrete passages where we may see it. It occurs in a contrast between this realm and an "eternal order": "The 'Something' which the Word of God creates is of an eternal order, wholly distinct from every 'something' which we know otherwise. It neither emerges from what we know, nor is it a development of it."[24] An opposition of time and eternity is implicit also in the contrast between the Creator and the creature: "Other than in the negation of the created, the position of the Creator and the *eternal* meaning of the created can never at all be known."[25]

However, the contrasts are not entirely negative, but even in their negations affirm the true significance of this world, including time:

> Strangely great, strangely powerful is the connection and relation between God and the world, between there and here. Precisely when it is known that the concretization and humanization of divinity in a particular history of religion or salvation-history is *no* connection to God, because God is thereby abandoned as God, at that point can it now also be noticed that everything appearing in the known world derives content and significance from the unknown God, that every impress of revelation is a pointer to revelation itself, that every experiencing endures within itself knowledge as its own Krisis and every time endures within itself *eternity* as its own dissolution [*Aufhebung*]. Judgment is not annihilation but establishment. Purification is not a clearing out, but fulfillment. God has not abandoned humanity, but God is true.[26]

This passage demonstrates another, more significant, time-eternity dialectic. One finds not merely a dialectic that holds time and eternity in opposition. Rather, one sees a dialectic between the *opposition* of time and eternity, on the one hand, and the God-activated *connection*

---

24. Barth, *Romans*, 102.
25. Rev. trans., emph. in original. *Römerbrief*, 67; *Romans*, 87.
26. Rev. trans., emph. added. *Römerbrief*, 58; *Romans* 78–79.

between time and eternity, on the other. It is, in other words, a dialectic of diastasis over against relationship. Moreover, as a *theological* dialectic, it is posed for a religious purpose. For Barth, *time* and *eternity* are another reminder that nothing of our own is ultimate, but, when confronted by the "Unknown God," time and eternity are brought to their true place. In the language of *Romans* II, the revelation, although just a crater, shows Revelation; judgment and the *Krisis* of God signify grace and justification; temporal existence comes to its limit and is brought beyond itself (that is, rendered dissolute or *aufgehoben*) not by its own essential character, but by *eternity*. What we see here, then, is an example of the dialectic of God's veiling and unveiling,[27] a dialectic in which the hidden God wills to be the revealed God, who can be known in no other way than by God's free act of revealing.

In this passage we may see also another purpose of the dialectic. That purpose is to call into question every assertion of a connection between time and eternity that is simply *given*, a feature of reality generally perceived as such and discoverable by disinterested observation. This dialectic implies that the connection of time and eternity is perceived much as are the connection of ethics and eschatology, of *Diesseit* and *Jenseit*, or of the self and God: by revelation, and through repentance.

This dialectical connection is reminiscent of the connection Calvin draws between knowledge of self and knowledge of God in the *Institutes*. For Calvin, the knowledge of self and the knowledge of God are intertwined, whereby one may not truly know God if one does not truly know oneself. But what does Calvin mean by

---

27. Cf. "The Humanity of God": "The *divinity* of God . . . is that mystery, comparable only with the impenetrable darkness of death, in which God veils himself at the very moment when he unveils himself to humanity, makes himself known, reveals himself," in Karl Barth, *Karl Barth: Theologian of Freedom*, ed. Clifford Green (Minneapolis: Fortress Press, 1991), 47. Bruce McCormack's work makes much of this dialectic.

knowledge of the self? It is quite clear from a close reading of Calvin's discussion that true knowledge of self indicates a knowledge of one's own sin and unworthiness before God. Such knowledge is certainly not a given, nor does Calvin intend it as a general anthropological principle.[28]

Likewise, with Barth's antithesis of time and eternity in *Romans* II we see a kind of religious epistemology, one that emphasizes (in a manner that at times seems to suggest not only Calvin, but also Kant) the *limits* of our knowledge of the ultimate.[29] A good example is the following passage from later in *Romans* II:

> *God* is righteous. *God* declares righteous. He himself, he alone. . . . From this critical position only one thing can no longer be understood, grasped, seen: entities, experiences, and persons that *in themselves*—without submitting themselves to the judgment of *God*, without awaiting the *divine* justification—are desired and affirmed to be great and in some sort of sense divine; jumblings of time and eternity; supposedly real projections into, befallings, appearances of the world of God in *this* world (to which belong also all such deep profundities and "higher worlds"!).[30]

All of these activities, which for Barth are all of one piece,[31] are antithetical to the "critical position" given by the recognition that God alone is just and justifies. Indeed, the critical position means that "we are deprived of the possibility either of projecting a temporal

---

28. Cf. John Calvin, *Institutes of the Christian Religion*, ed. John T. McNeill (Philadelphia: Westminster Press, 1960), 243–44 (II.I.3, "The Two Chief Problems of Self-Knowledge").
29. See Garrett Green, "Challenging the Religious Studies Canon: Karl Barth's Theory of Religion," *Journal of Religion* 75 (October 1995): 473–86. Green suggests that Barth has a theological "theory of religion" within §17 of the *KD* and, to a lesser but nonetheless real extent, within *Romans* II, one that should be studied alongside other theories. Prof. Green suggested the Kantian similarities in a presentation and discussion of that paper at the fall 1995 meeting of the Karl Barth Society of North America.
30. Rev. trans., *Römerbrief*, 89, 90; *Romans*, 107, 108.
31. Indicated by the subject of his "*Nur eines* ist von dieser kritischen Stellung aus nicht mehr zu verstehen, zu begreifen, zu sehen" (emph. added).

thing into infinity or of confining eternity within the sphere of time."[32]

For all the differences there are between the Barth of *Romans* II and the Barth of the *Church Dogmatics*, what is at issue in this passage is surely not one of them. This passage is striking, as are several of those we previously discussed, for how clearly present is what Hunsinger calls the motif of particularism, which emphasizes that our knowledge of God arises not out of general notions or principles, but from the very God who reveals God's own self specifically in Jesus Christ.[33] To a lesser extent, present also is the motif of objectivism. Based on what we have surveyed, then, I submit that the *theological conviction* of Barth expressed in the time-eternity dialectic of *Romans* II does not disappear, even given the changes in *theological expression*. "The infinite qualitative difference between God and humankind is never simply abandoned; *it is the always present, implicitly assumed, negative first moment of the theological method employed consistently throughout the Church Dogmatics.*"[34]

In the *Church Dogmatics*, Barth did not usually employ *time* and *eternity*, and their functionally parallel terms, as he did in *Romans* II: emblematically, symbolically, as a kind of theological shorthand to stress the crisis of humanity before God, or the radical diastasis between Creator and creature.[35] Rather he very often used these terms in quite different ways, with different referents, with a new emphasis on doctrines. Yet the theological convictions that gave rise to the earlier symbolic uses remained and strengthened over time. The distinction between humanity and divinity, known and bridged only by divine revelation, is a theological presupposition

---

32. *Romans*, 108; *Römerbrief*, 90.
33. See Hunsinger, *How to Read Karl Barth*, 32ff.
34. McCormack, "*A Scholastic of a Higher Order*," 118. (Emphasis is McCormack's.)
35. We will explore this further in chapter 6.

never abandoned by Barth, even if his manner of expressing it changed.

Theological Problems Raised by Diastasis

Despite the theological nuance dwelling, as it were, just below the surface, the dialectic of time and eternity as it was deployed in *Romans* II soon was seen as problematic, in that it seemingly promoted a one-sided concept of eternity. Although others pointed it out following the publication of *Romans* II, Barth himself came to recognize the problem, and explicitly addressed it in the *Church Dogmatics*. About his earlier statements in *Romans* II, Barth allows, "It was at this point that the objection could be made, as it was in fact made by both friends and critics, that while I had radically disturbed the optimism of the Neo-Protestant conception of time in itself it had really been confirmed by the extreme form it had been given by me."[36]

That admission comes as Barth is discussing the posttemporality of God, the third form in his threefold exposition of God's eternity. Each of the three forms of eternity, Barth argues, can be and has been emphasized in a one-sided fashion, to the neglect of the others. Barth describes a one-sidedness in the Reformers' emphasis on pretemporality, and in the neoprotestants' concentration on supratemporality. The problem with Barth's approach in *Romans* II, Barth acknowledges, is in his own one-sided concentration on posttemporality.

Such an emphasis was not, Barth insists, entirely wrong. He did it to combat the problems he saw with a liberal or neoprotestant overemphasis on supratemporality. "Expounding Rom. 8:24, I even

---

36. *CD* II/1, 635.

dared to say at that time: 'hope that is visible is not hope. Direct communication from God is not communication from God. A Christianity that is not wholly and utterly and irreducibly eschatology has absolutely nothing to do with Christ. A spirit that is not at every moment in time new life from the dead is in any case not the Holy Spirit. . . .' Well roared, lion! There is nothing absolutely false in these bold words."[37] Yet even though he viewed those early statements with some approval, what Barth did object to was his own one-sidedness, which led him to overlook the significance of God's pre- and supratemporality. In other words, in using posttemporality to combat the neoprotestant fixation on supratemporality, Barth wound up discarding both supratemporality and pretemporality. The result, as he later judged it, was that he thereby failed to speak of God rather than of some humanly posited concept. "The result was that we could not speak about the post-temporality of God in such a way as to make it clear that we actually meant to speak of God and not of a general idea of limit or krisis."[38]

Thus even for the actualism, objectivism, and particularism present in *Romans* II, it failed, by Barth's later reckoning, to show sufficient attention to the reality of God's revelation. Ironically, then, the tendency to turn eternity into a general concept or principle of reality shows up, not just in the nineteenth-century theological heritage of which he was critical, but also in Barth's own published criticism of that heritage, *Romans* II. As Barth insisted, whether that be the so-called early or late Barth, we must speak about the eternity of *God*, rather than about some concept or principle. For this reason, that the tendency should appear (if only implicitly) in *Romans* II is ironic indeed. The irony, as McCormack puts it, "is that in setting out to combat the supra-temporality of the Neo-Protestants, he has ended

---

37. Ibid., 634–35.
38. Ibid., 635.

with something very close to it. He has interpreted post-temporality as a future which never has come and never will come. Rather, eternity stands equally close to every moment in time, qualifying every moment with transcendental meaning."[39]

The problem came out, as he saw it, when he had to give positive content to his understanding, rather than in the no that he felt had to be said against the excesses of the time:

> That we had only an uncertain grip of the matter became apparent, strangely enough, in those passages of the exposition in which I had to speak positively about the divine future and hope as such. It emerged in the fact that although I was confident to treat the far-sidedness of the coming kingdom of God with absolute seriousness, I had no such confidence in relation to its coming as such. So when I came to expound a passage like Rom. 13:11f ("Now it is high time to awake out of sleep: for now is our salvation nearer than when we believed. The night is far spent, the day is at hand."), in spite of every precaution I interpreted it as if it referred only to the moment which confronts all moments in time as the eternal "transcendental meaning" of all moments in time.[40]

It may not be clear precisely what Barth's objection really is. Barth is not saying that we need to adopt a naive, fantastical, and speculative notion of the "end times." I have no doubt that Barth would find the dispensationalism widely and fervently held in American evangelicalism to be peculiar if not unintelligible. Rather, an adequate understanding of God's eternity must seriously include the sober notion that, except for God, there really will be an end to all things as they exist now. "Just as God is before and over time, so He is after time, after all time and each time."[41] All things have their appointed ends, and created reality as a whole has its appointed end. After all things, . . . God. It is an acknowledgment of this point, with

---

39. "*A Scholastic of A Higher Order*," 172–73. McCormack is drawing to *CD* II/1, 634–35.
40. *CD* II/1, 635.
41. Ibid., 629.

all its threat and promise, that Barth finds missing not only from "the utterly frivolous 'piety' of convinced 'Culture-Protestants,'"[42] but also from his own *Romans* II. The difficulty that the Barth of the *Church Dogmatics* has, it seems, is that when God's posttemporality is neglected, the resultant one-sidedness tends to turn eschatology into a general anthropological principle.

Perhaps we can understand some of Barth's later objection if we look closely at the relevant passage from *Romans* II. There, as indicated above, he is commenting on Romans 13, from which he translates verses 9b through 11 as follows: "If there be any other commandment, it is summed up in this word, namely, Thou shalt love thy neighbour as thyself! Love worketh no ill to his neighbour: therefore love is the fulfilling of the law. And this do, knowing the time, that now it is high time to awake out of sleep; for now is our salvation nearer than when we believed."[43] For the phrase, "this do," Barth understands τοῦτο as referring to ἐργάζεται in ἡ ἀγάπη τῷ πλησίον κακόν οὐκ ἐργάζεται, thus to the *act* whereby one loves the neighbor as oneself. Barth supplies the German verb *tun* in his translation, which one finds in some, but not all, German translations of the New Testament. So, we are to "do *this*," namely, "love the neighbor." But how, Barth asks, is it possible for us to do this, to "do the incomprehensible work of love?" He calls the fulfilling of this law an "impossible possibility" open to us. But how is it open to us? The impossible, he answers, happens as follows: "When we realize that time becomes like eternity and eternity like this time, *then* this possibility occurs."[44] With that strange sentence Barth is

---

42. Ibid., 635, quoting *Römerbrief*, 501.
43. I use Hoskyns' translation of the Scripture passage (*Romans*, 492) rather than a standard modern Bible translation (such as the RSV or NRSV) because using these fairly standard English translations may make it more difficult to understand Barth's exposition. Differences in translation of Rom. 13:11 seem to divide over how to render καί τοῦτο, which (as we discuss presently) is significant in Barth's commentary.

not eliminating the distinction between time and eternity. Nor is he making grace a human act. Rather he is pointing to a connection between the two, whereby every time may be qualified, "outside of" time, by eternity.

He continues: "[The possibility] occurs 'in perceiving the moment'.[45]—For there is a 'Moment' between the times, which itself is no moment in time. However, every moment in time can receive the full dignity of *this* moment. This moment is the *eternal* moment, the *now*, in which past and future stand still, the former in its going, the latter in its coming."[46] It may be this passage, which sounds somewhat Hegelian,[47] that later caused Barth concern. For "the moment" appears to be a general feature of reality, equally and unqualifiedly present to every moment, for it is "between the times." Such concern may have been heightened by what he says just a few sentences later:

> "*We* go along and flit from one year to the other'—*that* is the mystery of time, revealed in that eternal moment, which always and never is, revealed in the moment of revelation. Of this mystery we see a *parable* in the irrevocable scampering away of the past, the unstoppable coming of the future: the *irreversibility* of time. However, of this mystery we also see a parable in the complete hiddenness, opacity, and non-givenness of the *present* "between" the times.[48]

Remember that Barth was (as he later pointed out) supposed to be speaking about posttemporality, which amounts to eschatology. Yet

---

44. Römerbrief, 523; Romans, 497.
45. "In Erkenntnis des Augenblicks." This phrase is Barth's own translation from Rom. 13:11, εἰδότες τὸν καιρόν.
46. "Sie tritt ein 'in Erkenntnis des Augenblicks'.—Denn es ist ein 'Augenblick' zwischen den Zeiten, der selber kein Augenblick ist in der Zeit. Jeder Augenblick in der Zeit kann aber die volle Würde dieses Augenblicks empfangen. Es ist dieser Augenblick der ewige Augenblick, das Jetzt, in welchem Vergangenheit und Zukunft stillstehen, jene in ihrem Gehen, diese in ihrem Kommen." *Römerbrief*, 523. Cf. Romans, 497.
47. See above, in chapter 2.
48. *Römerbrief*, 524; *Romans*, 497

his description of this "moment between the times," even if it is a parable of eternity, certainly looks supratemporal. He does later connect the "moment" with posttemporality, by bringing in the concept of the kingdom of God: "Being the transcendent meaning of all moments, the eternal 'Moment' can be compared with no moment in time. *Salvation—the day*, the Kingdom of God—being the fulfilment of all time, is incomparable."[49] Yet even with this codicil, it seems that Barth would later judge that the damage had already been done.

We must note, however, what was behind Barth's eschatological reflections in *Romans* II, even if these were later judged by Barth to be inadequate. For Barth in *Romans* II gives the impression of trying to sail between the Scylla of liberalism and the Charybdis of naive speculation. To demonstrate this, let us turn to a passage in *Romans* II that is thematically similar to one found in *CD* III/2, §47.2, "Given Time."[50] There, Barth has this to say about time:

> Men are sold under time, its property. They lie like pebbles in the "stream of time," and backwards and forwards the ripples hurry over them. They do what they ought not; what they ought they do not. The qualified time, the time of withdrawal and of advance, the time of negative and positive ethical possibility, has yet to be. And yet, there are distinctions of time within this final separation between time and that strange "Moment" of eternity. There are times that are *near*, and there are times that are far; there is night-time and there is the time when the day begins to dawn; there are times of sleeping and there are times of awakening. There is therefore not only an eternal but also a chronological qualification of time. . . . There is always a tension between the "Then" of our unruffled existence and the "Now" of our disturbed recollection of non-existence.[51]

---

49. *Romans*, 498.
50. We discuss this above in chapter 2.
51. *Romans*, 499.

Yet those relative distinctions and qualifications are not the same as the distinction between our times and the eternal "Now," and are poor guides to understanding the eschatological judgment of God. "For the *hour* of awakening, the striking of the last hour, the time of fulfilment, which is here announced, certainly does not mean some succeeding chronological hour, as though the life which proceeds from death, the non-existence by which all 'existence' is dissolved, the *Now* which is between all past and all future, could be a period of time succeeding another period of time."[52]

In short, the eschaton is not a literal cataclysmic "end time." "The End of which the New Testament speaks is no temporal event, no legendary 'destruction' of the world; it has nothing to do with any historical, or 'telluric', or cosmic catastrophe."[53]

Following this, we then see how the understanding of the eschaton Barth urges is critical not only of sentimental fantasy but also of liberal complacency.

> What *delays* [the Eschaton's] coming is not the Parousia, but our awakening. Did we but awake; did we but remember; did we but step forth from unqualified time into the time that has been qualified; were we only terrified by the fact that, whether we wish it or not, we do stand at every moment on the frontier of time; did we, standing on the frontier, dare to love the Unknown, to apprehend and lay hold of the Beginning in the End—then, neither should we join the sentimentalists in expecting some magnificent or terrible FINALE, nor should we comfort ourselves for its failure to appear by embracing the confident frivolity of modern protestant cultured piety.

However, it is a criticism that, finally, retains the liberal assumption that the "end" of which Scripture speaks cannot be a real end, but must be understood existentially.

---

52. Ibid., 500.
53. Ibid.

> We should, then, refuse both methods of escaping so shamefully from the bitter earnestness of the Day that is *at hand*. But rather, knowing that the eternal "Moment" does not, has not, and will not, *enter in*, we should then become aware of the dignity and importance of each single concrete temporal moment, and apprehend its qualification and its ethical demand. Then we should await the Parousia: we should, that is to say, accept our present condition in its full seriousness; we should apprehend Jesus Christ as the Author and Finisher; and then we should not hesitate to repent, to be converted, to think the thought of eternity, and therefore to love. Apart from *knowing the time*, all this is, however, impossible; for without knowledge there is no love.[54]

For the Barth of *Romans* II, the "end" is "at hand," and not to be understood as the "sentimentalists" do, that is, as do those who expect a millennialist catastrophe. It is "at hand," so it is not to be shrugged off as he saw the "modern protestant cultured piety" around him doing. Yet it is not nor will it ever be a temporal event to be grasped like other temporal events, making it an inappropriate object of sentimental hopes for glory or revenge.[55] However, the older Barth of the *Church Dogmatics* asks whether by affirming this middle road he has indeed come up with a real alternative, and whether he has not in fact missed the central affirmation of Paul's witness: that God will indeed bring an end to all there is, and renew it according to God's plan.

Even after all the context and interpretation provided above, I find Barth's later criticism of himself a bit troublesome. For what content can one today give to the eschaton? Attempts to understand eschatology that result in projections of a literal end of time (and potentially experienceable by all) appear just as speculative and

---

54. Ibid., 500–1.
55. Such a theme suggests the Nietzschean critique of religious eschatological hopes being merely a cover for the resentments of the weak. For a good discussion of this from the perspective of a Christian philosopher, see Merold Westphal, *Suspicion and Faith: The Religious Uses of Modern Atheism* (Grand Rapids: Eerdmans, 1993).

fantastic as the "sentimentalism" Barth criticised. This struggle echoes Barth's opening comments on "The Limits of Angelology":

> In this sphere there has always been a good deal of theological caprice, of valueless, grotesque and even absurd speculation, and also of no less doubtful scepticism. *Vestigia terrent*—the lack of any sense of humour on the part of those who know and say too much, and the equal lack of any sense of humour on the part of those who deny or ignore too much. How are we to steer a way between this Scylla and Charybdis, between the far too interesting mythology of the ancients and the far too uninteresting 'demythologisation' of most of the moderns? . . . How are we to be both open and cautious, critical and naive, perspicuous and modest? There are no spheres of dogmatics where we are not well advised to take note of these questions. But there are reasons why they are particularly dark and oppressive in the doctrine of angels.[56]

The Barth of the *Church Dogmatics* wants some affirmation that there really will be an end, for without that emphasis a certain theological triumphalism and religious hubris tends to be the result. Well and good; but that emphasis has very little doctrinal and ethical content, and seemingly must be filled out by the "at hand" characteristic that Barth affirms in *Romans* II and that he later questions in the *Church Dogmatics*.[57] It may be that Barth's later criticism is better understood as a plea for eschatology to be more than merely a general anthropological principle (such as mortality) dressed up with a few theological trappings. One version of this that Barth criticized was understanding the eschaton to be (merely?) the end that comes to every human being, perhaps (as in *Romans* II) connected with the notion of *crisis* and a doctrine of revelation. Yet premillennial dispensationalism is also open to this criticism, as it dresses up barely concealed vengeance and religious chauvinism with wildly

---

56. *CD* III/3, 369.
57. For a full discussion of Barth's eschatology, see Gotthard Oblau, *Gotteszeit und Menschenzeit: Eschatologie in der Kirchlichen Dogmatik von Karl Barth* (Neukirchen-Vluyn: Neukirchener Verlag, 1988).

misinterpreted Biblical passages. In short, Barth himself appears never to have given eschatology any significant content beyond an outline. If he had, his efforts would need to be evaluated, in part, on how well he answers his own plea.

Finally, let us now consider one more question about the differences between *Romans* II and the *Church Dogmatics*. One of the primary features of Barth's mature understanding of eternity is how it locates the connection of time and eternity in Jesus Christ. This connection is placed in a clear Trinitarian context and supported by Barth's doctrine of revelation as expressed in the *Church Dogmatics*. It is, as others have recognized, perhaps Barth's most significant contribution to the concept of divine eternity.[58] The question to be asked here, then, is whether the christological angle on eternity is new, for Barth, in the *Church Dogmatics*, thus representing a radical departure from *Romans* II.

Although the christological concentration does not come to full and clear expression for Barth until the *Church Dogmatics*, hints of it do appear much earlier. Indeed, we can find these hints in *Romans* II. After all, one of the major themes of *Romans* is that God is known not by human initiative but by divine revelation, namely, Jesus Christ. More specifically, we see such a hint early on in *Romans* II, in Barth's discussion of Rom. 1:2–4. There he says that the gospel, "as the seed of eternity . . . is the fruit of time, the meaning and maturity of history—the fulfillment of prophecy" (28). This connects time and eternity by means of the Gospel. And then soon after,

Jesus Christ our Lord. This is the Gospel and the meaning of history. In

---

58. Counted among those who have noticed this may be Brian Leftow, in a response he wrote to George Hunsinger's article for the 1998 Barth Conference. Brian Leftow, "Response to *Mysterium Trinitatis*: Barth's Conception of Eternity," in *For the Sake of the World: Karl Barth and the Future of Ecclesial Theology*, ed. George Hunsinger (Grand Rapids: Eerdmans, 2004), 191–201.

this name two worlds meet and go apart, two planes intersect, the one known and the other unknown. The known plane is God's creation, fallen out of its union with Him, and therefore the world of the "flesh" needing redemption, the world of men, and of time, and of things—our world. This known plane is intersected by another plane that is unknown—the world of the Father, of the Primal Creation, and of the final Redemption. The relation between us and God, between this world and His world, presses for recognition, but the line of intersection is not self-evident. The point on the line of intersection at which the relation becomes observable and observed is Jesus, Jesus of Nazareth, the historical Jesus,—born of the seed of David according to the flesh.[59]

This is not yet the clear identification of Jesus as the God-Man who unites within himself time and eternity. However, the passage does hint at that later development. The concept of the identification is not alien to the passage. We see here a connection between time and eternity that is based not in creation or history or human achievement, but in the gospel, borne by Jesus Christ, indeed who "*is* the Gospel and the meaning of history," in whom "two worlds meet and go apart, two planes intersect."

Other hints may be found further on in *Romans* II:

[Christ's] life is the possibility which possesses all the marks of impossibility. His life is a history within the framework of history, a concrete event in the midst of other concrete events, an occasion in time and limited by the boundaries of time; it belongs to the texture of human life. But it is history pregnant with meaning; it is concreteness which displays the Beginning and the Ending; it is time awakened to the memory of Eternity; it is humanity filled with the Voice of God.[60]

And then even later: "The Epistle moves round the theme . . . that in Christ Jesus the Deus absconditus is as such the Deus revelatus. This means that the theme of the Epistle to the Romans—Theology, the Word of God—can be uttered by human lips only when it is

---

59. *Romans*, 29. Emphasis in original.
60. Ibid., 104.

apprehended that the predicate, Deus revelatus, has as its subject Deus absconditus."[61] Finally, we may note one last hint, this one found in the contemporaneous Calvin lectures: "Revelation *took place* in the other, in Jesus Christ. The intersecting of the human horizontal line by the divine vertical line *is* a fact. Time *is* related to eternity, this world to the next, I to Thou."[62]

Those hints are, however, merely hints. Barth would seek a more satisfactory way of expressing the relationship between God and time, one that moved beyond diastasis and its limitations. That way would become clear as he gave more and more theological attention to the person and work of Jesus Christ. Over time, the christological features of eternity hinted at in *Romans* II would become more developed, leading (although not in a straight line) to Barth's mature exposition of his doctrine of eternity in the *Church Dogmatics*. It is to this development that we now turn.

Beyond Diastasis

As we have seen, Barth's description of the relationship between God and time was, in *Romans* II, somewhat incomplete and weakened by certain problems. These were problems that he recognized by the time of the *Church Dogmatics*. However, as I have argued, already in *Romans* II he hinted at the solution to these problems, in particular, a thoroughgoing christological approach to the question of time and eternity.

The deployment of this approach was not sudden, appearing fully formed *sui generis* in the *Church Dogmatics*. Rather, we see the beginnings of a christological approach to the time-eternity problem

---

61. Ibid., 422.
62. Barth, *Theology of Calvin*, 61.

quite early: it was first hinted at in *Romans* II, and further suggested in works published in the years between *Romans* II and *CD* I/1 (1922 to 1932). I see two of these works as particularly representative of this development: his 1924 dogmatics lectures from Göttingen, *Unterricht in der Christlichen Religion*; and a relatively short article, first published around Christmas of 1930, "*Verheißung, Zeit,—Erfüllung.*"[63]

My task in this brief section is to note the intersection of christological themes and the question of time and eternity in these two works. From these we may see hints of the unfolding development of Barth's mature understanding of God and time. This development does not proceed in a straight line; we do not find progressively stronger christological approaches to time and eternity in the decade following *Romans* II. Rather, we find something simpler: in the years between *Romans* II and *CD* I/1, Barth became much clearer about the importance of the figure of Jesus Christ for dogmatics. This was certainly also the case for a Christian doctrine of time and eternity. Moreover, we do not find a radical break from the theological affirmations of *Romans* II. It is rather the case that the methodological and substantive changes in Barth's theology during the 1920s and early 1930s came about not only to correct certain problems in his earlier theology, but also (and more importantly) to clarify some fundamental theological insights of that theology.

Instruction in the Christian Religion

In 1924, Barth was still a relatively new professor at Göttingen (having started in 1921), preparing his first lectures in dogmatics. He had waited some time to teach dogmatics, as he held the position

---

63. Karl Barth, "Verheißung, Zeit—Erfüllung," *Zwischen den Zeiten* 9 (1931): 457–63. This source cites the original publication as being in "Münchener neuesten Nachrichten," Weihnachtsnummer 1930.

of Reformed Theology at the Lutheran-dominated University of Göttingen, where dogmatics lectures were usually the exclusive domain of Lutheran professors.[64] He was allowed to deliver these lectures only by calling them something besides *dogmatics*. Barth thus gave them the title *Instruction in the Christian Religion*,[65] the name of John Calvin's compendium of Christian doctrine, known to many by its English title, *Institutes of the Christian Religion*.

Barth was rather anxious about these lectures. In addition to feeling unprepared, he also felt, he later reported, completely alone, as he saw his contemporaries and recent precursors unable to lend good assistance in the task of a truly evangelical dogmatics.

> I shall never forget the vacation of early 1924. I sat in my study in Göttingen, confronted with the task of giving my first lectures on dogmatics. No one can have been more plagued than I was with the questions "Can I do it?" and "How shall I do it?" Alienated increasingly from the good society of contemporary theology and, as I saw more and more clearly, from almost the whole of modern theology, by the biblical and historical studies which I had hitherto undertaken, I found myself so to speak without a teacher, all alone in the vast field. I knew that the Bible had to be the master in Protestant dogmatics. And it was clear to me, as to other scholars of the time that in particular we had to take up the Reformers again.[66]

For that reason, Barth turned to a crusty old resource for help, one that turned out to be quite significant in his development at this stage: Heinrich Heppe's *Reformed Dogmatics*.[67] Barth's discovery of it is described as follows:

---

64. Eberhard Busch, *Karl Barth: His Life from Letters and Autobiographical Texts*, trans. John Bowden (London: SCM Press), 123.
65. Ibid., 155.
66. Ibid., 153.
67. Heinrich Heppe, *Die Dogmatik der evangelisch-reformierten Kirche, dargestellt und aus den Quellen belegt von Heinrich Heppe*, ed. Ernst Bizer (Neukirchen: K. Moer, 1935); Heinrich Heppe, *Reformed Dogmatics Set Out and Illustrated From the Sources*, ed. Ernst Bizer, trans. G. T. Thompson (London: Allen & Unwin, 1950).

Then it was that, along with the parallel Lutheran work of H. Schmid, Heppe's volume fell into my hands; out of date, dusty, unattractive, almost like a table of logarithms, dreary to read, stiff and eccentric on almost every page I opened; in form and content pretty adequately corresponding to what I, like so many others, had described to myself decades ago, as the "old orthodoxy."

Well, I had the grace not to be so slack. I read, I studied, I reflected; and found that I was rewarded with the discovery, that here at last I was in the atmosphere in which the road by way of the Reformers to Holy Scripture was a more sensible and natural one to tread, than the atmosphere, now only too familiar to me, of the theological literature determined by Schleiermacher and Ritschl.[68]

Why did Barth turn to Heppe? Quite simply because there Barth found the theological tools he needed. Through Heppe, as well as Schmid, the Lutheran counterpart to Heppe, Barth gave sustained theological attention to the Protestant orthodox theologians of the seventeenth century. He did this because those theologians showed Barth a serious biblical and thus *theological* focus on the issues of dogmatics. Consequently, and with regard to the topic of this study, Heppe (and Schmid) gave Barth the tools by which he could begin to give a theological interpretation of the relationship between time and eternity that was more positive in substance and that moved beyond the defects Barth would later note.

The influence of Heppe is quite apparent in the Göttingen lectures. Throughout them Barth drew heavily on the history of dogmatics, using Heppe to integrate the contributions of patristic, medieval, Reformation, and post-Reformation theologians. One finds frequent references to the Protestant orthodox in these pages, not always approvingly, but always respectfully.

One passage of significance that reflects this dependence on Heppe and Schmid, particularly with connection to the topic of God's

---

68. Barth in Heppe, *Reformed Dogmatics*, v.

eternity, is found as he considers Schleiermacher's definition of "eternity and omnipresence as the absolutely timeless and spaceless causality of God."[69] Barth is not satisfied with this definition, even though some might think that he would have approved of it and others that similarly take the relationship of time and eternity to be entirely negative. "If I were the theologian of negation I am rumored to be, I could hold a perfect orgy here."[70] His problem with the negative construal of Schleiermacher and others is that "with a mere negation of time and space we have not yet thought of God's eternity and omnipresence."[71] In Barth's estimation, "the older dogmatics," as he calls it, did not make that mistake, but was able to emphasize rightly the "positive relation" God has "to the limit of time and space" in such a way that God is not so "limited by them as the infinite is by the finite."[72] Barth then draws on several passages found in Heppe and Schmid, as well as Thomas's *Summa*, to call to mind classical definitions of eternity. They drive toward this clearly Boëthian allusion: "Eternity is the quality of God in virtue of which he contains in himself the meaning of time. Eternity is simultaneous duration."[73]

In this passage, Barth is concerned that the knowledge of God not be turned into an abstract consideration of concepts. Rather, Barth is insistent that God is personal, and that knowledge of God comes by the initiative of that divine person's act. This is a recurring theme in the *Göttingen Dogmatics*, and figures prominently in Barth's treatment of the divine attributes. Early on in that discussion, he says, "All that God is, he is as a person. He exists as a person. He is Father, Son, and

---

69. Barth, *The Göttingen Dogmatics*, 434.
70. Ibid., 435.
71. Ibid. So it is in these lectures that Barth apparently first criticizes Schleiermacher on the concept of eternity.
72. Barth, *The Göttingen Dogmatics*, 435–36.
73. Ibid., 436.

Spirit from eternity to eternity. Once we abstract away, even for a moment, from the speaking person that *addresses* us, that addresses *us*; once we dissolve the deity in a general truth or idea that is no longer a person, we are no longer thinking about God."[74] Some pages later, he offers this: "Is there really a knowledge of God's eternity apart from his holiness or love?"[75]

Hunsinger might call these emphases *personalism* and *actualism*, descriptions I accept, but will not develop here. Knowledge of God is connected with the actual acts of this personal God, and is not based on speculative concepts. "But now we must make a sharp turn here again and recall that if this is not to be all up in the air, if this coexistent eternity and this omnipresence that contains things in itself as in a most minute point are not to be metaphysical ghosts, everything depends on this being *God's* antithesis and relation to the limits of time and space that are at issue in the doctrine."[76] In other words, we must be certain that we are really talking about God, and not about concepts, metaphysics, and the like. Continuing directly: "God is personality. God reveals himself. Eternity and omnipresence in themselves, as concepts, break apart. In these concepts we do not get beyond infinity unless we know them in a here and now in which we are known by God, in which we encounter his holy, righteous, and merciful will, in which we are the objects of his love."[77]

Barth then arrives at his point with these words: "The limit of space and time is our limit, and the whole truth of the gospel and the law lies in the fact that in Christ time was fulfilled and the world was loved. . . . The point here is that the eternal light has risen, and the circle of the whole world cannot contain what now lies in the virgin's womb."[78]

---

74. Ibid., 368.
75. Ibid., 388.
76. Ibid., 437.
77. Ibid.

It is in the incarnation that the true understanding of God's eternity and our time are found. And so, here Barth makes explicit reference to Jesus Christ as the one in whom time is fulfilled. This is a doctrinal advance beyond what he had said of time and eternity in *Romans* II, in which diastasis was the prevailing theme. In short, with the *Göttingen Dogmatics*, Jesus Christ overcomes the diastasis of time and eternity. Here, and apparently for the first time, Barth draws on Christology as a corrective *theologoumenon* to our reflections on God's eternity.

Christology and Eternity

Such an appeal to Christology became for Barth a self-consciously chosen part of his theological method. Later, in reflecting on the changes in method during this period, he identified quite specifically this focus on Jesus Christ. "I had to change my own learning a second time. I simply could not hold to the theoretical and practical *diastasis* between God and man on which I had insisted at the time of *Romans*, without sacrificing it. . . . I had to understand Jesus Christ and bring him from the periphery of my thought into the centre."[79] The period to which Barth refers is actually that of his *Prolegomena zur Christlichen Dogmatik*, his lectures in dogmatics from his time in Münster.[80] These lectures were published in 1927, three years after he delivered the Göttingen dogmatics. Time does not allow us to explore fully the christological motifs present in his Münster *Prolegomena*. Barth's emphasis on Christology is apparent from even

---

78. Ibid., 438.
79. From Barth's 1964 *Selbstdarstellung*, cited by Busch, *Karl Barth: His Life from Letters and Autobiographical Texts*, 173.
80. Karl Barth, *Die christliche Dogmatik im Entwurf, vol. 1: Die Lehre vom Worte Gottes; Prolegomena zur christlichen Dogmatik*, ed. Gerhard Sauter (Zürich: Theologischer Verlag, 1982).

a cursory glance at the work. However, Barth identifies his turn to Christology as happening later than it actually had.

We should not be surprised if Barth's recollection of the precise time of his turn to Christology is telescoped somewhat, given that he makes his observation thirty-six years after the fact. Wilfried Härle has demonstrated that Barth had a kind of selective memory regarding his reaction to his former university professors at the time of the first World War.[81] Although Härle's point is judged by some to be overwrought, I find his basic observation convincing: that Barth's autobiographical recollections many years later may not be entirely accurate. It seems quite clear that they should not be taken at face value with regard to details. They say as much about the man recollecting as they do about the man recalled. In the case of Barth's recollection of a christological turn, I think it is clear that such a turn indeed took place, although it began earlier than Barth recalls in his 1964 essay. We see it already in the 1924 Göttingen lectures, and it continues in the 1927 *Prolegomena zur Christlichen Dogmatik*.

That Barth emphasizes Christology in the *Prolegomena* is clear. But there is little there that shows a connection of that emphasis with the question of God's eternity. It simply does not find a home in what he is doing in these lectures, in great part because the lectures are on prolegomena, and not on specific doctrines. For our purposes there is no need to go mining for what few passages there may be. It is adequate simply to indicate that the *Prolegomena* demonstrates the continuing focus on the doctrine of Jesus Christ as a resource for Christian dogmatics.

The christological emphasis does find a specific connection to issues of time and eternity in a little-known article Barth wrote for publication around Christmas in 1930, "Promise, Time, and

---

81. Wilfried Härle, "Der Aufruf der 93 Intellektuellen und Karl Barths Bruch mit der liberalen Theologie," *Zeitschrift für Theologie und Kirche* 72, no. 2 (1975): 207–24.

Fulfillment."[82] This article shows, almost ten years before *CD* II/1, the appearance of an incarnational focus in Barth's reflections on time.

The burden of this piece is to show how in the incarnation of Jesus Christ both time and the promise given to humanity were fulfilled. This fulfillment is in some sense complete, yet it is not complete in the sense that it has eliminated time or the passage of time, nor does it render the promise a thing of the past.[83] That is often the misunderstanding put forth even by those charged with preaching:

> Fulfillment is widely spoken of by those responsible for Christian proclamation as though with the appearance of Christ the promise has ceased to be promise, as though there were now no more time and no more waiting. "The promise is fulfilled" is thus understood to mean that the promise merely promised is now here, and can be adopted, possessed, and enjoyed by humankind or at any rate by certain human beings, namely by Christians.[84]

Barth is quite disdainful of such an understanding, and describes it rather scornfully. Continuing directly: "'The Time is fulfilled' is then understood in this way: where up til now there was mere time, becoming and passing, coming and going, the great waiting, there is now, given to humans beings or rather to those certain human beings, like an island in the sea, a piece of timeless presence, a piece of eternity."[85]

This a regrettable turn, in Barth's opinion, one that leads to an abandoning of a truly Christian understanding of the coming of Jesus Christ.[86] In short, we see here a continuation of the diastasis of time

---

82. Barth, "Verheißung, Zeit—Erfüllung."
83. Ibid., 457.
84. Ibid.
85. Ibid., 457–58.
86. Although he doesn't elaborate in this fashion, his objection surely would be of a piece with his concern for a genuinely theological understanding of God, one that sees eternity not as some independently knowable feature of reality, but that is rather a feature (or rather, an "attribute" or "perfection") of the very being of God.

and eternity that figures so prominently in *Romans* II. He goes on, "One cannot hide from oneself the fact that Christian proclamation today, that is, for about two or three hundred years, has predominantly spoken of the fulfillment *in just this way*. At the same time as this shift in the doctrine, with the tacit and express approval of the church and with its participation, the bourgeois Christmas practice came into fashion, or the old pagan solstice custom was taken up anew."[87] That is quite an indictment. We should recognize, however, that it is rooted in Barth's commitment to keep Christian proclamation focused on the particulars of what God has given and done, a commitment we have identified before as Barth's particularism and objectivism. We see this as Barth continues directly, "There can be no mistake: the more one thinks of fulfillment outside of promise and outside of time as a supposedly still pole in the flight of appearances, the more must paganisms of every kind move into the Christian realm again."[88]

No, with the appearance of Christ the promise continues, and so does time.[89] In short, time and promise go together; as long as we have time, we have promise, and vice versa.[90] The promise continues with the incarnation of Jesus Christ, and indeed is made more concrete in his appearance. It is indeed fulfilled, and in such a way it truly and more specifically endures as promise. In Jesus Christ the promise was fulfilled, but in such a way that the promise continues.[91] "Here is the future, the wealth of all future good, transplanted into the present, without ceasing therefore to be quite strictly future. Here we have, in Christ and not in us, and even therefore in a future manner [*zukünftig*], but in Christ for us and

---

87. "Verheißung, Zeit—Erfüllung," 458.
88. Ibid.
89. Ibid., 458–59.
90. Ibid., 457.
91. Ibid., 459ff.

thus really coming to us: divine sonship, communion of the saints, forgiveness of sins, an eternal life; in the hiddenness of the present, of the human, all too human, in the darkness of this age [*Weltzeit*]."[92]

Time does not break off with Christ, but is indeed fulfilled. And that fulfillment is a radically eschatological perspective on time, which grows out of faith in Jesus Christ and sees every moment of time as pointing to the end of time.[93]

What Barth has done in this essay is to connect the meaning of time with Christology. We thus see a complement to what he did in the Göttingen dogmatics: in those lectures he uses Christology to inform the doctrine of eternity, whereas in "*Verheißung, Zeit—Erfüllung*" he uses Christology (although in a preliminary and merely suggestive way) to inform his understanding of time.

Summary

In this chapter I have attempted to set Barth's reflections on time and eternity in the context of the development of Barth's theological thought. Understanding that development is important, for in that development we can see the emergence of certain themes that are exceedingly important in Barth's theological exposition of the concepts of time and eternity.

In the course of this exposition, I have sought to show that the story of Barth's development with respect to a theological understanding of time and eternity was not a quantum leap from one position to another radically different position. The notion of a radical break in Barth's development is one that has been discredited by other scholars. I accept their arguments and show how a more holistic understanding of Barth's development applies to an

---

92. Ibid., 462.
93. Ibid.

evaluation of Barth's concepts of time and eternity. There is continuity between *Romans* II and the Barth of the *Church Dogmatics*. However, my exposition hasn't demonstrated the opposite either, namely, an unbroken line of conceptual continuity leading from the Barth of 1922 to the Barth of 1940. The line is not a straight one. Nonetheless, we have seen that between the Barth of *Romans* II and the Barth of *Church Dogmatics* II/1 there is a trajectory, in great part marked out by a continuing emphasis on certain key themes and also by the clearer articulation of an enduring theological principle.

That enduring theological principle, present just as clearly in *Romans* II as in the *Church Dogmatics*, is that of the unknowability of God apart from God's condescension to reveal, that is, in God's willingness to be known and to provide the means to such knowledge, by and through Jesus Christ. That principle is a key theme in Barth's theological work throughout his life, and from it flow his different attempts at theological expression. Throughout the course of my exposition we have seen hints of it in several places in Barth's works over this period, and here I have drawn attention to it. In many ways, Barth's development was an ongoing attempt to be faithful to and consistent with this principle, to work it out within the sphere of dogmatics more faithfully and thoroughly. The same is true of the topics of time and eternity. In both *Romans* II and the *Church Dogmatics time* and *eternity* are deployed in ways that derive from Barth's insistence on this principle of God's unknowability apart from how God has chosen to be known, what we might call Barth's "revelational dialectic."[94] *How* they derive is different, but they complement each other precisely in their mutual genesis in and support of the revelational dialectic. At the risk of oversimplification, we may say that in *Romans* II, the concepts of *time* and *eternity* are

---

94. The revelational dialectic is discussed in the next chapter.

used to emphasize the unknowability side of the dialectic, while in the *Church Dogmatics* they are used to emphasize the knowability side. But in both *Romans* II and the *Church Dogmatics*, both sides of the dialectic are present.

Following *Romans* II, Barth grew to see that faithfulness to the central affirmations of the Christian faith leads beyond the profoundly negative emphasis in *Romans* II and requires rather more attention to the revelation of God in Jesus Christ. He believed that Christology should more deeply inform his theological method and his doctrinal exposition. Indeed, Christology is another one of the key themes that have emerged in my exposition. I have attempted to show how christological connections to time and eternity are present even in *Romans* II, and how such use of Christology can be found in works between 1922 and 1941. As a whole, they show a trajectory of theological thought that will become quite clear in the *Church Dogmatics*, when not only christological doctrines but also the doctrine of the Trinity and the doctrine of revelation will be drawn on quite deeply to form a thoroughly doctrinal understanding of time and eternity.

Barth's focus on these doctrines truly demonstrates the differences between the understanding of time and eternity in *Romans* II and their understanding in the *Church Dogmatics*. Yet the seeds of the later exposition, so different in many ways from the earlier, are found in the diastasis and crisis of *Romans* II. The focus on Christology, the doctrine of the Trinity, and the doctrine of revelation grew out of the theological affirmations of Barth's early work. It is to these that we now turn.

5

The Doctrinal Context

To this point, we have considered two contexts in which Barth's exposition of time and eternity may rightly be located. From these contexts, the conceptual and the developmental, one may more accurately perceive the contours and depth of Barth's theological reflection on divine eternality. We turn now to consider a third context: the doctrinal. Our investigation in this chapter focuses on the role that doctrine, and especially a few particular theological doctrines, plays in Barth's theological conceptions of time and eternity.

As we saw in the previous chapter, Barth's development as a theologian led him to a greater appreciation for doctrine and its importance for theological reflection. In particular, we saw in the preceding exposition Barth's increasing appreciation for certain specific doctrines, and for how these doctrines impact the whole theological enterprise.

Chief among those doctrines, we saw, was the doctrine of Jesus Christ. As Barth's theological outlook developed through the 1920s, he became quite clear that Christology should hold central importance for the entire theological task. One finds Barth's christological emphasis present in *Romans* II, more strongly stated in the *Göttingen Dogmatics*, and then so central in the *Church Dogmatics* that one can find it on almost every page. It should be no surprise, therefore, that in the *Church Dogmatics* Barth would deploy Christology to help elucidate a thoroughly Christian understanding of time and eternity.

In addition to Christology, two other Christian doctrines have tremendous importance for Barth in his later theology, as well as in his mature understanding of time and eternity. These are the doctrine of the Trinity and the doctrine of revelation. The doctrine of the Trinity seeks to articulate the nature of God; the doctrine of revelation endeavors to speak about God's relating to those beings that are not God. In Barth's hands each of them are christocentric both in form and in substance. Together they constitute the core of the dogmatic task in the *Church Dogmatics*, and lay the groundwork for the theological exposition that would proceed throughout it.

For Barth, each of these three doctrines—Jesus Christ, Trinity, and revelation—were deeply formative of his entire theological project in the *Church Dogmatics*. The same can be said of their influence on Barth's mature articulation of eternity and temporality. Barth's mature understanding of divine eternity is completely dependent upon his Christology, his articulation of the Trinitarian dogma, and his doctrine of revelation. Without understanding these doctrines and the context they provide, one can really not expect to have a sufficient understanding of the conceptions of time and eternity in the *Church Dogmatics*. Consequently, a description of these doctrines, particularly in their relationship to Barth's concepts of time and eternity, will be the primary task of this chapter.

The order in which we will consider these doctrines is not precisely the order in which they appear in the *Dogmatics*. An explanation for this decision is needed. It is clear from even a cursory reading of volume 1 that both the doctrine of revelation and the doctrine of the Trinity are closely related to Christology. It is also clear that Barth understands that the need for the doctrine of the Trinity arises out of God's act of revelation, which comes to primary focus in the person and work of Jesus Christ. Revelation, Trinity, and Christology together are the doctrinal core of Barth's mature theology, with Christology being central noetically, the doctrine of revelation being central ontically, and the doctrine of the Trinity arising with a kind of theological necessity from the revelation of God in Jesus Christ. Alternatively stated, out of Barth's understanding of Jesus Christ grows his doctrine of revelation, for the God who reveals is the one who chooses to reveal in Jesus Christ. And these two doctrines are the fertile soil from which springs his doctrine of the Trinity, which is not a bit of abstract speculation about God, but rather is grounded in the revelation of God in Jesus Christ, in whom we learn of God's nature.

Thus for the sake of clarity of exposition, we will first consider Barth's Christology, then his doctrine of revelation, then his doctrine of the Trinity. This order will, I hope, make it clear in the limited space available the great mutual dependence of these doctrines and their significance for understanding Barth's theology of time and eternity.

Jesus Christ

Without question, the figure of Jesus Christ is central in Karl Barth's theology. We saw in the previous chapter how this assertion is true, whether one speaks of the so-called early or later Barth. Of course, at a certain point in Barth's development (somewhere in the mid-1920s) Barth decided that he must allow Christology to have a more secure, even controlling, role in his theology. If one describes Barth's later theology as a "systematic" theology,[1] then this description is accurate only insofar as one understands that Barth wished all doctrines, and all theological assertions (including those regarding time and eternity) to be intentionally connected with what was for Barth the fundamental theological fact, the revelation of God in Jesus Christ.

This, of course, is the christocentrism of Barth's theology that many theologians have noted and a number of them reject. Certainly, one may raise objections about a theological method that allows Christology such a determinative role without committing oneself to a total rejection of Christology. For better or for worse, Barth gave Christology a controlling position in the theology of the *Church Dogmatics*, and particularly in his understanding of time and eternity. At this point in our discussion, however, we are going about merely a demonstration of this fact, and not an evaluation of whether Barth's christocentric method is valid or helpful.

The Christological Concentration of the *Church Dogmatics*

Barth states the christological determination of dogmatics quite plainly in §15.1, "The Problem of Christology." Here he defends the christological focus of the *Church Dogmatics*, and indeed the necessity of that focus for all dogmatics worthy of the name. "A church dogmatics must, of course, be christologically determined as a whole and in all its parts, as surely as the revealed Word of God, as attested by Holy Scripture and proclaimed by the Church, is its one and only criterion, and as surely as this revealed Word is identical

---

1. But cf. Barth's comments on "systems" and "systematic" in *Church Dogmatics*, trans. Geoffrey W. Bromiley et al (Edinburgh: T. & T. Clark, 1956–69), I/2, 861–69, and following, *passim*.

with Jesus Christ."[2] Christology is central to the task of dogmatics, and to its very method. It must be determinative of the whole and the parts, since Jesus Christ is the Word of God, which is the only criterion of dogmatics.

Consequently, when dogmatics does not operate determined by that criterion, both formally and materially, then, Barth believes, it must be operating according to a criterion alien to church dogmatics. "If dogmatics cannot regard itself and cause itself to be regarded as fundamentally Christology, it has assuredly succumbed to some alien sway and is already on the verge of losing its character as church dogmatics."[3] Moreover, that christological determination must not be implicit or incidental. "As a whole, i.e., in the basic statements of a church dogmatics, Christology must either be dominant and perceptible, or else it is not Christology."[4]

This christological concentration is true of the entirety of the *Church Dogmatics*, even though Christology is not, of course, everywhere subjected to doctrinal exposition. We find such formal exposition only in two sections, located in I/2 and IV/1. Yet even in volumes II and III, where there is no formal doctrinal exposition of Christology, one sees Christology's formative influence on Barth's theological work, indeed, the appearance of what may be called "mini-Christologies" or the exposition of topics that might appear, in another theology, with other topics under the heading of "The Person and Work of Jesus Christ."

Two examples readily suggest themselves. First, in Barth's reevaluation of the doctrine of election in II/2, we find a striking christological focus. In short, Jesus Christ is both the Electing and the Elected.[5] "In its simplest and most comprehensive form the dogma

---

2. *CD* I/2, 123.
3. Ibid.
4. Ibid.
5. Ibid., II/2, §33.

of predestination consists . . . in the assertion that the divine predestination is the election of Jesus Christ."[6] This, of course, is Barth's signal contribution to the doctrine of election in the history of doctrine (whether one agrees with his efforts here or not): to give an exposition of the doctrine that not only is connected with Christology (which would be rare enough), but is indeed grounded upon it and, in the end, directs attention to it.

A second example is one that is more directly relevant to the topic of this book. In his exposition of the doctrine of creation in volume III, the section titled "Man in His Time" (§47), the "Man" of whom Barth first speaks is not generic "Man," but Jesus Christ, the one who alone is "Very God and Very Man."[7] Only subsequently, after considering what we may learn about time from Jesus Christ, does Barth consider the place of human beings in time. "In order to see man in his time correctly, we have investigated the being of the man Jesus in His time." Jesus Christ is Lord of time, and his being in time is "true and genuine."[8] In comparison, we see that our being in time is so dissimilar to that of Jesus that ours is neither true nor genuine. Yet nonetheless in Christ we know that even our fallen temporality is under grace, even as in Christ we know the kind of temporality originally intended for us.

George Hunsinger has emphasized Barth's "particularism,"[9] and it is this christological focus that is especially denoted by Hunsinger's category. For Karl Barth, Christian theological reflection must be connected to and dependent on the "particulars" of how God has

---

6. Ibid., 103.
7. A phrase that recalls, not only the Nicene Creed, but the title of a part of *CD* I/2 (§15.2), in which Barth discussed the incarnation. In addition, the "Very God/Very Man/Very God-Man" formula is a major piece of Barth's exposition of Christology under the heading of the "Doctrine of Reconciliation," in *CD* IV/1, esp. §58.
8. *CD* II/2, 519.
9. George Hunsinger, *How to Read Karl Barth: The Shape of His Theology* (New York: Oxford University Press, 1991), 30–33.

revealed. Since God has revealed most decisively through Jesus Christ, then dogmatic science must look to Jesus Christ for the "particulars" of its judgments.

In short, the figure of Jesus Christ plays a significant role in Barth's exploration of doctrine. In the theological rhetoric of the *Church Dogmatics*, Jesus Christ is very often the One of whom a doctrine under discussion truly speaks, even when his name is not explicitly spoken. Indeed, as we have seen, for Barth it is from the person and work of Jesus Christ that need for any doctrine under discussion necessarily flows, and it is to that same Jesus Christ, his being and his deeds, that the doctrine necessarily must, in some way, point.

Christology, Time, and Eternity

Given the strong emphasis on Christology in the method and the particulars of the *Dogmatics*, we should not be surprised to find strong connections there between Barth's Christology and his understanding of time and eternity. To be sure, Christology exercises great influence on Barth's discussion of time and eternity. We see this influence in numerous places throughout the *Church Dogmatics*. In some of those places, we may see a few important theological assertions that result from this christological bearing. It is to a brief examination of these that we now turn.

For Barth, dogmatic reflection on eternity must begin with Jesus Christ, particularly with the incarnation. "Again, a correct understanding of the concept of eternity is reached only if we start from . . . the real fellowship between God and the creature, and therefore between eternity and time. This means starting from the incarnation of the divine Word in Jesus Christ."[10] Having begun

---

10. *CD* II/1, 616.

from that starting point, namely, from the revelation of God in Jesus Christ, dogmatic exploration of the concept of eternity leads to important insights about God's eternity. Following directly:

> The fact that the Word became flesh undoubtedly means that, without ceasing to be eternity, in its very power as eternity, eternity became time. Yes, it became time. What happens in Jesus Christ is not simply that God gives us time, our created time, as the form of our own existence and world, as is the case in creation and in the whole ruling of the world by God as its Lord. In Jesus Christ it comes about that God takes time to Himself, that He Himself, the eternal One, becomes temporal, that He is present for us in the form of our own existence and our own world, not simply embracing our time and ruling it, but submitting Himself to it, and permitting created time to become and be the form of His eternity.[11]

For Barth, the incarnation of Jesus Christ is the connection of time and eternity.[12] "In Jesus Christ God and man, eternity and time, converge and overlap in a temporal and time-transcending perfect willed and achieved by God."[13] That incarnational intersection of time and eternity is effected by the free loving act of God who loves in freedom. "As God was in Christ, far from being against Himself, or at disunity with Himself, He has put into effect the freedom of His divine love, the love in which He is divinely free." This divine love in freedom, the incarnation and mission of Jesus Christ, reveals the nature of God's eternity, which is itself characterized by freedom, and indeed by a kind of temporality, namely, "true time," which God not only *has* but *is*. "The eternity in which He Himself is true time and the Creator of all time is revealed in the fact that, although our time

---

11. Ibid.
12. "As the Mediator between God and humankind, between heaven and earth, Jesus Christ is also the Mediator between eternity and time." Hunsinger, "*Mysterium Trinitatis*: Karl Barth's Conception of Eternity," in *Disruptive Grace: Studies in the Theology of Karl Barth* (Grand Rapids: Eerdmans, 2000), 202.
13. *Perfect* here is a noun (*Perfekt*), not an adjective. CD III/1, 27.

is that of sin and death, He can enter it and Himself be temporal in it, yet without ceasing to be eternal, able rather to be the Eternal in time."[14]

"True time," of course, is what we see in Jesus Christ, as we mentioned above, the time Jesus has truly and genuinely. This is in contrast to a second kind of time, "lost time," which is neither true nor genuine, but is nonetheless the time that fallen humanity experiences and knows. Indeed, Barth's use of Christology yields three kinds of time: besides "true time" and "lost time," there is also "the time of revelation."[15] "But this different time is the new, third time, which arises and has its place because God reveals Himself, because He is free for us, because He is with us and amongst us, because in short, without ceasing to be what He is, He also becomes what we are."[16]

The time of revelation is exhibited primarily and decisively in Jesus Christ. "God's revelation is the event of Jesus Christ." Yet this time is not something that takes place apart from our time, in a realm having no contact with history and temporality. For Barth, revelation is not a "timeless truth" but is supremely temporal, originating in God's time and then exhibited in our time. "We do not understand [this time]

---

14. *CD* IV/1, 187ff.
15. The title of *CD* §14.
16. Ibid., I/2, 49. Here we see, in connection with temporality, Barth's use of the *anhypostasis/ enhypostasis* Christology so characteristic of traditional christological reflection, particularly that of the patristic period. Among those who have noted Barth's indebtedness to classical theological statements on Christology are Bruce McCormack, *Karl Barth's Critically Realistic Dialectical Theology: Its Genesis and Development, 1909–1936* (New York: Oxford University Press, 1995); and Thomas F. Torrance, *Theology in Reconciliation: Essays Towards Evangelical and Catholic Unity in East and West* (Grand Rapids: Eerdmans, 1975); also, Torrance, *Karl Barth: Biblical and Evangelical Theologian* (Edinburgh: T, & T, Clark, 1990). A very fine exposition of Barth's discussion of Christology in *CD* IV/1 may be found in Eberhard Jüngel, *Barth-Studien*, Oekumenische Theologie, Bd. 19 (Zürich Gütersloh: Benziger Mohn, 1982); E.T., Eberhard Jüngel, *Karl Barth: A Theological Legacy* (Philadelphia: Westminster Press, 1986). Barth discusses the anhypostasis/enhypostasis doctrine in *CD* I/2, 163 and IV/1, 49–50 and 91–92. McCormack in particular has shown how the classic doctrine of anhypostasis/enhypostasis becomes central in Barth's Christology.

as God's revelation, if we do not state unreservedly that it took place in 'our' time." But this time nonetheless is not to be understood as equivalent to or coterminous with our own, fallen, time. Rather, it is the appearance of God's own time within our time, and so manifests the Boëthian simultaneity of past, present, and future, a living, true temporality.

> Conversely, if we understand it as God's revelation, we have to say that this event had its own time; in this event it happened that whereas we had our own time for ourselves as always, God had time for us, His own time for us—time, in the most positive sense, i.e. present with past and future, fulfilled time with expectation and recollection of its fulfilment, revelation time and the time of the Old Testament and New Testament witness to revelation—but withal, His own time, God's time; and therefore real time.[17]

This is surely a Boëthian cast to a christologically informed understanding of God's relation to time, in which God's life is the "perfect possession" of past, present, and future "all at once."[18]

> The incarnate Word of God *is*. But this means that it was and will be. But again it was never "not yet," and it will never be "no more." On the contrary, it is "now" even as it is "once" (and to that extent "no more"); and it is also "now" even as it is "then" (and to that extent "not yet"). It is a perfect temporal present, and for that very reason a perfect temporal past and future. It enters fully into the succession and separation of the times which together constitute time, and transforms this succession and separation into full contemporaneity.[19]

In Jesus Christ, then, God's time intersects our time. But it does so not out of necessity, but out of freedom; not as judgment only, but

---

17. *CD* I/2, 49.
18. Boëthius's definition is discussed above in chapter 2.
19. *CD* III/1, 73–74. Brian Leftow says something similar, although in a more philosophical context: "If God is timeless and at some time becomes incarnate, then since the incarnation cannot constitute a change in Him, He is from all eternity incarnate, notwithstanding that *in time* He becomes incarnate only at a certain date." Leftow, *Time and Eternity* (Ithaca, NY: Cornell University Press, 1991), 322, n12.

THE DOCTRINAL CONTEXT

as reconciliation. "It is with this lost man, who has only this lost time, who in reality has not time at all, that God in His time—at the beginning of His time of grace—has concluded His covenant."[20] The gracious and free intersection of God's time with lost time in the time of revelation is an act of grace and healing. For Jesus "does not extinguish time. . . . He normalizes time. He heals its wounds. He fulfils and makes it real. And so He returns it to us in order that we might have it again as 'our time,' the time of the grace addressed to us, even when we had lost it as 'our' time."[21] In the incarnation, God "masters time. [God] re-creates it and heals its wounds, the fleetingness of the present, and the separation of past and the future from one another and from the present."[22]

As a result, we have the opportunity, by grace and at second hand (that is, through Jesus Christ), to experience real time. Jesus "invites us in faith in Him to become contemporaries of genuine time, so that in Him and by Him we, too have real time." To have real time, and to have it really, is to live in the new reality of Jesus Christ, to participate in the reconciliation made possible by him.

> Really to have time is to live in Him and with Him, in virtue of His death and resurrection in the present which is the turning point in which the sin and servitude and condemnation and death of man . . . lie behind us as the past, in which they can be present only in Him, . . . and in which man's innocence and obedience and justification and sanctification and felicity lie before us, but are already present in Him.

That is the life of real time, which we have only by participation in Jesus Christ, whose past, present, and future are for him simultaneous, and so to whom we can and may look for our future, as a present reality. "Really to have time is to be in Him and with Him, in virtue

---

20. *CD* III/1, 72.
21. Ibid., 74.
22. Ibid., II/1, 617.

of our participation in His present, on the road from this past into this future."[23]

In Christ, then, there is the possibility that lost time, the time of fallen human beings in their fallenness, may be lifted up and blessed with a sense of God's time, God's eternity. "Jesus has more than just His own time. He lives in His time, and while it does not cease to be His time, and the times of other men do not cease to be their times, His time acquires in relation to their times the character of God's time, of eternity, in which present, past and future are simultaneous."[24]

The foregoing is sufficient to demonstrate that the figure of Jesus Christ is decisive for Karl Barth's understanding of time and eternity in the *Church Dogmatics*. Without a doubt, Christology is, for Barth, a foundational doctrine, not only in the *Dogmatics*, but also in his theological articulation of the meaning of time and eternity.

Revelation

Second in our series of doctrines to explore is revelation. Revelation is the act by which God makes God's self known to God's creatures. For Barth, revelation is always the act of God. Knowledge of God is never something the creature achieves on it's own. It is always the act of God and therefore the gift of God. As is well-known (although perhaps for reasons not as well-known), Barth had a low opinion of the idea of "general revelation," as well as the project of "natural theology."[25] As Barth understood it, knowledge of God was never *a given*, but rather was always *given by God*.

---

23. Ibid., III/1, 74.
24. Ibid., III/2, 440.
25. See Brunner's essay "Natur und Gnade" and Barth's response "Nein" in Emil Brunner, *Natur und Gnade: zum Gesprach mit Karl Barth* (Zurich: Zwingli-Verlag, 1935); Emil Brunner, *Natural Theology: Comprising "Nature and Grace,"* trans. Peter Fraenkel (London: Centenary, 1946).

The Christological Particularism of Revelation

It is for this reason that for Barth in the *Church Dogmatics*, revelation *is* Jesus Christ. Barth's statement from I/2 that we cited above is relevant here: "God's revelation is the event of Jesus Christ."[26] Such an emphasis is present throughout Barth's work. But it came to particularly clear focus in the *Church Dogmatics*. "Revelation in fact does not differ from the person of Jesus Christ nor from the reconciliation accomplished in him."[27] Revelation is the means by which God is known. And for Barth that revelation is at all points either specifically Jesus Christ, or is related to him as promise is to fulfillment or as parable is to meaning. But revelation is not only the means by which knowledge of God is conveyed; it is also the content of such knowledge. That content is not mere information about God. Indeed, it is God's very self. This is what the incarnation of Christ means, and what it reveals: Immanuel, God with us.

Thus in a Barthian framework *revelation* may be understood to mean specifically and perhaps even exclusively *Jesus Christ* because, for Barth, this is the means by which God has chosen to be known. This has important implications for Barth's theological method, and for the task of dogmatic theology as he conceived it. For to seek knowledge of God outside of God's actual means of revealing is to engage in speculation.

Such an emphasis, a form of "particularism" as Hunsinger might call it, is not far removed from the understanding of revelation in *Romans* II. McCormack has observed that "strictly speaking,

---

26. *CD* I/2, 49.
27. Ibid., I/1, 119. When, during his 1962 tour of the United States, Barth was asked whether revelation may occur outside of Christianity, Barth replied no. In his elaboration, he said, "Revelation does not mean only that there are signs of God's presence but that God himself is speaking." Karl Barth, "Gespräch in Princeton I," in *Gespräche, 1959–1962*, ed. Eberhard Busch, vol. 4, Gesamtausgabe, IV, Gespräche 25 (Theologischer Verlag, 1976), 504–5.

revelation for Barth in Romans II is the resurrection and only the resurrection."[28] Certainly, more than the resurrection is considered in the *Church Dogmatics*. Yet the focus on the specifics of Christian proclamation when revelation is in view is a characteristic of all of Barth's theological output, and it has a more thorough impact on Barth's method in the *Church Dogmatics*. It is a controlling theme throughout it.

The Revelational Dialectic

In revelation, God makes known God's mystery, which is not removed by revelation. The revelation does not demystify God, but rather imparts the understanding that God is always for us shrouded in mystery. The importance of this is that Barth at all times wants to hold together these two important affirmations: we really have true knowledge of God, but we do not have complete knowledge of God. Indeed, under God's own control, part of what we are given to know is God's mystery. "Revelation in the Bible means the self-unveiling, imparted to men, of the God who by nature cannot be unveiled to men."[29] Revelation is a making known of God that preserves this distance, and even makes this distance known. "Revelation itself is to be understood . . . as the revelation of the free loving-kindness of God," a revealing that remains a gracious concealing.[30] It is God's "concealment even in [God's] revelation."[31] In the New Testament, far from being a departure from the Old Testament witness to God's mystery, "it is now supremely true that God conceals Himself in revealing Himself."[32] As Barth states it in the opening to the second

---

28. McCormack, "A Scholastic of a Higher Order: The Development of Karl Barth's Theology, 1921–31," (PhD diss., Princeton Theological Seminary, 1989), 138.
29. *CD* I/1, 315.
30. Ibid., 322.
31. Ibid.

volume, the content of revelation "is the existence of Him . . . who remains a mystery to us because He Himself has made Himself so clear and certain to us."³³

This duality of hiddenness in the midst of revealedness we might call the "revelational dialectic." Barth is often called a dialectical theologian, but it has often been overlooked that there is more than one kind of dialectic.³⁴ This revelational dialectic is another species of dialectic in Barth's mature work, one that arises out of the same theological convictions as Barth's other dialectics.³⁵ As McCormack puts it, "The time-eternity dialectic . . . gives rise to a further sub-class of dialectic, the dialectic of veiling and unveiling in God's self-revelation."³⁶

That revelational dialectic might be described as follows. In revelation, God reveals God's self. But the revealing is not a complete emptying, an evaporating of mystery. It is a revealing of the self, and thus of the mystery. It is an unveiling of that which remains veiled. For Barth, God's act of self-revelation yields true knowledge of God, and part of that knowledge is that some of God's being is and will remain a mystery. Economy and theology, God's acts and God's essence, the works of God *ad extra* and the being of God *ad intra*: these are shown in revelation to be connected to each other; but their connection does not exhaust the mystery of God nor deny the freedom of God.

---

32. Ibid., 323.
33. Ibid., II/1, 3.
34. To correct this oversight is among the burdens and contributions of works such as Ingrid Spieckermann, *Gotteserkenntnis: Ein Beitrag zur Grundfrage der neuen Theologie Karl Barths* (München: Chr. Kaiser, 1985); Michael Beintker, *Die Dialektik in der "dialektischen Theologie" Karl Barths: Studien zur Entwicklung der Barthschen Theologie und zur Vorgeschichte der "Kirchlichen Dogmatik,"* Beiträge zur evangelischen Theologie (München: C. Kaiser, 1987); McCormack, "Scholastic of a Higher Order"; and McCormack, *Critically Realistic*.
35. An expansion and extension of this point is, in great part, the burden of chapter 4.
36. McCormack, "Scholastic of a Higher Order," 171–72.

God's freedom, of course, is a major concern of Barth's, and it is what he sees as implicit denials of God's freedom that he finds objectionable in the classical liberal theologians he so often criticizes. More positively, Barth's focus on God's freedom points to another dialectic, that of divine freedom and divine love. He considers these in detail in his discussion of the attributes of God in II/1, where he proceeds under the section headings "The Perfections of the Divine Loving" (§30) and "The Perfections of the Divine Freedom" (§31).

Quite likely, this dialectic of divine freedom and love is related to a dialectic in the human sphere likewise important to Barth, that of human freedom and obedience. As one example from the context we are exploring at this point, that of revelation and Trinity, we find this comment of Barth's on dogmatic method: "The freedom of dogmatic method is the freedom of obedience. This obedience will not be the obedience required, if it is not rendered freely, and if it does not leave freedom to others. Nor will the freedom be the freedom required, if it makes possible anything other than obedience, and does not therefore summon all others to render obedience in freedom."[37] One may rightly ask why the human dialectic is not likewise freedom and love. Yet the typically paired terms for Barth, I suggest, are *freedom* and *obedience*. A helpful contribution to Barth scholarship would be an exploration of these two dialectics: divine freedom and love, and human freedom and obedience. In any case, obedience is quite obviously an important theme in Barth's work, both early and late.[38]

---

37. CD I/2, 861.
38. For a discussion of the importance of freedom in the work of Karl Barth, see Clifford Green's introduction to Barth, *Karl Barth: Theologian of Freedom*, ed. Clifford Green (Minneapolis: Fortress Press, 1991). See also Clifford Green, "Freedom for Humanity: Karl Barth and the Politics of the New World Order," in *For the Sake of the World: Karl Barth and the Future of Ecclesial Theology*, ed. George Hunsinger (Grand Rapids: Eerdmans, 2004), 95–108.

Returning to the revelational dialectic, we may summarize it as follows. Barth understands God's act of revelation as expressing both God's hiddenness and revealedness, so that God's being and God's act are always (ontically) identical and always (noetically) distinct, never separate and yet never collapsed into one another. Use of this dialectic in the *Church Dogmatics* typically and frequently takes the form of pairs pointing to the reality of God "inward" and "outward," *ad intra* and *ad extra*.

This revelational dialectic, the pattern of *ad intra* and *ad extra*, is such an important aspect of Barth's understanding of revelation, and thus of the task of dogmatic theology, that it pervades the entirety of the *Church Dogmatics*. It is also of vital importance for his understanding of eternity.[39] Indeed, that pattern lies behind other paired or dialectically linked terms that are characteristic of Barth and are found throughout the *Dogmatics*: *being* and *act*, *theology* and *economy*, *ontic* and *noetic*, *hidden* and *revealed*, and, of course, *time* and *eternity*. These terms express in a variety of ways the revelational dialectic, the scheme of *ad intra* and *ad extra*. Time and Eternity is another way of conveying that dialectic; it is, in a way, a shorthand for it. We see evidence that Barth intended this equation to be made in §31: "Time which is in a sense the special creation of the 'eternal' God is the formal principle of His free activity outwards. Eternity is the principle of His freedom inwards."[40]

Finally, as we might expect, this revelational dialectic, even when expressed in connection with the question of time and eternity, is for Barth clearly linked with Christology. Indeed, it is self-consciously developed with regard to the person and work of Jesus Christ as the

---

39. "The distinction between God's being in and for itself and God's being in relation to the world will be of great importance in understanding Barth's conception of eternity," Hunsinger, "*Mysterium Trinitatis*," 197.
40. *CD* II/1 609.

focus of God's revelation. "He, Jesus Christ, is the free grace of God as not content simply to remain identical with the inward and eternal being of God, but operating *ad extra* in the ways and works of God."[41] Such an emphasis we see in Barth's Christology.

> We have to do with the eternal beginning of all the ways and works of God when we have to do with Jesus Christ—even in His true humanity. This is not a "contingent fact of history." It is the historical event in which there took place in time that which was the purpose and resolve and will of God from all eternity and therefore before the being of all creation, before all time and history, that which is, therefore, above all time and history, and will be after them, so that the being of all creatures and their whole history in time follow this one resolve and will, and were and are and will be referred and related to them. The true humanity of Jesus Christ, as the humanity of the Son, was and is and will be the primary content of God's eternal election of grace.[42]

Trinity

We turn now to a discussion of a third doctrine of Barth's, one that is also central to Barth's mature theology and that is essential for his theological understanding of time and eternity. This is his doctrine of the Trinity. We begin with Barth's own words concerning that doctrine. "The doctrine of the Trinity is what basically distinguishes the Christian doctrine of God as Christian, and therefore what already distinguishes the Christian concept of revelation as Christian, in contrast to all other possible doctrines of God or concepts of revelation."[43]

---

41. Ibid., 95.
42. Ibid., IV/2, 31.
43. Ibid., I/1, 301.

Meaning and Function

From a Roman Catholic perspective influenced by both Rahner and Barth, Walter Kasper says that the doctrine of the Trinity "is the Christian form of speaking about God."[44] Such a statement could readily have been affirmed by Barth, for whom the doctrine of the Trinity is the Christian doctrine of God. Kasper goes on to say, "The trinitarian confession is therefore the recapitulation and summary of the entire Christian mystery of salvation, and with it the entire reality of Christian salvation stands or falls. . . . Becoming a Christian, like being a Christian, is unconditionally linked to the trinitarian confession."[45] For Barth, the doctrine of the Trinity addresses the question, "Who is God?" and thus deserves to be given "the first word" in dogmatics. "What we are trying to bring to practical recognition by putting [the doctrine of the Trinity] first is . . . that this is the point where the basic decision is made whether what is in every respect the very important term 'God' is used in Church proclamation in a manner appropriate to the object which is also its norm."[46] Barth makes quite clear that he intends to give the doctrine of the Trinity a clear and controlling role in his *Dogmatics*, "that its content be decisive and controlling for the whole of dogmatics."[47]

For Barth, to say that God is triune is to speak of God's revelation; the two are intimately connected. That connection is seen very clearly when Barth, near the beginning of his discussion of "The Place of the Doctrine of the Trinity in Dogmatics,"[48] says, "*God reveals Himself. He reveals Himself through Himself. God reveals Himself.*"[49] Later, when Barth comes to discuss "The Root of the

---

44. Walter Kasper, *The God of Jesus Christ* (New York: Crossroad, 1992), 233.
45. Ibid.
46. *CD* I/1, 301.
47. Ibid., 303.
48. The title of §8.1, ibid..
49. Ibid., 296.

Doctrine of the Trinity,"[50] he asserts that "the basis or root of the doctrine of the Trinity . . . lies in revelation."[51] The doctrine of the Trinity is an unfolding of "the statement that God reveals himself as the Lord,"[52] an unfolding that makes clear the pattern of revelation to which Scripture witnesses. Because of that intimate connection with revelation, which is, after all, the sole criterion of and warrant for dogmatics, the doctrine of the Trinity has an extremely important role to play in Barth's theology.

Barth approaches the doctrine of the Trinity from two directions, the unity by means of the trinity and the trinity by means of the unity. A brief look at each of these will suffice.

First, Barth focuses on the unity of God that is revealed in God as Trinity. Precisely in the threeness of God, the unity of God is affirmed. Barth insists that the threeness by no means entails three essences, but a threeness of "persons" that affirms the unity.[53] As Barth notes, "The name of Father, Son and Spirit means that God is the one God in threefold repetition, and this in such a way that the repetition itself is grounded in His Godhead, so that it implies no alteration in His Godhead, and yet in such a way also that He is the one God only in this repetition."[54]

Second, Barth approaches God's triunity from the other side, by emphasizing the trinity that is revealed in God's unity. This unity is not simply any unity, but God's *revealed* unity. Consequently, the unity includes a threefold distinction within the essence of God between the three modes of being.[55]

---

50. §8.2, ibid.
51. Ibid., 311
52. Ibid., 306
53. Ibid., 349–50.
54. Ibid., 350.
55. Ibid., 353–55.

Barth prefers to speak of these distinctions as the three *modes of being* (*Seinsweisen*) of God, rather than as the three *persons*, the traditional term. He does not reject the term *persons*, but usually encloses it in quotes. His reason for doing so appears to be out of concern that *persons* might imply, in the modern usage of the word, distinct personalities.[56] Nonetheless, some interpreters have jumped on the phrase *modes of being* as evidence that Barth is a modalist.[57] One can so read Barth, however, only by leaving vague or undefined the term *modalism*.[58]

Most properly, *modalism* refers to the belief in Trinitarian matters that the distinctions between the persons of the Trinity are economic only, and do not apply to God's essence or being. This is surely the meaning of *modalism* against which orthodox dogma developed, and it implied of God (as the orthodox saw it) that the persons were simply "masks" of God, chosen in the divine economy merely to represent God, "the monarch." In the classic heresies of modalism,

---

56. Ibid., 351. However, Walter Kasper has suggested that the modern view of personhood is actually helpful in understanding the Trinity, and that Barth (as well as Rahner) rejected the term *person* because of an insufficiently modern understanding of the notion of person and of personhood. As Kasper saw it, Barth and Rahner had in mind only an extreme individualistic corruption of the notion of personhood. "For what Rahner describes is in fact not at all the full modern understanding of person but rather an extreme individualism in which each person in a center of action who possesses himself, disposes of himself and is set off over against others." For Kasper, a more accurate understanding of the modern concept of person is to say "that person exists only in relation; that in the concrete, personality exists only as interpersonality, subjectivity only as intersubjectivity" (Kasper, *God of Jesus Christ*, 289). This understanding of personhood allows Kasper to hold to an understanding of God as eminently personal. To reject three consciousnesses in God does not compel us to reject three centers of one consciousness: "For according to the traditional terminology, we must say that the one divine consciousness subsists in a triple mode. . . . We have no choice, then, but to say that in the Trinity we are dealing with three subjects who are reciprocally conscious of each other by reason of one and the same consciousness which the three subjects 'possess', each in his own proper way" (ibid.).
57. As does, apparently, Catherine Mowry LaCugna, who says of Barth's reflections on the doctrine of the Trinity, "The result is a form of modalism; whether this modalism is Sabellian could be debated." Catherine Mowry LaCugna, *God For Us: The Trinity & Christian Life* (San Francisco: HarperSanFrancisco, 1991), 252.
58. Alan Torrance is helpful on this point: Alan Torrance, "The Trinity," in *The Cambridge Companion to Karl Barth*, ed. John B. Webster (Cambridge: Cambridge University Press, 2000), especially 85 and 90, n24.

the modes were seen as economic only, as a presentation of the undifferentiated unity within the essence of God. Hence the name *modalistic monarchianism* is how these heresies have often been designated. The problem for the orthodox was that this made a radical distinction between the God whom we encounter in revelation and the "true" God, or, one might say, between the God who is revealed and the God who reveals. In a passage that should make clear this important distinction from modalism, Barth says, "If we are dealing with His revelation, we are dealing with God Himself and not, as Modalists in all ages have thought, with an entity distinct from Him."[59]

Given that definition, it is simply incorrect to claim that Barth is a modalist. For Barth, the three *Seinsweisen* are "always very distinctive," and "the threeness is grounded in the one essence of the revealed God."[60] Even in the *Göttingen Dogmatics* one finds a strenuous objection to conceptions of the Trinity that posit the threeness as economic or external only, the idea "that the whole business of person is simply a matter of arrangement, condescension, or economy, a mode of revelation for our sake, that the three divine persons, *hypostases*, or *prosopa* are not more than masks, or means of manifestation, or modes of subsistence, and that behind them God's essence is concealed as something different and higher, the one true substance."[61]

Thus for Barth the threeness of God's modes of being apply to eternally immanent relations within the essence of God.[62] As Hunsinger puts it, "Modalism can be charged against Barth only

---

59. *CD* I/1, 311.
60. Ibid., 360.
61. Barth, *The Göttingen Dogmatics: Instruction in the Christian Religion*, ed. Hannelotte Reiffen, trans. Geoffrey W. Bromiley, vol. 1 (Grand Rapids: Eerdmans, 1991), 101, cited in McCormack, *Critically Realistic*, 358.
62. *CD* I/1, 361, cf. 353.

out of ignorance, incompetence, or (willful) misunderstanding."[63] Assuredly, Barth affirms a true Trinity of eternal relations, which is the Trinity revealed in the economy, an immanent as well as an economic Trinity. However, the distinction between the modes of being cannot be based on neat divisions in the economy of God. Barth draws here upon the ancient assertion *opera trinitatis ad extra sunt indivisa*.[64] What then are we to make of the distinctions between the modes of being? They are to be distinguished "in terms of their distinctive relations and indeed their distinctive genetic relations to one another." The distinctions are equal, even as they are dissimilar. "Father, Son and Spirit are distinguished from on another by the fact that without inequality . . . they stand in dissimilar relations of origin to one another."[65]

The three *Seinsweisen* of the Trinity are thus intimately in relation with yet distinguished from each other. In God's triunity there is a definite and complete "participation of each mode of being in the other modes of being."[66] Barth draws on the ancient doctrine of *perichoresis* for support, which "states that the divine modes of being mutually condition and permeate one another so completely that one is always in the other two and the other two in the one."[67]

Perichoresis is an exceedingly important doctrine for Barth. It enables him to speak of both the threeness and the oneness of God's being in act. Barth frequently draws upon it, if only implicitly, as he "relates" and "distinguishes" doctrinal elements. Indeed, Barth explicitly relates the doctrine of perichoresis to his understanding of eternity, near the end of his discussion of the divine perfection of eternity. It will be helpful to cite a sizable portion of the passage:

---

63. Hunsinger, "*Mysterium Trinitatis*," 191.
64. *CD* I/1, 362.
65. Ibid., 363–64.
66. Ibid., 370.
67. Ibid.

> God *lives* eternally. It is for this reason that He has the distinctions mentioned. It is for this reason that they are not to be evaporated or assimilated to one another. . . . It is for this reason that God is equally truly and really pre-temporal, supra-temporal, and post-temporal. But since He is God, He is all this in divine perfection. Thus "before" in Him does not imply "not yet"; "after" in Him does not imply "no more"; and above all His present does not imply any fleetingness. In each of the distinctions of perfection He has a share in the others. His beginning includes not only His goal and end, but also the whole way to it. In His present there occurs both the beginning and the end. At God's end, His beginning is operative in all its power, and His present is still present. At this point, as in the doctrine of the Trinity itself, we can and must speak of a *perichoresis*, a mutual indwelling and interworking of the three forms of eternity.[68]

The perichoretic rhythm would be obvious even if Barth had not explicitly named that doctrine and thus explicitly drawn the connection. That Barth did in fact name perichoresis as a model for conceptualizing the kind of threefold eternality for which he argues demonstrates how important he thought the doctrine of the Trinity to be for a properly theological understanding of God's eternality. The connection is not incidental, nor accidental. As Barth uses it in the above passage, the doctrine of perichoresis (with its Trinitarian resonances) is not simply a heuristic device or a nifty illustration for describing divine eternality. To recall again Walter Kasper, for Barth the doctrine of the Trinity *is* the Christian doctrine of God. Eternity is a perfection or attribute of God. To attempt to speak about eternity is to attempt to speak about this God, who is not a frozen, undifferentiated unity but whose being is a living triunity.

In short, *of course* eternity and Trinity are connected for Barth, because it is of *God* that both doctrines speak. Indeed, we would expect the same of the other two doctrines, as well. For the doctrine

---

68. Ibid., II/1, 640.

of the Trinity arises out of God's revelation, which is, as we have seen, focused on and finds fullest expression in Jesus Christ.

Revelation and Trinity

We will benefit from a brief consideration of the connection between the doctrine of the Trinity and the doctrine of revelation. For Karl Barth, these are intimately related. Indeed, the doctrine of the Trinity is coinherent with revelation, for it is the Triune God who reveals to us the divine nature, which does not only *appear* to be triune, but intrinsically *is* triune. As Barth saw the matter, "The Christian concept of revelation already includes within it the problem of the doctrine of the Trinity."[69] Revelation leads to and necessitates a doctrine of the Trinity. "The statement . . . that God reveals Himself as the Lord, or what this statement is meant to describe, and therefore revelation itself as attested by Scripture, we call the root of the doctrine of the Trinity."[70]

Barth's insistence on such a complete doctrine of the Trinity, both economic and immanent, reflects, as we said, Barth's insistence that revelation is a making known of the true God, a making known that really reveals, and yet conceals even as it reveals. It is thus very important to understand what Barth is insisting on in the doctrine of the Trinity: that God has truly revealed to us God's own being. The doctrine of the Trinity indicates that God's revelation is a revelation of act and being, of being by means of and in the form of act; that what God *does* in revelation is to make known God's *essence*. In short, Barth's doctrine of the Trinity is a doctrine not only of God's economy, but of God's inner being; a doctrine not only of

---

69. Ibid., I/1, p. 304.
70. Ibid., 307.

an economic Trinity, but of an immanent Trinity, that is, of eternal Trinitarian relations within God's very being.

The importance of this becomes quite clear when we compare Barth's doctrine of the Trinity with Schleiermacher's, against which Barth developed his own.[71] Let me briefly sketch Schleiermacher's discussion of the doctrine of the Trinity. As he does with all other doctrines, Schleiermacher wishes to avoid a speculative approach to the doctrine of the Trinity. This concern proves determinative for the very shape and major features of his doctrine. For Schleiermacher, as for Barth, "speculation" was a major concern, and a problem against which his theological efforts were directed (although, without a doubt, what Schleiermacher and Barth meant by *speculation*, and their means of avoiding it, differed greatly[72]). Schleiermacher sought to safeguard against speculation by his careful placement of the doctrine of the Trinity in his system, not at the beginning, but rather at the end.[73]

The reason for this placement is that, for Schleiermacher, the doctrine of the Trinity was not itself "an immediate utterance concerning the Christian self-consciousness,"[74] but rather was a combination of the essential points of Christian doctrine, themselves immediate utterances. Those points had primarily to do with "the doctrine of the union of the Divine Essence with human nature, both in the personality of Christ and in the common Spirit of the Church."[75] In other words, the doctrine of the Trinity arises out of the conviction of faith that the divine, and truly the divine, was in

---

71. See Robert F. Streetman, "Some Questions Schleiermacher Might Ask about Barth's Trinitarian Criticisms," in *Barth and Schleiermacher: Beyond the Impasse?*, ed. James O. Duke and Robert F. Streetman (Philadelphia: Fortress Press, 1988), 114–37.
72. This was addressed also in chapter 2.
73. *The Christian Faith*, ed. H. R. Mackintosh and J. S. Stewart (Edinburgh: T. & T. Clark, 1986), 749-50. Hereafter referred to as *Chr. F.*
74. That phrase is characteristic of Schleiermacher's theological method throughout *Chr. F.*
75. Ibid., 738.

Jesus Christ and continues to be present to the church through the Holy Spirit.

It is this conviction that gives rise to the doctrine of the Trinity. It follows naturally, even imperatively, from all the other core affirmations of the Christian faith. Indeed, the doctrine of the Trinity, as Schleiermacher understood it, was "the coping-stone of Christian doctrine," for it expresses quite neatly God's union with Christ and with the Church.[76] Schleiermacher's statement here is extremely significant, for if all interpreters kept it in view, then perhaps we would have fewer repetitions of the incorrect and rather unhelpful criticism to the effect that Schleiermacher thought so poorly of the doctrine of the Trinity that he relegated it to an appendix. Such appeared to be the view of Claude Welch, in his otherwise masterful treatment of nineteenth-century theology: "Even the doctrine of the Trinity has to come in an appendix, though it expresses all that is essential in the explication of the consciousness of grace."[77] There surely are problems with Schleiermacher's doctrine of the Trinity (as I will show), but this old saw (unthinkingly repeated by students surely far less knowledgeable than Welch) is so inaccurate and misleading that it should be banished simply in the name of scholarly honesty.

Schleiermacher's concern with speculation, however, causes him to stop here in his approval of the doctrine of the Trinity as developed in the Church's theological tradition. He halts at the spot where the doctrine proceeds to speak of Trinitarian distinctions within the very essence of God. "The assumption of an eternal distinction in the Supreme Being is not an utterance concerning the religious consciousness, for there it never could emerge."[78] In other words, Schleiermacher approves of and argues for a doctrine of economic

---

76. Ibid., 739.
77. Claude Welch, *Protestant Thought in the Nineteenth Century, vol. 1: 1799–1870* (New Haven: Yale University Press, 1972), 72.
78. *Chr. F.*, 739.

Trinitarian relations (an "economic Trinity"), but rejects a doctrine of immanent Trinitarian relations (an "immanent Trinity") as involving many contradictions and tending to speculation. The *pro nobis* of God is available to us, but not the *a se*, the noetic but not the ontic, the *ad extra* but surely not the *ad intra*.

Such a brief exposition of Schleiermacher's doctrine of the Trinity should suffice here for highlighting the distinction between Schleiermacher and Barth. For Barth, as I noted above, insisted that the doctrine of the Trinity is not a doctrine about God's works alone, a doctrine of a simply economic Trinity, for which God's essence is disconnected from God's activity. As Barth understood things, the doctrine of the Trinity can and must speak of a distinction in God's essence and not only in God's works. Even here, a primary concern of Barth's was our knowledge of God. He believed it fatal for a theology to split knowledge of God's being from knowledge of God's act, leaving us with knowledge of the act but no knowledge of the being, or with the illusion that we have knowledge of the being apart from knowledge of the act. Yet Barth believes that in the economy of God we really have to do with the true God, and not with something else; there is not another God hidden behind God. "There is no such thing as Godhead in itself. Godhead is always the Godhead of the Father, Son and Holy Spirit."[79] George Hunsinger puts it well: "Like the turtles in another story, the being of God, for Barth, is trinitarian 'all the way down.'"[80]

Here it may become even clearer that Barth's understanding of revelation and his doctrine of the Trinity are integrally connected. For Barth, the "God [who] reveals Himself as Lord" is precisely the Triune God: Revealer, Revealed, and Revealedness.[81] The doctrine

---

79. *CD* II/2, 115.
80. George Hunsinger, "Election and the Trinity: Twenty-five Theses on the Theology of Karl Barth," *Modern Theology* 24, no. 2 (April 2008): 9.

of the Trinity, for Barth, is the church's reflection on the pattern of revelation in Scripture, the pattern that reflects the reality and the content of God's self-revelation to God's people. In the doctrine of the Trinity, the church reflects on not only the fact of God's revealing, but also on who God really is. Thus the doctrine of the Trinity, for Barth, is not simply a doctrine of a triune economy, the one God acting toward us in three ways, but a doctrine of an immanent Trinity, of the very eternal distinctions that Schleiermacher rejected. "The content of the doctrine of the Trinity . . . is not that God in His relation to man is Creator, Mediator and Redeemer, but that God in Himself is eternally God the Father, Son and Holy Spirit."[82] Barth insists that if revelation is really revelation, if it is to be trusted, then here, in the doctrine of the Trinity, it is true that revelation has to be a revelation of who God really is, and thus a revelation of God's inner being, for otherwise in revelation God would be deceiving us. "The doctrine of the Trinity . . . affirms securely that in the Father, the Son and the Holy Spirit, as they meet us in His revelation as Creator, Mediator and Redeemer, we have to do with the essence and the truth of the living God, not with mere appearances or emanations, not with demi-gods or deified creatures."[83]

Thus for Barth, the trustworthiness of revelation means a full-blown doctrine of the Trinity, both *ad intra* and *ad extra*. The doctrine of the Trinity speaks of God, not only of God's works (the economy), but of the being of God as well. In Barth's view, this is a matter of proper theological method, which always must proceed along the path laid out by the Word of God, which is to say "revelation."

---

81. See *CD* I/1, 296.
82. *CD* I/2, 878.
83. Ibid., 878–79.

In short, the doctrine of the Trinity, because of its close connection with revelation (and Christology), is central to the theological project of Karl Barth's *Church Dogmatics*. For Barth, this doctrine is and must be determinative for dogmatics, both in its overall structure and in its details.

Trinity and Dogmatic Structure

Let us consider that structure for a moment. Upon examination, it becomes clear that the structure of the *Church Dogmatics* is connected with the doctrine of the Trinity. Indeed (as we will see), the structure bears the appearance of having been determined by that doctrine.

The method Barth uses to structure his dogmatics is the classical method of the *loci*, which typically (in its numerous exemplars) moves through a series of doctrines in an order reminiscent of the Apostles' Creed, without necessarily subjecting these doctrines or this order to a single unifying principle. Barth says of them that "the *Loci* of the older orthodoxy were in fact basic dogmatic tenets which did not pretend to proceed from a higher unity than that of the Word of God itself, or to express any higher syntheses than arise out of the Word of God, or to be rooted and held together in any higher system than that of the Word of God."[84]

For example, the order might typically look, rather unspectacularly, something like this:

1. The One God
2. The Triune God
3. Revelation
4. Creation
5. Fall

---

84. Ibid., 870.

6. Sin
7. The Person of Christ
8. The Works of Christ (including justification)
9. The Holy Spirit (including sanctification)
10. The Church
11. The Last Things

In Barth's view, this method, that of the *loci*, "is the only truly scholarly method in dogmatics" even though it had been "wrongly set aside as unscholarly by the more progressive of the contemporaries of J. Gerhard and A. Polanus."[85]

Barth's uses the *loci* method, with some slight adaptations, and structures his *Dogmatics* around four *loci*: God, creation, reconciliation, and redemption. Under these *loci* the other traditional *loci* would be discussed. Before those, however, Barth devotes volume I to an explication of the doctrine of revelation, from which all dogmatics proceeds. The plan for the *Dogmatics*, then, was this:

Volume I: The Doctrine of the Word of God

Volume II: The Doctrine of God

Volume III: The Doctrine of Creation

Volume IV: The Doctrine of Reconciliation

Volume V: The Doctrine of Redemption[86]

---

85. Ibid.
86. Volume V, of course, was never written, although it was part of the original plan Barth had for his dogmatics. See Ibid., 881–883.

This is the structure Barth used for his *Dogmatics*. "The content of this Word of God" (initially explored in volume I) would be "unfolded" "in these four specific *Loci*,"[87] namely, in the subsequent four volumes, on God, creation, reconciliation, and redemption. Those four *loci* would be comprehended in two steps: first, an exploration of the nature of God, whose being and act are one (volume II), and second, the works of God (volumes III through V). Those works, although understood perichoretically, are nonetheless appropriated to each of the persons of the Trinity: the doctrine of creation appropriated to the Father (in whose work the Son and the Holy Spirit join); the doctrine of reconciliation appropriated to the Son (in whose work the Father and the Spirit participate); and the doctrine of redemption appropriated to the Holy Spirit (in whose work the Father and the Son cooperate).[88] This may be seen in the headings of the subsections in which Barth discusses each of the persons or *Seinsweisen* of the Trinity:

- 10. God the Father
- 10.1. God as Creator
- 11. God the Son
- 11.1. God as Reconciler
- 12. God the Holy Spirit
- 12.1. God as Redeemer

Furthermore, recall how the titles of volumes III through V correspond to these subsections:

    Volume III: The Doctrine of Creation

---

87. Ibid., 878.
88. "It is meaningful and right to designate God the Father in particular (*per appropriationem*) as Creator, and God the Creator in particular (*per appropriationem*) as the Father." Ibid., III/1, 49.

Volume IV: The Doctrine of Reconciliation

Volume V: The Doctrine of Redemption

In short, there is a clear Trinitarian cast to the structure of the *Dogmatics*, one that is by no means accidental but is rather part of Barth's intended (and stated) design.

Because of this, one might think that the structure of the *Church Dogmatics* arises out of the doctrine of the Trinity, and that what we have here, contrary to Barth's antipathy to an *a priori* determination of doctrine by a single principle and to his rejection of systematization, is the subjection of dogmatics to a *concept* or *principle*, namely, that of the doctrine of the Trinity itself. "The question arises whether behind the unfolding of the content of this Word of God in these four specific *Loci*, there is not implied a fundamental principle from which these four *Loci* may be systematically developed, viz., the dogma of the unity and trinity of God, which we have placed at the head of our doctrine of the Word as the revelation of God."[89]

Yet Barth rejects that as a misunderstanding of his method. "We did not derive our differentiation of the *Loci* from the doctrine of the Trinity." The origin of his method is the same as "the root of the Doctrine of the Trinity,"[90] namely, the revelation of God who freely and graciously reveals Godself. "We derived the doctrine of the Trinity itself from the same source as that from which is now derived the differentiation of the *Loci*, viz., the work and activity of God in His revelation."[91] It is not the doctrine of the Trinity that comes first, or is most basic in the *Dogmatics*. Rather it is "the fact of revelation" that comes first. It is that fact that precedes the doctrine of the Trinity

---

89. Ibid., I/2, 878.
90. That is the title of Ibid., §8.2 (I/1, 304–33).
91. Ibid., I/2, 878.

and all other doctrines. "The essence of this fact [of revelation] is that God confronts us as Creator, Mediator and Redeemer, that as such He speaks and deals with us, that He is therefore God and Lord in this threefold way."

The doctrine of the Trinity, as it were, is but the church's obedient reflection on that basic fact, the being of God as revealed in God's act. "This being of God in His work and activity is not a dogma, or a basic view, or a controllable principle which can be used as such for the construction of a system." To treat a doctrine that way would indeed be to put an alien criterion in place of the determinative fact of all Christian theological reflection, which does not build upon first principles but reflects on the revelation of God, indeed, "the Word of God, freely preceding and underlying all views and dogmas."[92]

Barth understands his structuring of the *Church Dogmatics* in *loci* fashion as a form of theological obedience that looks primarily to the word of God, the act of God's revelation, to its particularity, and to its unique structure. "We attained our differentiation of the *Loci* by reference to this actuality and not to the doctrine of Trinity, although inevitably it both confirms the latter, and is confirmed by it." Indeed, Barth sees the doctrine of the Trinity as essential to his theological task. For without it, the distinction and the connections between the constitutive *loci* of volumes II through V would be, in Barth's view, theologically impossible to articulate.

> How can we affirm so definitely the interconnexion and yet also the independence of the doctrines of creation, atonement and redemption, if we are not instructed by the doctrine of the Trinity itself that the *opera trinitatis ad extra sunt indivisa*, and that the Father, Son and Holy Spirit as we recognize them in these *opera* are independent modes of the being of God Himself, and therefore irreducible to any higher unity?[93]

---

92. Ibid., 879.
93. Ibid., 879.

Contrary, then, to what some might assume to be the role of the doctrine of the Trinity in the *Church Dogmatics*, in fact, "the organising and controlling centre of dogmatics is not . . . the doctrine of the Trinity." Rather, that center "stands outside the series of *Loci* to which the doctrine of the Trinity belongs, as part of the doctrine of God."[94]

Nonetheless, the doctrine of the Trinity plays an exceptionally important, indeed, determinative role in the *Dogmatics*. As we have seen, the structure of the *Dogmatics* may be called Trinitarian, in a way that is intentionally connected with the deep theological import of that doctrine, and, moreover, with the divine reality to which that doctrine points and that, indeed, gives rise to that doctrine.

Trinity and Temporality

That Trinitarian structure of the *Dogmatics* has important implications for Barth's understanding of divine eternality. We will discuss this more in the next chapter. For now, it will be sufficient briefly to draw the connection between, on the one hand, the doctrine of the Trinity with the *loci* that Barth says are implied in that doctrine discuss, and, on the other hand, Barth's concept of God's eternity, which he develops in volume II/1, §31.3.

That concept of divine eternality is threefold: God's eternity is to be understood as God's pretemporality, supratemporality, and posttemporality. Yet one should not dismiss that threefold cast of eternity as incidental or cute. Barth has "good reason to give clear emphasis to this truth and therefore to the concepts of the pre-temporality, supra-temporality and post-temporality of the eternal God." This reason goes to the heart of Christian theology. "For a great deal depends on this truth and on the legitimacy of these

---

94. Ibid., 879.

concepts." The emphasis has deep connections with the core of church doctrine, as indeed do the very concepts of pretemporality, supratemporality, and posttemporality. These all, the emphasis and the concepts, in turn have implications for the doctrines that flow from that core, in other words, the *loci* that form the heart of volumes III through V.

> It is only if they are true and legitimate that the whole content of the Christian message—creation as the basis of man's existence, established by God, reconciliation as the renewal of his existence accomplished by God, redemption as the revelation of his existence to be consummated by God (and therefore as the revelation of the meaning of His creation)—can be understood as God's Word of truth and not as the myth of a pious or impious self-consciousness.[95]

There Barth draws a connection between the forms of divine temporality and particular doctrines, namely, those doctrines that are the *loci*, the exposition of which will be the focus of volumes III and IV, as well as volume V had he made it to that point. In other words, we may see a connection between pretemporality and the doctrine of creation, supratemporality and the doctrine of reconciliation, and posttemporality and the doctrine of redemption.

The connection is more implicit than explicit.[96] Nonetheless, the plain implication of his remark (cited two paragraphs above) regarding the basis of his threefold understanding of divine eternality is to point to the *loci* he will discuss in the subsequent volumes. Indeed, he explicitly points to future pages in his *Dogmatics*, promising that such forthcoming work will spell out in a doctrinal

---

95. Ibid., II/1, 620.
96. Similarly, with regard to the correlation that may be drawn between the threefold temporality of God and the persons of the Trinity, Hunsinger has this to say: "Note that Barth does not mean to imply . . . that beginning, middle, and end can be simply equated with Father, Son, and Holy Spirit. Although there may be a loose correlation here, it is not strict. The trinitarian parallel is much more nearly formal than substantive." Hunsinger, "*Mysterium Trinitatis*," 198.

manner his understanding of divine eternality, with these words: "In the future course of dogmatics we shall often have occasion to think of both the distinction and the unity in God's eternity."[97]

Summary

In this chapter, I have discussed three doctrines of great importance for the *Church Dogmatics*. Those three are the doctrine of the Trinity, the doctrine of revelation, and the doctrine of the person and work of Jesus Christ (Christology). I have shown how these three doctrines are closely related to each other, how they influence the structure of the *Church Dogmatics* (to the point of being determinative for it), and that this influence is of great importance for the concept of God's eternity in the *Dogmatics*.

---

97. *CD* II/1, 640.

6

Eternity and Time in the Church Dogmatics

As we enter this chapter, we complete the first step of this book's argument and turn to the next. We have been about preparation, to the end that we may engage in exposition. Such preparation has been the special burden of chapters 2 through 5. Of course, it is not as if there has been no exposition. On the contrary, the preparation has contained much that was expository and interpretive. Nonetheless, we turn now to the heart of the exposition, oriented by the concepts explored in the previous chapters.

In this chapter I will seek to state Barth's mature understanding of God's eternity. I will build toward this statement by means of a close reading of the portion of the *Church Dogmatics* that offers Barth's most complete statement on eternity. In the course of my exposition of this passage, the work from the earlier chapters will be recalled in order to make clear Barth's theological objective in his statement on eternity. In the end, I argue, it is clear how deeply doctrinal this statement is.

Following this expository section, I will then offer three sets of observations in light of Barth's mature articulation of a theology of eternity. The first offers an understanding of Barth's argument in this section of the *Church Dogmatics* and links it with his work from the early 1920s. The second set seeks to clarify the precise relationship between Barth's concept of divine eternality and the Christian doctrines with which he connects it. The third set argues for a particular interpretation of what God's "temporality" might mean for Barth. I will then offer a summary of the main insights offered in the chapter.

The Path Thus Far

A word about where our journey has taken us would be helpful. The argument I have pursued in these pages has been, one might say, about context and understanding: how one depends on the other; how the former gives rise to the latter; how understanding of context leads to understanding of that which arises from the context. To have a full understanding of Karl Barth's concept of divine eternality, you must understand certain contexts for that concept. Conversely, without understanding the contexts, you will not truly understand what Barth has to say.

Such an argument is not, in its elemental features, anything particularly new. It is a commonplace of hermeneutics that context is essential for understanding, irrespective of the particular "text" being interpreted. The contribution of this book thus far is the description of three contexts and the demonstration of their importance for understanding Barth's theological understanding of time and eternity.

The first context we explored was the *conceptual*, those different ways, found in the history of ideas, of describing time or eternity that provide an important background for appreciating Barth's contribution. The burden of chapters 2 and 3, then, was to describe that context and to demonstrate its bearing on Karl Barth's understanding of time and eternity. That context consists of two parts, which were covered in separate steps.

The first part (chapter 2) dealt with those concepts, and the historical figures who are identified with those concepts, with which and with whom Barth was in conversation as he developed his own concepts of time and eternity. This is certainly the most important part of the context, for Barth was explicitly in conversation with the work of each of the six figures covered in chapter 2, drawing on the insights of some, criticizing most of them at least in part, and incorporating elements from a few into his own conceptuality.

Together, these figures, and the concepts of time and eternity they represent, truly provide important background against which one may more fully appreciate Barth's contribution. Indeed, I believe that failure to recognize these concepts and follow Barth's use of them leads interpreters to misreadings and misstatements of Barth's understanding of time and eternity. Such errors in interpretation at this juncture usually arise through overstatement, in which Barth's approach to the question of time and eternity is mistakenly understood as a radical rejection of "the traditional concept," and not, as I demonstrated, a continuation and appreciative reworking of certain elements of the tradition.

Among those whose ideas Barth appreciatively reworked, Boëthius must count as receiving the most favorable treatment. In particular, Barth found extremely useful Boëthius's definition of eternity, and drew from it two concepts to which he returned again and again: *life* and *simultaneity*. Save what could be read as a caution not to take Boëthius in a direction Barth would find unfortunate ("Provided it is not at all the eternity of being, but the eternity of *God*"[1]), Barth appears to offer no criticism of Boëthius's concept of eternity. He picks up the elements he approves, returning to them subsequently, while choosing not to mention points of disagreement.

Other figures, however, received treatment from Barth that is not entirely approving. Some of them come in for pointed criticism of their understanding of eternity or of time, yet it would be a mistake to focus only on the criticism, as if that told the whole story. As I demonstrated in chapter 2, each of the six classical figures considered there had elements in their reflections on time or eternity that Barth either took up, perhaps only implicitly, or that in arguing against he was able to clarify further his own approach to the problem.

For example, Barth explicitly criticized Augustine's view of time. However, as I demonstrated in chapter 2, that criticism centered on the limitations Barth saw in the theological usefulness of Augustine's understanding of time for an exposition of the time of revelation, or God's time for us. Yet in several passages Barth sounds thoroughly Augustinian when speaking of time, or rather, a specific kind of time, namely, "lost" time, showing that his rejection of Augustine was not complete but targeted, with regard to its usefulness for understanding a particular (although important) aspect of theology. Finally, it is that question of usefulness, or rather, sufficiency, that Barth probes to some extent in most of the six figures we examined. In each of them, it was this question, or one quite similar, which pointed us to what was really at stake for Barth, the deeper theological issues in the question, and thus to a greater understanding of Barth's theological conception of time and eternity.

The second part of the conceptual context (addressed in chapter 3) describes those concepts that have contributed greatly to the

---

1. *Die kirchliche Dogmatik* (Munich: Chr. Kaiser, 1932, and Zurich: EVZ, 1938–65), II.1, 688–89; *Church Dogmatics*, trans. Geoffrey W. Bromiley et al (Edinburgh: T. & T. Clark, 1956–69), II/1, 611. Cited above in chapter 2.

discussion of eternity since Barth. In some ways, this chapter serves as an appendix to the work of chapter 2. For, clearly, Barth did not draw on these concepts, as their promulgation occurred after Barth. Thus they could not serve as "context" for understanding Barth's work, not in the sense that they are Barth's own context. Rather, they provide greater context for us in understanding the theories and concepts of chapter 2. For the conversation about the nature of time and eternity continues, and those joining in that conversation have answered the classical thinkers with questions and rejoinders, rejection and approval. These contributions to the conversation cannot be ignored by those who wish to understand any serious attempt to articulate a theory or a theology of eternity, including that of Karl Barth. For this reason, the conceptual context appropriately includes figures whose theological or philosophical work came after Barth.

In chapter 3, then, I suggested that, for our purposes, we could understand the contributions of these later figures as falling into two categories: the *temporalist* and the *atemporalist*. I argued for the cogency and, indeed, the superiority of the modern atemporalist position against the more widely accepted temporalist position. Furthermore, I argued that the modern atemporalist position provides a better vantage point from which to understand Barth's concept of eternity.

The second context we explored was the *developmental*, meaning the ways in which Barth's theology changed, and, in particular, the specific changes and continuities one may observe in his understanding of time and eternity. In chapter 4, I sought to describe those changes and continuities, especially those between *Romans* II and the *Church Dogmatics*. I especially tried to show how certain changes were the result of a clearer articulation of enduring theological principles. Barth's thought did indeed change. The issue of time and eternity is one example of that change. But these changes were not radical breaks or quantum leaps. Rather, they resulted from Barth's ongoing reflection on theological principles that remained basic for him, and on the theological implications of those principles.

The third and final context we explored was the doctrinal. There I sought to describe those central doctrines of the Christian faith that were deeply formative of Barth's understanding of time and eternity and with which Barth attempted to bring that understanding into conformity. These doctrines are the christological doctrines of the incarnation and the person of Christ, and the doctrines of revelation and Trinity. My task in chapter 5 was to describe these doctrines, to make clear the role they play in the *Dogmatics*, and to suggest their relevance for Barth's concepts of eternity and time.

What became quite clear in that exposition was not only the importance of these doctrines for Barth's understanding of time and eternity, but even more their importance for the entire theological project of the *Church Dogmatics*. Indeed, what is most important for Barth is not his theological understanding (much less "doctrine") of time and eternity. It can not be called foundational. Christology, revelation, and Trinity certainly might have claim to that appellation, for they surely are much more important for Barth, and are formative for his theological conception of time and eternity. But even these doctrines are not, in the end, *most* important for Barth, nor do they constitute the *a priori* starting point for his *Dogmatics*. Rather, as Barth would have it, these doctrines are important only as they point to the reality that gives rise to them, the word of God, God's free act of love in turning to that which is not God. It is this realty to which all theological reflection, including that on time and eternity, must be obedient.

Yet it is quite clear that this doctrinal context of revelation, Trinity, and Christology is deeply formative for Barth's theological understanding of time and eternity. Both formally and materially, in their shape and in their details, Barth's conception of God's eternity as well as his understanding of time in its three forms are greatly dependent upon his understanding and exposition of these three central doctrines. Moreover, it is obvious that this context, the doctrinal, is more determinative for Barth's reflections on time and eternity than are the other contexts, the conceptual and the developmental.

Within these three contexts, then, Barth's mature understanding of time and eternity was formed. From them, to be sure, we may better understand his theological reflections on eternality and temporality, and indeed his theology as a whole. Oriented and prepared by our exploration of these contexts, we can focus on Barth's direct contribution to the topic. We turn now to a close examination of his theology of time and eternity, as he expresses it in the *Church Dogmatics*.

Exposition: God's Perichoretic and Temporal Eternality

The defining theological *locus* of Barth's reflections on eternity is his exploration of the attributes, or, rather, "perfections" (*Vollkommenheiten*) of God, in volume II/1 of the *Church Dogmatics*, §31, "The Perfections of the Divine Freedom." It is here that Barth offers his clearest doctrinal statement of God's eternity. Although we have touched on this passage several times in these pages, the exposition at this stage now compels us to explore it closely and thoroughly. Thus in what follows, I will engage in a close reading of this core passage of the *Church Dogmatics*.

That passage, as I said, occurs in Barth's lengthy discussion of the perfections of God. Barth enumerates twelve perfections elucidated in three pairs for each of two divisions. The first division, those he calls "The Perfections of the Divine Loving" (§30), include the attributes of grace and holiness, mercy and righteousness, patience and wisdom. The attributes of the second division are discussed under the title "The Perfections of the Divine Freedom" (§31), and include these attributes: unity and omnipresence, constancy and omnipotence, eternity and glory. The two divisions, divine loving and divine freedom, encompass attributes typically described in earlier theologies under the rubrics of, respectively, "communicable" and "incommunicable" attributes, although Barth offers only limited acceptance of the terms.[2]

Divine Loving	Divine Freedom
Grace and Holiness	Unity and Omnipresence
Mercy and Righteousness	Constancy and Omnipotence
Patience and Wisdom	Eternity and Glory

Barth's theological exposition of eternity, then, occurs in the last pairing of the second division, in the subsection titled "The Eternity and Glory of God." Straight away, Barth affirms that the divinity of God's freedom "consists and confirms itself in the fact that in Himself and in all His works God is eternal and therefore glorious."[3] Although it is easy to overlook, much is packed into that brief statement. That in God *and* in all God's works God is eternal points to the distinction and the unity of the being and the act of God, a dialectic that we have seen repeatedly. Barth is telegraphing in these opening statements of the subsection that eternity must be understood as something about

---

2. "Even the distinction favoured by the Reformed between *attributa incommunicabilia* and *communicabilia* can be admitted only as distinction, but in no sense a separation. For which of the attributes of God, in which as Creator, Reconciler and Redeemer He allows His creatures to share, is not, as His own, utterly incommunicable from the creaturely point of view, i.e., communicable only by the miracle of grace?" (*CD* II/1, 345).
3. Ibid., 608.

God that is true not only within God but outside of God as well. Eternity is not to be relegated solely to the inner nature of God.[4]

Barth then proceeds to build his description of divine eternity. God's eternity, says Barth, "is a quality of God's freedom." Moreover, eternity is "pure duration," "the simultaneity of beginning, middle, and end."[5] This is what distinguishes eternity from time, for which such duration "is lacking." Time has past, present, and future, but past and future show that the present has no duration. Eternity, however, has this duration. "Eternity has and is the duration which is lacking in time. It has and is simultaneity."[6] Eternity, then, is not merely an infinite extension of time, what some call *sempiternity*. No, eternity is this simultaneity, distinguishing it fundamentally from time as well as from "sempiternity," a merely enduring existence through time in the sense of an infinite series of existing moments.

This emphasis on the diastasis between eternity and time is readily found in classical theologians, and Barth cites approvingly some classic statements of this diastasis (in sequence, Augustine, Anselm, and Polanus). The tradition, he notes, was quite accurate in highlighting the contrast found between the lack of duration in time, and the perfection of duration in eternity. Such an emphasis, Barth says, rightly reflects the biblical witness.[7]

This duration, Barth insists, is a matter of God's freedom. Referring to one of the two prior perfections considered (constancy), Barth has

---

4. A process or Hartshornian approach might accept eternity as an attribute of the abstract pole of the divine being, and temporality of the concrete pole, as discussed in chapter 3. Barth's opening statement demonstrates a theological outlook at odds with a theory that relegates fundamental aspects of God's being, and thus of God's activity, to an "abstract" pole alone. For Barth, God is being-in-act. "God's being cannot be described apart from the basic act in which God lives. Any attempt to define God in static or inactive terms, as is customary in certain theologies and philosophies, is therefore to be rejected," in George Hunsinger, *How to Read Karl Barth: The Shape of His Theology.* (New York: Oxford University Press, 1991), 30.
5. "Die Ewigkeit ist dieses Einmal und Zugleich von Anfang, Mitte, und Ende und eben insofern: reine Dauer." *KD* II/1, 685; *CD* II/1, 608.
6. *CD* II/1, 608.
7. Ibid., 608–9.

this to say: "The reason why He is free to be constant is that time has no power over Him. As the One who endures He has all power over time." This freedom through and in eternity means that eternity is God's exclusive possession, even as God gives to someone else a share in that eternity. "In its fellowship with God the creature is permitted to taste it in one way or another, but it does not on that account itself become God and therefore eternal." Freedom is the hallmark of eternity: a freedom over and against time, yet indeed a freedom with and even in time, a freedom to be and to act, internally and externally, under no external compulsion. "Time—which is in a sense the special creation of the 'eternal' God—is the formal principle of His free activity outwards. Eternity is the principle of His freedom inwards."[8]

Barth again points to statements from the Bible that support his argument. In Scripture, God's eternity is a matter of God's freedom: a freedom not only *from*, distinguishing God from that which is not God; but also a freedom *for*, an utter presence to and complete power over the human person. God is eternal *so that* God may be present to us, and freely so.[9]

That God is free as God is eternal means that eternity cannot adequately be described as time's opposite. "It is a poor and short-sighted view to understand God's eternity only from the standpoint that it is the negation of time." The positive quality is essential: "As true duration, the duration of God Himself is *the* beginning, succession and end." Indeed, God's duration is the ground of all beginning, succession, and end. God's eternity cannot be described as simply the negation of time, for time is possible only because the possibility of time lies within God. "By the terms *olam* and αἰών the Bible understands a space of time fixed by God, and eternity

---

8. Ibid., 609.
9. Ibid., 609–10.

is generally ascribed to God under the categories of beginning, succession and end. The biblical writers do not hesitate to speak of God's years and days, or to describe these as eternal."[10]

Theologically, then, the standard distinction between time and eternity takes us only so far. As a matter of theological method, one does not arrive at a true understanding of eternity by starting "here," with our experience of time, and then reasoning by negative inference, *via negationis*, to "there," to eternity. We know eternity not by understanding time, with its attendant limitations, and postulating eternity's radical discontinuity with time, but by knowing God, the "possessor of interminable life." To start with a diastasis of time and eternity leads to a theological standpoint for which God's readiness for time is a puzzle.

> Eternity is the *nunc* [now] which is undoubtedly not subject to the distinctions between past, present and future. But again, it is not subject to the abolition of these distinctions. The usual way of treating the concept of eternity in theological tradition leads to the dangerous position that there appears to be no eternity if there is no time and if eternity cannot be non-temporality; and that there appears to be no knowledge of eternity except through time, in the form of a negation of the concept of time.[11]

Barth, then, makes quite clear that the typical way of construing time and eternity (one that he himself had implicitly followed[12]) must be abandoned. "The theological concept of eternity must be set free from the Babylonian captivity of an abstract opposite to the concept of time."[13] A positive relation must be described, because that relationship is itself the very demonstration of God's act toward

---

10. Ibid., 610. The first term is the Hebrew עוֹלָם (*olam*), as found in, e.g., Gen. 21:33, Isa. 40:28, and Jer. 31:2.
11. *CD* II/1, 611.
12. See above, ch. 4.
13. *CD* II/1, 611.

that which is not God, toward the creature of God. Eternity is not simply "over against" time, because the possibility of time and the possibilities within time are grounded in eternity.

Eternity, then, must not be seen as merely the negation of time, but as the ground of time. "God's eternity is itself beginning, succession and end." Moreover, eternity "has" beginning, succession, and end, and is "not conditioned by them." Indeed, "God has time because and as He has eternity."[14] Eternity and time are in an asymmetrical relationship with each other, both noetically (in how eternity is known) and ontically (in how it really is). From the perspective of time, the relationship of eternity and time cannot but be known and experienced as a diastasis. Nonetheless, from God's side, time is not simply the negative of eternity, but rather eternity is the ground of time, encompasses it, is the occasion for it, and is the perfection to which it aspires. God has time for us, not because time is ready for eternity, but because eternity is there for time. Because of this, Barth insists that eternity must not be construed as "timeless," characterizing this as "an illegitimate anthropomorphism."[15] God eternally has time. Within the being of God this enduring sequence of beginning, succession, and end is a kind of time; indeed, it is "true time."

It is important that we understand what Barth is arguing here. Barth is not saying that there is no distinction between eternity and time, nor is he saying that God is temporal as we are temporal. That is precisely his point. God's eternity means that God can be temporal in ways that we cannot. If "time" means solely the durationless sequence of moments that we experience, then of course Barth would agree that God is not temporal and that eternity must be construed as

---

14. *CD* II/1, 611.
15. Ibid., 612. It might be that Barth is intending some irony here. The opposite statement, that to construe eternity as temporal is an illegitimate anthropomorphism, could readily be said by many theologians, perhaps even by Barth in his earlier days.

timeless. However, he is not willing to accept this as the sole definition of time. Rather, he asserts that God's eternity is a kind of temporality, one that does not suffer from the disunity of before, during, and after, but for which pure duration is its fundamental characteristic.

> What distinguishes eternity from time is the fact that there is in [God] no opposition or competition or conflict, but peace between origin, movement and goal, between present, past and future, between "not yet," "now" and "no more," between rest and movement, potentiality and actuality, whither and whence, here and there, this and that. In [God] all these things are *simul*, held together by the omnipotence of [God's] knowing and willing, a totality without gap or rift, free from the threat of death under which time, our time, stands.[16]

What Barth is seeking, then, is "a positive relation to time which is the special possession of eternity." He finds this lacking in what he calls "the older theology," the classical theologies whose emphasis on the opposition of time and eternity he finds a necessary first step that must not at all be the only step. Theology can and must say more about eternity, "without cancelling or blurring the distinction between [time and eternity], or imposing upon eternity the limitations of time."[17] It can and must, because the diastasis rests upon an openness to time grounded not in time itself, but in eternity, in the very being of God. "Eternity is the negation of time only because and to the extent that it is first and foremost God's time and therefore real time, in the same way as God's omnipresence is not simply the negation of our space, but first and foremost is positively God's space and therefore real space."[18]

The emphasis, Barth insists, must fall on the positive. "For, rightly understood, the statement that God is eternal tells us what God *is*,

---

16. Ibid., 612.
17. Ibid., 613. As I see it, that is precisely what the "temporalists" have done.
18. Ibid.

not what [God] is not."[19] The negative has its place, and that is to emphasize the perfection of God, who has created our time. But time has its place, too; it "is not simply nothing." It is grounded in eternity, which is absolutely real time; consequently, because of its being grounded in eternity, our time is relatively real time. "As the eternal One who as such has and Himself is absolutely real time, He gives us the relatively but in this way genuinely real time proper to us." God can do this because God has time, not merely our time, but God's own time: "How can He be and do all this if as the eternal One He does not Himself have His own time, superior to ours, undisturbed by the fleetingness and separations of our time, simultaneous with all our times, but in this way and for this reason absolutely real time?"[20]

To express this, Barth offers some illustrations that may have been familiar to his contemporaries: "As the tree on the river's bank is always beside it, yet does not flow with it; as the Pole Star is at the zenith of the vault of heaven, yet does not move around with it; and as the ocean surrounds the land on all sides and yet is not land itself—so the eternal God co-exists with the time created by Him."[21] But right away Barth rejects these illustrations as imperfect: "For God is the Creator and Lord of our time, and therefore eternity is the *tota simul et perfecta possessio vitae*, and co-exists with time and all it contains with a superiority which the tree cannot have over the river or the Pole Star over the vault of heaven or the ocean over the continent." Such "coexistence" as implied in the illustration does not truly fit the God-creature relationship. There is more to that relationship than is expressed in those illustrations, and indeed the illustrations suggest something that does not apply to God's eternity. "Consequently the statement that God co-exists with our time cannot

---

19. Ibid., emph. in *KD* II/1, 691.
20. *CD* II/1, 613.
21. Ibid., 614.

be reversed, as is possible with the elements in the illustrations." Eternity's coexistence with time cannot be turned around so that we could say that time coexists with eternity. "We glorify God by seeking the basis of our temporal existence in His eternity. But we do not glorify Him if we try to use His eternity in its character as the basis of our temporal existence as a pretext for giving our temporal existence the character of something analogous to His eternity, as is obviously the case if we allow ourselves to make this reversal."

In short, Barth insists that the relationship between eternity and time is asymmetrical. This emphasis on asymmetry is very important, and recurs frequently in §31. As we noted above, the asymmetry of eternity and time is noetic and ontic. Eternity corresponds with time, but time does not in and of itself correspond with eternity; eternity possesses time, but time does not possess something of eternity; eternity comprehends time, but time can not comprehend eternity.[22]

Barth then makes an important step in his exposition by making an explicit connection to the doctrine of the Trinity. The German is enthusiastic and direct, and a retranslation, with the addition of some line breaks, will be of some help:

> The right understanding of the positive side of the concept of eternity, protected against improper results, is gained once one is clear in this:
>
> We are speaking of the eternity of the *triune* God:
>
> of the God who is eternally the *Father*, without origin or begetting himself origin and begetter and so inseparably beginning, continuation and end, and thus himself in his essence together the All!—
>
> of the God who indeed is also eternally the *Son*, begotten as such of the Father and now to be sure of the same essence with him, as begotten

---

22. This asymmetry arises out of the same concern that drove Barth to reject natural theology.

of the Father also inseparably beginning, continuation and end and so in his essence together the All!—

of the God who indeed is also the *Spirit*, as such proceeding from the Father and the Son, and now to be sure of the same essence with them, as the Spirit of the Father and of the Son he is also inseparably beginning, continuation and end and so in his essence together the All!

That one, *this* is the eternal God. Truly the *eternal* God; for the All is pure duration, free from all fleetingness and from all ruptures of what we call time, the *nunc aeternitatis*, which cannot come into being nor pass away, which is determined by no distinctions, which in its unity is disturbed and interrupted neither by its threeness nor through its inner movement (this begetting of the Father, this being begotten of the Son, this being sent of the Spirit by both) but already through the All in its unity is grounded and established.[23]

Thus God's eternity, Barth argues, is understood rightly on the basis of the doctrine of the Trinity. For this eternity is not a general philosophical concept. It is a perfection of God. It exists only as it is a perfection of the eternal God who exists, and it is known only as it is known from the eternal God who acts in giving such knowledge to those who are not God, in the grace of revelation. This God is the God who is Father, Son, and Holy Spirit, not only appearing to be such, but truly *is* these three in one. To understand that God is triune is, for Barth, to take a big step forward in understanding the positive side of eternity, because it is to understand that eternity is, although superior to our time, for that reason open to our time. Because God in God's own being has these distinctions of origin, begotten, and sent without suffering disunity, it is fully consonant with this that God would have within God's own being the supremely temporal distinctions of beginning, succession, and end without suffering loss of duration.

23. *KD* II/1, 693; *CD* II/1, 615.

Again, Barth wishes to arrive at a correct understanding of eternity by starting on the positive side. That means to start with the being of God who is Trinity. It also means to start with the supreme and decisive act of God in making God's own self known. This is to say that we must start with the doctrine of the incarnation. Thus the next step in Barth's exposition is to draw on that very doctrine. "A correct understanding of the concept of eternity is reached only if we start from the other side, from the real fellowship between God and the creature, and therefore between eternity and time. This means starting from the incarnation of the divine Word in Jesus Christ."[24]

Barth's method, we recall, is to start, not with first principles or general theories, but with the particulars of God's acts in their concreteness. In this case, such concreteness is sought in the incarnation. "The fact that the Word became flesh undoubtedly means that, without ceasing to be eternity, in its very power as eternity, eternity became time." In the incarnation, Barth sees further demonstration of what he had seen with the doctrine of the Trinity: the capacity of eternity for time. Continuing directly:

> Yes, it became time. What happens in Jesus Christ is not simply that God gives us time, our created time, as the form of our own existence and world, as is the case in creation and in the whole ruling of the world by God as its Lord. In Jesus Christ it comes about that God takes time to Himself, that He Himself, the eternal One, becomes temporal, that He is present for us in the form of our own existence and our own world, not simply embracing our time and ruling it, but submitting Himself to it, and permitting created time to become and be the form of His eternity.[25]

In the incarnation, God becomes human. Anticipating the pattern of humiliation and exaltation in *CD* IV/1, Barth emphasizes that in the

---

24. *CD* II/1, 616.
25. Ibid., 616.

incarnation God remains God even as God takes human form. The incarnation "does not mean that He who is utterly above us ceases to be who He is in His superiority. But while He is still this, He humbles Himself and lifts us up by becoming one of us, like us in all things." Yet the form in which human beings exist is time. Thus if in the incarnation God becomes "one of us, like us in all things," then this must include time, the temporality that is a constitutive part of our existence. "For our being, as created human being, has this form, and He could not assume our being, could not become and be like us and reconcile us to Himself, without taking time also and concealing and revealing His eternal being in it."[26]

The incarnation, then, is evidence of the positive aspect of eternity that Barth is compelled to demonstrate. "This is just what takes place in Jesus Christ. His name is the refutation of the idea of a God who is only timeless. His name describes a divine presence which is not only eternal but also temporal"[27]

In all this as well, we are talking about the freedom of God. The incarnation means that "from this standpoint too we cannot understand God's eternity as pure timelessness." Proceeding directly, "Since it [eternity] became time, and God himself, without ceasing to be the eternal God, took time and made it His own, we have to confess that He was able to do this. He was not only able to have and give time as the Creator, but in Jesus Christ He was able Himself to be temporal."[28]

Let us pause here to recall what Barth has been arguing. He has been putting forth the case for a "positive side" to the concept of eternity. This positive side is in addition to the negative side offered in traditional theology (and, indeed, even in Barth's own

---

26. Ibid. Note the revelational dialectic, in the language of "concealing and revealing."
27. Ibid., 616–17.
28. Ibid., 617.

theology from some years before). Yet the negative side is not to be abandoned. Barth does not say that it is an error to see eternity and time as distinct or even opposed. He does say that it is inadequate to remain there and to see nothing further. He does not say it is wrong to describe eternity as timeless; rather, it is wrong to say *only* that. Jesus Christ "is the refutation of the idea of a God who is *only* timeless." Timelessness of some sort is truly affirmed of God. It is not, however, the only thing to be affirmed regarding God's eternity. In a way possible only because it is God of whom we speak, we must say that eternity is in some sense timeless and in another sense temporal. So it is that God

> is timeless in that the defects of our time, its fleetingness and its separations, are alien to Him and disappear, and in Him all beginning, continuation and ending form a unique Now, steadfast yet moving, moving yet steadfast. He is temporal in that our time with its defects is not so alien to Him that He cannot take it to Himself in His grace, mercy and patience, Himself rectifying and healing it and lifting it up to the time of eternal life.[29]

Thus far, Barth has said that he wants a positive conception of eternity. For Barth, such a conception will not abandon the important distinction between eternity and time that the standard negative conceptions make. More importantly, this positive conception will arise out of theological insights of the doctrine of the Trinity and the doctrine of the incarnation.

All of this is preparation for Barth's statement by which he introduces the heart of his exposition of divine eternity. "Defined and delimited in this way against misuse, the temporality of eternity may be described in detail as the pre-temporality, supra-temporality and post-temporality of eternity."[30] Such a description, he believes, is

---

29. Ibid., 617–19.
30. Ibid., 619.

close to Scripture, for which God is known and described in positive connection with time and yet not as subject to time. In the Bible, God is distinguished from time, but in that distinguishing the Bible also makes clear the positive relationship of God to time, "describing God as the One who is not conditioned by time, but conditions it absolutely in [God's] freedom." The positive asymmetry of eternity's relationship to time is recognized in Scripture, and described very directly and without embarrassment. God precedes time's beginning. God accompanies time's duration. God exists after time's end.[31]

Eternity, then, is not merely not-time, nor does it stand strictly over against time. Eternity is not alien to time: in God's freedom eternity is open to time. "What is certain is that God and eternity must be understood as the element which surrounds time on all sides and therefore includes its dimensions."[32] However, this does not mean that eternity needs time in order for eternity to exist, any more than God needs creation in order to be God.[33] Such asymmetry is a characteristic of what Hunsinger would call *objectivism*. "The being of God in act is a being in love and freedom. God, who does not need us to be the living God, is perfectly complete without us. For God is alive in the active relations of love and freedom which constitute God's being in and for itself."[34]

The same is true for eternity, and Barth makes it clear that he holds it be true. "God would [not] be any less eternal if time did not

---

31. Ibid.
32. Ibid.
33. Notions of asymmetry and ontological priority figures prominently in George Hunsinger's critique of Bruce McCormack. For example: "Barth's whole point in stressing that God would be the Holy Trinity without us was that God does not need the world to be God, nor, furthermore, does God need it to be constituted as the Holy Trinity, because God just is the Holy Trinity prior to and independently of the world. It would be hard to imagine a view more contrary to Barth than one that makes the Holy Trinity a mere function of God's relationship to the world." George Hunsinger, "Election and the Trinity: Twenty-five Theses on the Theology of Karl Barth," *Modern Theology* 24, no. 2 (April 2008): 17.
34. Hunsinger, *How to Read Karl Barth*, 30.

exist outside Himself." It is much the same as with other perfections of God's freedom, such as God's omnipresence, omnipotence, and unity.

> In relation to all spaces God is the original and proper space, the Omnipresent; in relation to all powers He is the original and proper power, the Omnipotent; and in relation to all unities He is the original and proper One, unique and simple. And He is all these things even if apart from Him there was no space or power or unity. It is in this way that eternity has and is a positive relationship to time, . . . it is itself temporal, and would be so even if no time existed apart from it.[35]

Eternity, then, is to be understood as God's pretemporality, supratemporality, and posttemporality. Such a formulation affirms both the distinction of time and eternity as well as the (revealed) readiness of eternity for time over against time's incapacity for eternity. This threefold understanding of eternity has fundamental importance for Christian doctrine and, even, proclamation. "For a great deal depends on this truth and on the legitimacy of these concepts."[36] Indeed, what depends on it are core affirmations of the Christian faith. The very doctrines that will be the focus of the subsequent volumes of the *Church Dogmatics* are at stake. "It is only if they are true and legitimate that the whole content of the Christian message—creation as the basis of man's existence, established by God, reconciliation as the renewal of his existence accomplished by God, redemption as the revelation of his existence to be consummated by God . . . —can be understood as God's Word of truth."[37]

The assertion here is the very one bound up with Barth's doctrine of revelation, and with the character of his doctrine of the Trinity as affirming both economic and immanent triunity: that in revelation

---

35. *CD* II/1, 619–20.
36. Ibid., 620.
37. Ibid.

God reveals not only an appearance of God but God's true self. "This sign does not point away into space, to a God who, in fact, is neither past, present nor future."[38]

Thus Christian faith and the integrity of Christian proclamation of the word of God depend on this threefold statement of God's eternal temporality (that God is before, above, and after our time) being true. Not only that, Barth continues, but a somewhat converse assertion is also true: that the affirmation of God's threefold eternality depends on God's word. "The concepts of pre-temporality, supra-temporality and post-temporality are legitimate because they simply spell out and analyse what the Christian message guarantees to be the Word of God and therefore the truth."[39] It is not the case that this understanding of God's temporal eternality, God's active being as before, above, and after our time is a mere inference from other theological statements or from Scripture. The simple proclamation of the Christian message necessarily involves the proclamation of these statements about God: that God, in being present to and for us, is before, above, and after us: "The Gospel itself and as such cannot be spoken and take shape without these statements being made and this understanding of the divine eternity forcing itself upon us . . . directly, because the Gospel must either remain unproclaimed or be spoken in the form of these statements."[40]

Having given this explanation of the basis and necessity of the threefold description of God's eternity, Barth then turns to an explanation of each one. "We shall go through them quickly," he says, "to remind ourselves of the two aspects—that the truth of God's Word depends on their truth, and that they themselves are based on and preserved by the truth of God's Word."[41]

---

38. Ibid. See my discussion of "modalism" and "modalistic monarchianism" above in chapter 5.
39. Ibid., 621.
40. Ibid.

Taking him at his word, let us note what Barth "quickly" says about these three aspects of God's eternity:

- *Pretemporality* indicates that God exists before all: all other beings, all other times. There is nothing that existed before God. From that pretemporality all other times have their movement. Here, in the beginning, God's temporality is open to our time, as its origin, freely and under no compulsion by us or our times.

- *Supratemporality* emphasizes the accompaniment of God's temporality to our time. Here, too, in the middle, God's temporality is open to our time as that which is above and with it, freely and under no compulsion by us or our times.

- *Posttemporality* indicates that God is after all time. God's temporality is the goal toward which all beings and all times are going. Here, too, at the end, it is open to our time as that which welcomes it at the conclusion, freely and under no compulsion by us and our times.

Such is the "quickly" developed explanation of Barth's threefold description of eternity's temporality. Under those three divisions, of course, Barth goes into much greater detail, using the excurses for such development. In those excurses we find two common features. Most apparent is Barth's attempt to show that theologians of certain periods were prone to stress one of the forms of eternity to the neglect of the others. For example, the Reformers and the Protestant Orthodox (especially those within the Reformed tradition) gave great stress to pretemporality, particularly with regard to the doctrines of

---

41. Ibid. "Quickly" might strike one as wildly inaccurate or as an attempt at self-deprecating humor, for the discussion that follows takes many pages. Notice, however, that excurses comprise the bulk of the remainder. If he was referring to the main text rather than the excurses, then Barth likely was not joking when he said he would "go through them [each of the three parts of eternity] quickly."

election and providence, but paid little attention to supratemporality or posttemporality. In the nineteenth century, Protestant liberalism gave great stress to supratemporality to the total exclusion of the other two forms of eternity. Movements more recent for Barth gave greater attention to posttemporality, but these, too, had become "a one-sided reaction."[42] In short, we see that Barth believes that divine eternity is not understood at all except as an eternity of all three forms of temporality. For emphasizing only one form leads, inevitably, to a misunderstanding even of the one that is emphasized.

The other feature one may find in these excurses is both more doctrinal and more subtle. There Barth develops an elegant interaction of the three forms of eternity with each other and with signal doctrines that highlight, in perichoretic manner, the distinctiveness and interdependence of each form. Each form is illustrated by a particular doctrine, but is also shown to be perichoretically related to other doctrines, and with the whole of the *Church Dogmatics*.

So, then, pretemporality is rightly illustrated by the doctrine of election, yet it is not thereby alienated from other doctrines and thereby from other affirmations of the good news. "It is because God is pre-temporal that He does not owe us anything: either our existence" (pointing to the doctrine of creation), "or that He should establish and maintain fellowship with us" (the doctrine of reconciliation), "or that He should lead us to a goal in this fellowship, to a hereafter which has a place in His own hereafter" (the doctrine of redemption).[43]

---

42. Ibid., 633.
43. Ibid., 621. The important dispute between George Hunsinger and Bruce McCormack is centered in the relation of election and the being of God as triune. See especially, Hunsinger, "Election and Trinity," and Bruce McCormack, "Election and Trinity: Theses in Response to George Hunsinger," *Scottish Journal of Theology* 63, no. 2 (2010): 203–24.

Likewise, supratemporality is illustrated by a distinctive doctrine, in this case the incarnation. This is seen in the beginning of the excursus on this form, as Barth recalls the account of Christ's birth and the message of the angels in the second chapter of the Gospel of Luke: "Glory to God in the highest and on earth, peace, good will toward men" (Luke 2:14 KJV). The incarnation, says Barth, is decisively important for a Christian understanding of eternity. "The birth of Jesus Christ. It is in this that time is secured in eternity. It is in this that time has its meaning immediately to God."[44] The appearance of Jesus Christ is the revelation of God, and thereby it is also the revelation of eternity. "In the appearing of the Messiah King in time . . . eternity is revealed, or, as we should now say more specifically, the supra-temporality of God as His presence in time."[45] Moreover, this form of eternity, too, is perichoretically connected with the other forms and with other doctrines: "It is as God is supra-temporal that He realises His love, giving us that which He is under no obligation to give us—our existence, fellowship with Him, and in this fellowship a living hope."[46] Supratemporality is thus graciously bound with pretemporality and posttemporality, as well as the doctrines of creation ("to give us . . . our existence"), reconciliation ("fellowship with [God]"), and redemption, the promise of eschatology ("and in this fellowship a living hope"). The presence of Immanuel, God with us, as realized in the incarnation is a presence that joins together past and future. To live in Christ is to live in that presence, and so to live, even in our time, without regret for the past or anxiety over the future.[47]

By the time Barth gets to the excursus on posttemporality, he has already shown several times that he understands that it is most

---

44. *CD* II/1, 625.
45. Ibid., 625–26.
46. Ibid., 624.
47. Ibid., p. 628–29.

naturally connected with eschatology. In Barth's opinion, interest in eschatology among continental theologians had waned for many years, and notwithstanding the single-minded overemphasis that, in Barth's opinion, the doctrine had recently received, the doctrine is rightly included in dogmatics, in equality with the doctrines of creation and incarnation. Here, too, there is perichoretic warrant for this.

> Without detriment, then, to the necessary recognition of God's post-temporality, His pre-temporality was again perceived, though it had been neglected in the 18th and 19th centuries no less than His post-temporality. Everything depends on there being no new rivalry between these conceptions. In the truth of God there is certainly dynamic particularity, but for that reason there is no rivalry, and therefore we have no right to ride hobby horses in its exposition and proclamation.[48]

What we have in these excurses, then, is a thoroughgoing perichoretic interweaving of doctrines and themes, with certain doctrines being "appropriated" to particular forms of divine eternity in a manner similar to the doctrine of divine appropriations, and others being tied in by means of dialectical inclusion. Pretemporality is illustrated by and appropriated to election, supratemporality to incarnation, and posttemporality to eschatology or consummation. Additionally, each of these forms of eternity interact with the structural doctrines of the *Church Dogmatics*: creation, reconciliation, and redemption. It is not just God's pretemporality that is seen in God's work of creation, but also the presence and promise of God as well. And reconciliation encompasses aspects of God's pre- and posttemporality, and not only the abiding presence of God's supratemporality, as known supremely in the incarnation of Jesus Christ. Finally, redemption is also dynamically, not statically, particular, as it is the hope in the One who, in election and

---

48. Ibid., 637.

incarnation, determined that Jesus Christ would be the revelation of God's being in act and thus the promise for which all creation yearns.

Observations

Having walked through a detailed exposition of the central text for Barth's description of eternity, I will now offer some further observations of what he has done.

The Shape of Barth's Argument

First of all, there is the matter of the argument itself. The course of Barth's theological reasoning in this section (§31) is directed toward establishing a positive definition of eternity. He begins by citing traditional theologies that emphasize the diastasis between eternity and time, stressing the negative aspect of eternity, namely, in how it is not time. He cites those sources affirmatively, to a point. Yet he finds these negative definitions of eternity lacking. A positive concept of eternity (one, however, that does not completely abandon the insight of the negative concepts) is surely needed.

From that point on, Barth develops this positive concept, drawing on those doctrines he sees as especially close to the proclamation of the gospel: Trinity, incarnation, and revelation. From these, Barth develops an understanding of eternity as a unique (because it is divine) form of "temporality," so that eternity is distinct from time without being alienated from time, as it is truly open to time.

Recalling my exposition of Barth's developmental context (chapter 4), I believe it is apparent that what Barth is attempting in §31 is something he had sought for some time. In the early 1920s, as he was lecturing in Göttingen, he had made it clear that a more positive statement about eternity was needed. He saw his own *Romans* II as an example of the negativity he wanted to overcome, without abandoning its core theological affirmations and outlook. In this section of the *Church Dogmatics*, Barth develops the positive understanding of eternity he was seeking in his Göttingen lectures.

Eternity, Perichoresis, and Doctrine

A second issue concerns the deep interconnection of Barth's concept of eternity with doctrines throughout the rest of the *Church Dogmatics*. That interconnection gives the appearance of a close relation between the structure of eternity and the structure of the *Dogmatics*. Yet what kind of relation is it, and what are those doctrinal interconnections?

Without question, the doctrine of the Trinity is deeply formative for Barth's concept of eternity. Furthermore, as I have demonstrated in the previous chapter, the doctrine of the Trinity, perichoretically understood and developed, becomes the pattern for the structure of the *Church Dogmatics*. As God exists eternally in a triunity of Father, Son, and Holy Spirit, and as the works of the divine persons are appropriated to one divine person or another (yet never to the full exclusion of the others), so Barth sees it fitting to discuss the doctrinal *loci* in a manner and sequence that makes clear these appropriations: creation (vol. III) appropriated to God the Father, reconciliation (vol. IV) appropriated to God the Son, and redemption (in the vol. V Barth had hoped to write) appropriated to God the Holy Spirit.

What becomes apparent is that Barth understands the three forms of eternity to have a close connection with the three doctrines of God's economy, which are the focus of the anticipated subsequent volumes. Because God is pre-, supra-, and posttemporal, the truth of the Christian message is established.

> We have good reason to give clear emphasis to this truth and therefore to the concepts of the pre-temporality, supra-temporality, and post-temporality of the eternal God. For a great deal depends on this truth and on the legitimacy of these concepts. It is only if they are true and legitimate that the whole content of the Christian message—creation as the basis of man's existence, established by God, reconciliation as the renewal of his existence accomplished by God, redemption as the revelation of his existence to be consummated by God . . . —can be understood as God's Word of truth.[49]

Yet it is not accurate to say that these *loci* are *equivalent* to certain individual forms of temporality. Creation does not equal pretemporality. Supratemporality is not the same as reconciliation. Redemption is not the only thing that can and must be said about God's posttemporality. There is more to be said of any form of eternity than can be encompassed under one doctrinal heading. Each of those *loci* expresses realities that connect with more than one form of eternity. It is not the case, and I am not proposing, that each one of the three forms of eternity line up singularly with one of the three major structural *loci* of creation, reconciliation, and redemption.

As becomes clear in the excurses for each of the three forms of temporality, Barth is positing something more subtle and intricate. What he does is suggest a correspondence between each of the three forms of eternity and three other doctrines, a correspondence that is akin to the doctrine of divine appropriations. These corresponding forms and doctrines, these appropriations, are as follows: pretemporality with election, supratemporality with incarnation, and posttemporality with eschatology.

---

49. Ibid., 620.

One might fairly ask why these doctrines are appropriated to the three forms of eternity, while creation, reconciliation, and redemption are not. Barth does not address this question, yet I believe that a likely answer is close at hand. For Barth, each of those doctrines that are lifted up as somehow illustrative of the three forms of eternity are, in his theological exposition, supremely and distinctively about Jesus Christ. They, more than the other doctrines, are about the act of God in, upon, and with the person of Jesus. Thus election is primarily and supremely the election *of Jesus Christ*.[50] The incarnation is the becoming flesh of God *in Jesus Christ*. Eschatology is the consummation and redemption of all things *in Jesus Christ*. Each of these doctrines are in Barth's hands either singularly or supremely and thus distinctively about God's act in Jesus Christ.

The same cannot be said of the other doctrines. Although "dogmatics must actually be Christology and only Christology," it is "not Christology in this rather limited sense of the term; not as if the revelation of the Father by the Son and of the Son by the Holy Spirit is in fact identical with the action of God in overcoming human rebellion and human need."[51] Creation, reconciliation, and redemption are God's act toward us. To be sure, Barth holds that the meaning of these three are made known, revealed, by God in Jesus Christ. ("Dogmatics must actually be Christology and only Christology.") But they are not equivalent to the triune relationship of Father to Son and Holy Spirit. These three, creation, reconciliation, and redemption, are God's act toward us. The creature is created. The sinner is reconciled. The world is redeemed. In each of these events, God acts graciously toward the creature, and the God who acts is always the *triune* God, and thus the *eternal* God, in

---

50. While this may not be true of many, if not most, doctrines of election, it is certainly the case for Barth's.
51. *CD* I/2, 872.

whom before, during, and after suffer no disunity, from whom it is revealed that to be in fellowship with this God is to acknowledge the One who is before, with, and after us. For this reason, all three of those *loci*—creation, redemption, and reconciliation—will contain the impress of all three forms of the divine eternity.

My suggestion, then, that Barth appropriates the three forms of eternity to the doctrines of election, incarnation, and eschatology arises out of what I observe Barth himself doing with those doctrines. There is a clear correspondence and interconnection between those doctrines and the three forms of eternity. Yet it is not a static interconnection. As is typical in Barth's theology, the correspondence between the three forms of eternity and the doctrines of election, incarnation, and eschatology is dynamic. That dynamism is enhanced by the further connections Barth establishes with the three *loci* he intends to explore in the remaining volumes. The interconnections of doctrines and motifs all demonstrate the doctrinal, Trinitarian, and perichoretic understanding of God's eternity that Barth is proposing.

God's Time and Our Time

A third and final issue I wish to address concerns Barth's understanding of time, particularly as shown in his concept of God's eternity.[52]

In short, there is no one thing as Barth's "concept of time." The lack of specificity in such an interpretive banner leads inexorably to rhetorical excess whenever it is unfurled. Barth does, however, speak of time in certain characteristic ways, for example (and perhaps not exhaustively) time as given by God in creation, time as unredeemed

---

52. Portions of this section also appear, in abbreviated form, in Daniel M. Griswold, "Time," in *The Westminster Handbook to Karl Barth*, ed. Richard Burnett (Louisville: Westminster John Knox Press, 2013), 209–11.

humanity experiences it, and time as may be experienced when known in God's grace through Jesus Christ.

That second manner of describing time, the time of unredeemed humanity, may be understood as a middle state between the other two. It is time apart from God and unfulfilled by eternity. Barth calls this kind of time by several different names. There is *lost time*, as he describes it in his doctrine of creation:

> The first counterpart of the time of the history of creation in the time of the subsequent history of the covenant is "our" time in the stricter sense of the concept, i.e., the time of man as isolated from God and fallen into sin. It is the time whose flux has become a flight. It is the time in which there is no real present and therefore no real past and future, no centre and therefore no beginning and no end, or a beginning and end only as the appearance of a centre which is in reality the one and only thing and in one respect or another is not true and proper time. . . . It is time without any recognizable ground or meaning in eternity. This is how time appears and must appear when it is no longer an order established by God and to be appropriated and acknowledged by man, but a human work and institution. . . . As the time of lost man it can only be lost time.[53]

There is *empty time*, which is what time is apart from eternity: "Because, in this occurrence, eternity assumes the form of a temporal present, all time, without ceasing to be time, is no more empty time, or without eternity."[54] And there is *wounded time*, that which is in need of healing by Jesus Christ: "When [God, in the incarnation of Jesus Christ] subjects Himself to time He does freely what He does not have to do. [God] masters time. [God] re-creates it and heals its wounds, the fleetingness of the present, and the separation of past and the future from one another and from the present."[55]

---

53. *CD* III/1, 72.
54. *CD* II/1, 626.
55. Ibid., 617.

All of these terms express, in different ways, the same fundamental character of the same kind of time. This is time as it is not intended to be, time that is far from ideal. Without God, time simply cannot be what it should be. The human being who is lost will experience time itself as lost. Such time is in need of healing, just as those who exist in that time are in need of healing. This kind of time can hardly even be called *time*, for it has so little substance, but abides primarily in its discontinuity and exists in its lack of existence.

Clearly, such metaphors as *lost* or *empty* or *wounded* time express, not scientific assertions, but theological convictions. For Barth's theological purposes, particularly in *CD* III, "time" is not so much a physical entity as the manner in which one exists. As Gotthard Oblau puts it, time is the "form of being," the *Daseinsform*, of the human being. To this he immediately adds, of course, that eternity is the *Daseinsform* of God.[56] In short, "time," just as "eternity," is not a "thing" apart from those who possess it. Both time and eternity are, rather, the very means by which these two very different categories of beings, God and the human being, exist with and over against their "environment," or all that is not them.

The picture that emerges from all this appears to be as follows. Barth understands human time to be fundamentally flawed, as long as such time and those who experience it are isolated from God. Yet such time is described, mostly, in a way that expresses well the fundamental character of time as it really is: flowing, evanescent, ever changing, a mode in which "past" and "future" do not exist because they are not "present." Speaking of our own "relatively real" time, Barth says that "in contradistinction from eternity time is just this division into present, past and future."[57] This would appear to be

---

56. Gotthard Oblau, *Gotteszeit und Menschenzeit: Eschatologie in der Kirchlichen Dogmatik von Karl Barth* (Neukirchen-Vluyn: Neukirchener Verlag, 1988), 120.
57. *CD* III/1, 71.

what most people mean by *time*. Barth, however, seems to be taking the position that the true character of time is not found in "our" time's lack of existence, but rather in something else, something abiding. Time's true character is seen in a tri-unity found within the being of God, in whom there is a (supreme) beginning, middle, and end in which those distinctions do not give way to each other but endure together.

For Barth, eternity and time are distinct, but, from eternity's perspective, they are not the antithesis of each other. Rather, as we have seen, eternity is the ground of time and its basis. Eternity is not timeless, but possesses time, and is indeed "temporal." "Time is not eternity. Eternity itself is not timeless. It is thdoe simultaneity and coinherence of past, present and future. Thus eternity is the dimension of God's own life, the life in which He is self-positing, self-existent and self-sufficient as Father, Son and Holy Ghost. It is this in contrast to time as the dimension of our life—the dimension in which past, present and future follow in succession."[58]

This "coinherence" of past, present, and future within God is of the very same coinherence that characterizes the relationship of Father, Son, and Holy Spirit. Barth's understanding of eternity's temporality is expressly and deeply a Trinitarian understanding of eternity. God, in God's eternity, is not timeless but "temporal," because God is the Triune God.

Yet it is clear that *temporal* means something different here than what it typically means. Eternity may be "temporal," but not in the same way that creatures are temporal. What, then, does Barth mean when he speaks of God's *temporality*? It all rests on Barth's apparent insistence that *time* can mean more than just the time that we know, in which past, present, and future are alienated from each other.

---

58. Ibid., III/2 526.

Commonly speaking, time *is* the coming into existence of things that had not been, after which they cease to be. There may be a continuity of moments that, in our perception, memory, and anticipation form a whole that we designate by the singular noun *time*. But we don't pretend that the reality is different than our experience, namely, that the past exists no longer, the future not yet, and the present is but the quantum distance between the two. Barth, however, wants to assert a theological definition of time that is different from our common understanding that arises out of our own experience, a definition that applies supremely and truthfully only to God.

Thus when Barth speaks of God's temporality, he has not collapsed the distinction between Creator and creature, but rather has sought to express God's freedom *vis-à-vis* time. God's threefold eternality/temporality is the device Barth uses to express a positive relationship of God to time that is recognizably Christian.

The roots of such a Christian expression of God's relationship to time may be noticed in Barth's understanding of eternity. For Barth, God's eternity is always an eternity in relation: either in relation with God's own self, among the Father, Son, and Holy Spirit; or in relation with God's creatures. Divine eternality in its connection with our temporality is likewise at every point relational: election, incarnation, consummation.

Even though Barth seeks to find time's true meaning in God, rather than in human experience, nonetheless he does (as we have seen) look at time, and this he does theologically. Time, as experienced by human beings, does become, in Barth's hands, the focus of theological exposition. His understanding of human time arises out his theological description of the human creature in *CD* III. What becomes apparent there is that Barth expresses several different meanings, or contexts that point to different meanings, for the word *time*. Each of these is marshalled to express a theological point. When he speaks of *lost time*, therefore, he is describing in another way the fallenness of the human creature.

Hunsinger rightly suggests, however, that Barth does not correlate lost time with sin, and thus the healing of fallen time with salvation from sin. Rather, Barth correlates lost time with creatureliness, which is by nature transitory and imperfect. "Time's wounds, as here set forth, are inherent in the good creation. They may be exacerbated and corrupted by sin, but they are not identical with it, nor are they hostile to God. When measured by eternity, they are merely imperfections, not corruptions."[59]

While it may be true that, for Barth, time has "wounds" or "imperfections" that are given to it in creation, nonetheless time becomes deeply problematic for the human creature because of sin. Time's "wounds" do seem to be identical with human sin, or rather a wounding caused by sin, as perpetrator to victim. The problem with time, then, is more than just creatureliness; it includes sin. As time is the *Daseinsform* of the human being, time is affected by the fall of that human being. In a sense, time is fallen because we are fallen. "The difference which emerges between our general being in time and that of the man Jesus does not seem to be one which is original or natural."[60] This is something more. The problems with our experience of time may not all be attributed to creation. Continuing directly:

> On the contrary, when we make this comparison between Jesus and ourselves . . . the antithesis between Jesus and ourselves points not merely to the contrast between man and God, creature and Creator, eternity and time, but to God's judgment upon man; not merely to the nature and order of God and man, but to God's indictment against

---

59. George Hunsinger, "*Mysterium Trinitatis*: Karl Barth's Conception of Eternity," in *Disruptive Grace: Studies in the Theology of Karl Barth* (Grand Rapids: Eerdmans, 2000), 204.
60. *CD* III/2, 517.

man, to His sentence and punishment, and to man's existence under His wrath. What we have been describing is *sinful* man in time.[61]

Regardless, then, of whether time's "imperfections" are inherent aspects of its created nature as given it by God, or are the result of the fall, time as experienced by human beings is not the same as God's "time," nor can our temporality be a valid guide for the nature of God's "temporality."

Time, then, is described by Barth in various ways. Several of them, as we have seen, emphasize the limitations of time as experienced by human beings, and highlight the difference between Creator and creature. What becomes apparent from those passages where that distinction is emphasized and human time is described according to its imperfections is that such imperfections do not define what time really is. Rather, for Barth, time is defined not by its imperfections, but rather by the character of God's time. Barth conceives of something he understands as "time" in which before, during, and after exist all at once, without one passing away and giving way to another. For Barth, God has something like (indeed, something superior to) our time, with its contours of past, present, and future. Yet for God these contours endure and do not pass away. Whereas we merely experience time, God possesses time: the time unique to God, and for that reason also the time we experience, which, by God's free act of grace, is healed of its imperfections, delivered from its alienation.

Summary

Although Barth's understanding of eternity is articulated in a number of places found throughout his massive theological corpus, it finds

---

61. Ibid.

its most definitive expression in a particular section of the *Church Dogmatics*: §31.3, "The Eternity and Glory of God," which constitutes the concluding portion of his exposition of the "perfections," or attributes, of God. That core theological text has provided the focus for this chapter, in which I have attempted to give a detailed exposition of Barth's primary, mature statement of God's eternity.

My exposition took the form of a close reading of this portion of §31.3, one that traced the contours of Barth's theological argument. I sought to show that Barth was here making his way to the "positive" understanding of God's eternity he had been seeking for some time. The progress of Barth's argument finds him, from the very start, showing that a number of theologians in the tradition got eternity right, but only partly so. They correctly distinguished between God's eternity and our time. However, to place them in opposition, as so many did, and to do no more than that, was theologically inadequate. Negative expositions of eternity do not adequately express the nature of God's eternity. Indeed, they likely are merely the corrupt theological procedure against which Barth inveighs so often, the one that begins with the facts of human experience or with human ideals and then either extrapolates them into an imagined infinite dimension or simply negates them.

Barth's exposition in §31.3 stresses that we cannot be content with the merely negative definitions of eternity typical of much theology. More is needed, and that "more" must begin with the God whose eternity we seek to understand, an eternity that is related to time not merely negatively, but asymmetrically, both positively (from God's side) *and* negatively (from the creature's side). The God with whom our proper understanding of eternity must begin is the triune God, who is known as and truly is Father, Son, and Holy Spirit, Three in One, in a union and distinction that endures in love, the parts persisting together and not giving way or passing away one to another.

That threefold union, the perichoretic relationship of dynamic particularity distinctive of God, is the proper model for understanding eternity *and* time. Moreover, for Barth, not only is the Trinity the basis for *understanding* eternity and time. It truly *is* the basis, ontically, for eternity and even for time. Without God possessing a kind of time, *true* time, there could be no time as enjoyed by the creature.

Just as an adequate understanding of eternity must begin with the God who is triune, so too must such an understanding begin with the God who took human form. Here Barth insists that the incarnation shows that we cannot describe God's eternity as merely timeless. Rather, for Barth, Jesus Christ is the demonstration of God's positive embrace of time.

Having laid out those preliminary concerns, Barth proposes his definition of eternity: God's pretemporality, supratemporality, and posttemporality. This formulation, Barth believes, arises out of the witness of Scripture. There, God's bearing toward time is not only distinct, but also positively (yet asymmetrically) oriented, and is seen as God's existing before our time, alongside and yet superior to our time, and after our time. God, whose eternity is pre-, supra-, and posttemporal, is open to time yet distinct from it; this eternal God chooses to embrace time, but such an embrace remains a choice, for God's existence is not dependent upon time.

That threefold definition of eternity is, for Barth, not merely a useful thought experiment. Rather, it encapsulates the core affirmations of the Christian faith. For the definition asserts that God is before our time, with our time, and after our time. As Barth understands it, if these assertions were not fundamentally true then what the doctrines of creation, reconciliation, and redemption articulate likewise could not be true.

These three forms of eternity are not understood as static, disconnected states. Rather, they are understood in dynamic interconnection. Indeed, Barth understands these to be related much as are the persons of the Trinity related to each other: with unity and distinction, in a manner that I have been calling *perichoretic*. Such use of perichoresis continues in Barth's exposition of the forms of eternity. Each form is distinct, yet each is also directly related to the others. When one form is emphasized to the neglect of the others, the underlying theological understanding of eternity is necessarily inadequate, as is also the understanding of God. Barth insists, even as he demonstrates, that an adequate, thoroughly Christian understanding of God's eternity will acknowledge the dynamic particularity and interconnection of God's pre-, supra-, and posttemporality, and thus the perichoretic relations of the doctrines that are illustrative of these forms of eternity: election, incarnation, and eschatology. The forms of eternity as well as the doctrines must be understood in their relation to each other.

So it is that Barth articulates his mature understanding of God's eternity: as an attribute or "perfection" of God, one that is not merely the negation of time but is God's very readiness for time. This readiness has its ontological basis in the "internal" perichoretic relations of Father, Son, and Holy Spirit. The economic expression of this readiness can and must be articulated in the core doctrines of the Christian faith—election, incarnation, and eschatology—as well as in those doctrines that articulate the divine economy and that help to form the structure of the *Church Dogmatics*: creation, reconciliation, and redemption.

7

Conclusion

Throughout these pages I have sought to describe Barth's understanding of divine eternality. I placed his concept of eternity in context, indeed, in three contexts, for apart from acknowledgment of those contexts there can be only limited understanding of Barth's position. Following that context-setting work of exposition and interpretation, I offered a close reading of the core passage for Barth's concept of God's eternity. I now conclude with observations concerning three areas of concern in this project: the distinctly Trinitarian cast to Barth's understanding of eternity, how notions of temporalism and atemporalism play out in the case of Barth's doctrine, and the intersection of human experience and a doctrine of divine timeless eternality.

Eternity as Triune

The Trinitarian concept of divine perichoresis truly holds central importance in Barth's understanding of eternity. The eternality that belongs to and *is* God truly is Trinitarian, and, more specifically, perichoretic. Barth's mature definition of eternity in §31.3 makes deep and extensive use of the doctrine of divine perichoresis.

Barth's concept of eternity is thoroughly perichoretic in two ways. First, it arises from a perichoretic doctrine of God. For Barth, the God of whom Christian theology must speak is truly triune. God not only is known as or appears to be triune; God exists as Trinity. The persons of Father, Son, and Holy Spirit are not appearances, nor are they successive and mutually exclusive modes. Rather, God truly *is* these three persons, in their distinction and in their unity. The doctrine of the Trinity is the affirmation of a reality that is both noetic and ontic; it speaks not only of God's dealings with us but also of God's very being.

This triune God both exists and acts as a loving unity of the three persons, each one participating with and in the others. God can be truly known only as this God, who exists and acts as these three in a pattern of dialectical inclusion. God *is* three in one; the triunity lies at heart of God's being.

All of this is decisive for Barth's mature articulation of divine eternity. For Barth, eternity is an attribute (or, as he prefers to call it, a "perfection") of God. It is not a "place" in which God exists, nor is it a "thing" through which God acts. It is an attribute of God, and therefore it can rightly be said that eternity *is* God, or, more properly, that God is God's eternity. Eternity is an aspect of God's very nature. Since God's nature is triune, and must be understood not modalistically but rather perichoretically, then so too must eternity be understood, for eternity is an attribute of the God who is triune. The understanding of eternity that Barth proposes is based on and deeply informed by a doctrine of a perichoretically triune God that is the center of Barth's entire theological project in the *Church Dogmatics*.

In short, Barth offers a theological description of eternity that arises from a rich doctrine of the Trinity as the real and not merely apparent coinherence of divine persons. This doctrine, in its deep and essential connection with the doctrine of Jesus Christ and the doctrine of revelation, is the formal basis for Barth's understanding of eternity as a likewise triune, indeed, perichoretic reality.

The second way in which Barth's concept of eternity is rightly described as perichoretic is with regard to its "parts." Primarily, this is seen in the dynamic interrelations of the forms of eternity. Pre-, supra-, and post-temporality must be understood, not in isolation, but in their interactions with and mutual dependence upon each other. Barth is very clear about this in his exposition of the three forms of eternity. He sees the dogmatic affirmations that God is prior to, with, and after us to be necessarily interconnected. He makes his opinion plain: a theology that acknowledges only God's pretemporality, for instance, and gives no or little regard to God's supratemporality or posttemporality is a theology that will become one-sided and thereby fail to be adequate.

By extension, a similar relation of parts can be seen in the doctrines Barth uses to illustrate the forms of eternity. The doctrines of election, incarnation, and consummation are dynamically, even perichoretically, interconnected. Christian theology cannot adequately express one of these in isolation from the others. Even as they must, as a matter of rhetoric and clarity, be described in turn and not all at once, they still must mutually inform each other and be understood in their mutual relationship and interdependence.

We also see the perichoretic relationship of dogmatic parts to each other and to the forms of eternity in those doctrines of God's economy that are central to the structure of the *Church Dogmatics*: creation, reconciliation, and redemption. All three are perichoretically related to each other, and to the three forms of eternity.

In those two ways Barth's mature statement of eternity in *CD* II/1 is perichoretic: as it arises from and is determined by the doctrine of the Trinity; and as its components are dynamically related to each other, directly and by means of certain doctrines Barth connects to these components.

One other perichoretic aspect should be named here. Heretofore, I have noted the coinherent aspects of Barth's theology of *eternity*. Moreover, it seems that this understanding of eternity likewise yields a perichoretic understanding of *time*. Both God's time (that is, eternity) and consequently our time may be understood perichoretically. Of course, in Barth's hands it is God's time that has theological priority, both ontically and noetically. God's time is a blessed simultaneity of duration, a holy unity of beginning, middle, and end, that is the very identity of "true time" and the ontological basis for any and all temporality. The perichoresis in God's time is the dynamic inclusion of the three forms of eternity, the coinherence of God's beginning, middle, and end. Our time, on the other hand, is a *derived* temporality based on God's temporality. As derived, it is not equivalent to God's time, and so does not have eternity's simultaneity of duration. Yet as it is blessed by God and as, by God's grace and initiative, it participates in God's time, our time may be blessed by this God who has taken up our time into the divine being and has healed its wounds. The God who possesses past, present, and future as comprehended together is free to give us a sense of that same reality.

It might fairly be asked why I do not simply say throughout that Barth affirms a thoroughly Trinitarian understanding of eternity. To be sure, Barth's concept of eternity is deeply rooted in his articulation of a classical doctrine of the Trinity. He develops his theological statement of eternity in self-conscious connection with a creative yet orthodox Trinitarian doctrine of God. There would be nothing incorrect with saying that Barth has a Trinitarian concept of eternity.

I choose to employ as well the less familiar term *perichoretic*, however, for the simple reason that the term *Trinitarian* may not on its own convey the deeply triune, nonmodalistic understandings of God's being and act that Barth intends. For far too many, a trinity is simply a sequence of three, one whose parts may succeed one to another with no interaction at all. One may find trinities all over, in such a perspective. What Barth has in mind with the divine perfection of eternity, however, is much more than a successive sequence of three parts. He understands these parts in a way that is modeled, intentionally, on his doctrine of God, for whom existence is as Father, Son, and Holy Spirit in loving and unending unity in distinction. The dynamic interaction of the persons and of the forms of eternity is appropriately called *perichoretic* to indicate the kind of trinity that is meant. Barth's understanding of divine eternality, as is his doctrine of God, is Trinitarian in this perichoretic sense.

Atemporalism and Barth's "Temporalism"

Throughout this book, I have made it clear that I do not accept the still-dominant theological preference for a temporalist understanding of God. Some might find a stance such as mine to be a problem, if only in the context of interpreting Barth. How, one might ask, can one affirm an atemporalist understanding of God and also accept Barth's theory of eternity? Does not Barth reject atemporalism?

Some might call my position contrarian. I believe, however, that I have good reasons for resisting the tide of theological opinion that takes it as obvious that God is temporal and not atemporal, and for resisting a distinct, although related, current that assumes Barth promotes a temporalist understanding of God and rejects an atemporalist understanding. My reasons for both of those points of resistance arise from my reading of Barth and my reading of the historical and modern philosophical treatment of the theory of God's timeless eternality. These readings I have defended throughout these pages. In short, I reject a temporalist understanding of God and a temporalist reading of Barth because one of them misunderstands Barth and both of them misunderstand atemporalism, in its classical and recent forms.

Modern philosophical retrievals of atemporalist positions understand temporality to be characterized and defined by incompleteness and the transitory. To be sure, they share that understanding with other outlooks, philosophical, theological, and experiential. Barth does not reject that understanding of time, insofar as it applies only to creatures. Indeed, he affirms it. The human creature, in particular, is afflicted by the *distentio animae*, and our time is in need of "healing." From a Barthian standpoint, creaturely time, understood as this "falling apart" of past, present, and future, requires a strong diastasis between that time and eternity, at least from the temporal side. Throughout Barth's theology, he wants to maintain the distinction between God and creature. That distinction would apply also to the mode of temporality. Barth would not accept an understanding of God's relationship to time that saw God as subject to the same *distentio animae* we experience.

However, Barth wants to provide for an understanding of a kind of "time" that begins, not with our experience, but with the nature of God. This understanding of time is thus very different from either philosophical, scientific, or even common understandings of time. Barth has in mind a kind of time that is not at all marked by the transitory, for which the distinctions of past, present, and future are not absolute, as these do not pass away and give way to each other. God is open to time, our time, because within the divine being God has time, God's own time. These two kinds of time, ours and God's, are not equivalent. Yet the existence of our time, and any possibility for the fragility of time to be overcome, depends on God having God's own time.[1]

The modern atemporalists on which I draw provide a philosophical affirmation of the notion of God's "openness" to time without God being temporal in all and only the ways in which we are temporal. For them, God is not temporal, and it is important to remember that their understanding of temporality points to the entirely successive nature of time. Barth, however, has an understanding of time that is (in the divine case) not wholly successive but, as Stump/Kretzmann and Leftow would say, atemporally durational, , for it is truly the kind of "genuine duration" that is "fully realized duration—not only extended existence . . . but also existence *none* of which is already gone and *none* of which is yet to come."[2] This enduring and durational form of time, a kind of true or *ur*-time, as it is true duration, belongs to God.

All of this is to say that I affirm what I said in the introduction to this study: in different senses, God is neither temporal nor atemporal, and, in yet still different senses, God is both temporal and atemporal. God is not temporal in the sense that God is not subject to the lack of duration that is characteristic of creaturely temporality, and so is, in that respect atemporal. Yet God *is* temporal in the sense that God has within the being of God a distinction of origin, continuance, and goal that is a distinction in unity, and this "temporality," the *timeliness* of Father-Son-Holy Spirit, is the basis for God's openness to time, and so is in that sense not atemporal.

---

1. For Barth, "eternity is a sort of temporal plenum from which time takes its reality." John C. Yates, *The Timelessness of God* (Lanham, MD: University Press of America, 1990), 113.
2. Stump and Kretzmann, "Eternity," *Journal of Philosophy* 78 (1981): 445.

Eternity and Human Experience

The issue that has been behind this book throughout, the question of how God is related to time, has found frequent mention in theology over the last several decades. Much of the work is very interesting. Some of it engages modern physics, analytic or process philosophy, or even comparative religions.[3] Yet some of it seems to lapse into less than careful ways of dealing with the issue of God's eternity. One type of inadequacy tends to arise when attempts are made to bring a doctrine of eternity into proximity with human experience.

The theological impulse of our day appears to be closely connected with a certain religious longing, namely, for God to be a companion throughout life's temporal journey, perhaps even a fellow sufferer with the individual throughout life's temporal trials. So those who view God as temporal often seem to base that view and the theological decisions that support it on the sense that if God is to be caring, a companion to life's temporal difficulties, then God must likewise be temporal. Conversely, it is believed, a God outside of time must be too far removed from the temporal aches of creatures to be concerned about them.

I understand that impulse, and believe that the human needs from which it arises must be taken seriously. Those needs are not irrelevant to Christian doctrine. Surely, if God is the Merciful One of whom the Bible, the Christian tradition, and indeed a good number of other religious traditions speak, then that God is concerned about the temporal triumphs and sufferings of God's creatures. Nonetheless, this still-current theological impulse that emphasizes God's temporal companionship typically seems to proceed along ill-chosen paths.

---

3. See, e.g., Robert Cummings Neville, *Eternity and Time's Flow* (Albany: State University of New York Press, 1993).

First, it is a questionable theological procedure to construct our idea of God based on the highest ideals of the age. Such a theological method leads right into Feuerbach's criticism of theology and religion: that God is nothing but the projection of human wants and desires to the nth degree. As Barth memorably put it, by saying "*Mensch*" in a loud voice one has not thereby said "God."[4] Whereas some previous ages may have valued quiet perseverance or heroic independence as ideals, our age appears to lift up (with good reason) virtues such as compassion, sympathy, and intuitive concern for others. We, as our predecessors, are tempted to attribute to God the values that we ourselves hold. There is, of course, likely some correspondence. The God who creates and declares good, the Glorious One from whom all beauty and virtue flow, surely embraces within the divine being something of the virtues we have been given, we believe, by God's own hand. Yet too often, history shows, the fine virtues we wish to place on God turn out to be boxes that cannot fully contain the divine reality. Must God's compassion be understood merely as human sympathy raised to the highest level?

Second, it is not clear that God's being "outside" of time would make God "far" from human experience. My difficulty here is the reliance upon spatial metaphor. To talk about God being "outside" of time implies a picture of "time" as a geometric solid. An object, presumably even a divine object, "outside" of time would thus be distant from all points "within" time, indeed more distant from some (those at the "center"?) than from others. The curiosity of such an assertion can be seen if we lay aside spatial metaphors for time, and instead focus simply on space itself and God's relationship to it. In its classical formulation, the doctrine of God's omnipresence

---

4. Cf. *Die kirchliche Dogmatik* (Munich: Chr. Kaiser, 1932, and Zurich: EVZ, 1938–65), II/1, 302; *Church Dogmatics*, trans. Geoffrey W. Bromiley et al (Edinburgh: T. & T. Clark, 1956–69), II/1, 269.

affirms that God is present to all space and yet located at none.[5] This understanding of God's relationship to space grows out of theological convictions fundamental to theism. As God is "zero-spatial," God is not definable in spatial terms, and so for that reason is near to every spatial point.

When God's relationship to space is considered by means of this understanding of omnipresence, it becomes apparent that to speak of God "outside" of space is to deploy a metaphor, one intended to express the religious conviction and theological instinct that God is near at hand and yet not spatially locatable, measurable, or determined. But that metaphor is no substitute for a careful theological definition. For when one says, in the context of systematic theology, that God is "outside" of space, then God's relationship to space is itself conceived spatially: there is space, and there is some "distance" (a spatial term) between God and space. Yet if God is nonspatial, then the relationship between God and space cannot be conceived as spatial pure and simple, as in the picture of two spheres.

When we move back to discussing God's relationship to time, perhaps it is clear how careful we need to be with spatial metaphors. Here, the Zero Thesis provides us with a helpful way of conceiving the relationship. Thus God is atemporal, in the sense that God exists at no point in time and cannot be measured temporally. And yet God is able to be proximate to any point in time, near at hand to the temporal triumphs and sufferings of God's creatures.

Perhaps these reflections indicate why I believe we do not need to accept the judgment that God's care and sympathy for temporal creatures require that God be temporal. It is by no means clear that atemporalist views of God are deist. Much theology, however, assumes that atemporalism does lead to deism. Indeed, Barth would

---

5. Recall also my discussion above, in chapter 3, of Brian Leftow's concept of the "Zero Thesis."

likely find some forms of atemporalism as having a tendency toward deism. Yet there is much in his theology, as I have shown, that should lead one to challenge the shallow understanding of omnipresence and eternity implicit in charges that atemporalism leads either to deism or to a God incapable of sympathy or care.

Truly, the only way for us to be engaged with reality is to be "in" time in Heidegger's sense, to exist as temporal creatures and to deal positively with the reality that we are temporal creatures. From a religious standpoint, a life lived well and to the glory of God is one that sees all our opportunities lying within the temporality of creaturely existence. One who lives life that way will recognize, for instance, that care for one's sister or brother is *limited* by time just as it is possible only *in* time. The presence of one human being to another is temporal, transient, capable of growth and decay. All these things are true of human compassion and sympathy. These highly important characteristics of creaturely care are fundamentally temporal, but not simply because the activity is temporal. The agent (that is, the human creature) is temporal as well, in the sense that for such a being the present is both possibility and threat, a fleeting existence accompanied by a discontinuity of experienced time that induces something much like what Augustine would call a *distentio animae*.

Yet it should be asked whether discontinuity is the only way to understand creaturely time. Jeremy Begbie has helpfully questioned this, and, in the context of theology and music, has suggested an understanding of temporality that is not dominated by the idea of the radical discontinuity of discrete and tiny quanta. For Begbie, music facilitates an experience of time that points to an overcoming of discontinuity, creatively and provisionally, in which by memory and anticipation the past is not completely past and the future is already in some sense present.[6]

Music does this by means of several tools, most of them unique to it, such as rhythm and meter. For the most part, all of these are temporal, deeply so. Music takes time, as rhythm and meter and development and resolution take time. Their temporality gives music its shape. It is in great part why music is so enjoyable.

There is a subtle aspect to music's temporality that many overlook. It has to do with the notes themselves. Pitch is fundamentally about time. That's because pitch, how high or low a note is sounding, is possible because something is vibrating. A string, a column of air in a trumpet or an organ pipe, a vocal chord, a drum head: when they sound, they vibrate, and the rate at which they vibrate, their *frequency*, is what makes them sound high or low. Frequency is how these pitch vibrations are measured. In other words, they are measured in time. The note to which an orchestra tunes is an A vibrating at 440 cycles per second, or hz. The average range of human hearing is 20 to 20,000 hz. The point is this: without time, there is no vibration. If there is no vibration, there is no pitch. Sound is possible because there is time. The very nature of music as ordered sounds is deeply connected to temporality.

But pitch in not the only way in which temporality is embedded in the sounds that constitute music. For music also has tone, or timbre. Why is it that we can tell the difference between a clarinet and a trumpet playing the same note? Timbre. It is timbre that makes a Les Paul guitar sound different than a Stratocaster, Bonnie Raitt sound different than Lady Gaga, and Willie Nelson sound *very* different than Luciano Pavarotti. The distinctive timbres of violas and cellos, respectively, is why it is so effective, indeed moving, when the cellos play the melody higher than the accompanying violas in the third

---

6. See Jeremy S. Begbie, *Theology, Music and Time* (Cambridge: Cambridge University Press, 2000), especially chapters 4, 5, and 6.

CONCLUSION

movement of Mahler's *Fourth Symphony*. This all depends on that characteristic of musical sounds we call tone, timbre, or "color."

Just as is pitch, timbre is likewise a matter of frequencies. A note with a certain timbre is not just that single frequency but is "colored" by several other less prominent tones pitched above it, a series of "overtones," each with their own frequency. The timbre of a sound is formed by the distinct combination of overtones upon the fundamental pitch, each overtone having its own frequency, yielding a colored sound that is a complex interaction of resonating tones and intersecting frequencies. Every note, not just in its pitch but also in its tone, is deeply and distinctly temporal.

This easily overlooked aspect of music's temporality contributes greatly to its enjoyment. Indeed, it is one reason why music must truly be heard, and not just read off of the page and then imagined.[7] Music's beauty is a complex interaction of metrical, rhythmic, melodic, and tonal components. All of these require time and take time. The multifaceted temporality of music demands that we take time to take it in.

Does the performance and enjoyment of music as an inherently temporal experience require me to retract my mostly negative description of creaturely time as characterized primarily by discontinuity, so prominent in this book? I do not believe it does.

First of all, even Begbie's excellent highlighting of multiple continuities within music does not *eliminate* temporal discontinuity. By Begbie's reckoning, music highlights the potential of time to exhibit a complex interaction of multiple continuities.[8] In addition, music makes use of, and even depends on, temporal discontinuity.

---

7. Perhaps he was joking, but Arnold Schoenberg said that "music need not be performed any more than books need to be read aloud, for its logic is perfectly represented on the printed paged." Cited in Begbie, *Theology, Music and Time*, 56.
8. See especially chapter 2.

Musical tension and resolution are not possible absent time, both its continuities and its discontinuities.

Second, in Barth's mature theology the discontinuity within creaturely time is not emphasized as a theological end in itself. To make it such would run the risk of working in a theological direction quite the opposite of what Barth believes is proper and even possible. Noetically, neither temporal continuity nor discontinuity can be the certain theological starting point for a proper understanding of God's eternity, either *via negationis* or *via eminentiae*. By neither of these can we leverage our way to God. There's an ontic aspect to this as well: neither eternity nor the being of God (of which eternity is one perfection) is dependent upon time, not in its continuities, not in its discontinuity. God does not need our time in order to be God. Within a Barthian framework, the theological importance in emphasizing discontinuity would appear to be mainly as it makes clear the distinction between Creator and creature and the asymmetry between God's eternity and our time. To make more of it would be to make too much of it.

Perhaps this can all be stated less technically and more personally. I experience time as both opportunity and burden. I know well time's distinctive wounds: the sense of loss as time carries what was loved and lovely into my past, as well as the anxious feeling of helplessness at the approaching unknown. Likewise, I know time's distinctive joys: the deepening of love, the growth of children, the sheer pleasure of music.

None of these, however, can provide me the perfect fulcrum by which I can leverage my way into certain knowledge of God, neither by elevating time's joys nor by a conceptual negation of time's burdens. The route there is not a matter of human reasoning but rather of divine action. Indeed, theology cannot really provide the way. It can only describe the way that has been made. Indeed, the problem of time is, for me, just as much soteriological as it is theological. Time, my time, must be redeemed.

As a matter of faith, I know that it both has been redeemed and is being redeemed. God—who, as Father, Son, and Holy Spirit, lives and loves from all eternity—freely chooses to embrace creaturely time. God can do this, not because of something within that time, but because God has a kind of time, superior and perfect to my own, within God's own being. That time is complete within itself; God does not need to create or experience another kind of time in order to be God or to become even more divine. Yet God chooses to give created time to creatures. Even more, God chooses to redeem time and to heal its wounds by means of taking up creaturely time in a decisive way, through the incarnation of the Son. By means of the Son's work, the time of human beings—indeed, even my time—is blessed, and forgiven, and healed, and above all brought into even closer proximity to the time God has within God's own self.

At this point, none of this is complete or direct. The full redemption of my time is, from my perspective, still in the future. Yet there are hints of it in the here and now: in the blessings of creation; in forgiveness experienced from God and from others; in the celebration of the Eucharist, which reflects the weaving together of God's past, present, and future with my own. All of these strike me as signs, or perhaps echoes, of the dynamic eternity that is uniquely God's own, an eternity that is radically distinct from time and yet that is free to embrace time, indeed, my time.

Such has been the theological and personal impetus for this book: to offer, and defend, an interpretation of Karl Barth's understanding of God's eternity that is true to Barth, theologically coherent, and religiously authentic. In short, Barth's theology of eternity flows from and communicates an understanding of God as the one who is not comprehended by our time, yet who comprehends our time.

Bibliography

References from Barth

Barth, Karl. *Anselm: Fides Quaerens Intellectum—Anselm's Proof of the Existence of God in the Context of His Theological Scheme*. London: SCM Press, reprinted by Pickwick Publications, 1960.

_____. *Die christliche Dogmatik im Entwurf. Vol. 1: Die Lehre vom Worte Gottes: Prolegomena zur christlichen Dogmatik*. Edited by Gerhard Sauter. Zürich: Theologischer Verlag, 1982.

_____. *Church Dogmatics*. Translated by Geoffrey W. Bromiley et al. Edinburgh: T. & T. Clark, 1956–69.

_____. *The Epistle to the Romans*. Translated by Edwyn C. Hoskyns. London: Oxford University Press, 1976.

_____. *Fides quaerens intellectum: Anselms Beweis der Existenz Gottes im Zusammenhang seines theologischen Programms*. Zollikon: Evangelischer Verlag, 1958.

_____. "Gespräch in Princeton I." In *Gespräche, 1959–1962*, edited by Eberhard Busch. Gesamtausgabe, IV. Gespräche 25. Theologischer Verlag, 1976.

_____. *The Göttingen Dogmatics: Instruction in the Christian Religion*. Edited by Hannelotte Reiffen. Translated by Geoffrey William Bromiley. Vol. 1. Grand Rapids: Eerdmans, 1991.

_____. *Karl Barth: Theologian of Freedom.* Edited by Clifford Green. Minneapolis: Fortress Press, 1991.

_____. *Die kirchliche Dogmatik.* Munich: Chr. Kaiser, 1932, and Zurich: EVZ, 1938–65.

_____. *Letters, 1961–1968.* Edited by Jurgen Fangmeier and Hinrich Stoevesandt. Translated by Geoffrey W. Bromiley. Grand Rapids: Eerdmans, 1981.

_____. *Der Römerbrief. 2nd edition, 1922.* Zürich: Theologischer Verlag, 1989.

_____. *Die Theologie Calvins 1922.* Edited by Hans Scholl. Zürich: Theologischer Verlag, 1993.

_____. *The Theology of John Calvin.* Translated by Geoffrey W. Bromiley. Grand Rapids: Eerdmans, 1995.

_____. *Unterricht in der Christlichen Religion. Vol. 1: Prolegomena, 1924.* Edited by Hannelotte Reiffen. Karl Barth Gesamtausgabe. Zürich: Theologischer Verlag, 1985.

_____. *Unterricht in der Christlichen Religion. Vol. 2: Die Lehre von Gott/Die Lehre vom Menschen, 1924/1925.* Edited by Hinrich Stoevesandt. Zürich: Theologischer Verlag, 1990.

_____. "Verheißung, Zeit—Erfüllung." *Zwischen den Zeiten* 9 (1931): 457–463.

Other Works

Anselm. *Saint Anselm: Basic Writings—Proslogium, Monologium, Gaunilon's On Behalf of the Fool, Cur Deus Homo.* Translated by Sidney Norton Deane. LaSalle, IL: Open Court, 1962.

_____. *Theological Treatises.* Edited by Jasper Hopkins and Herbert Richardson. Vol. 3. Cambridge: Harvard Divinity School Library, 1967.

Aquinas, St. Thomas. *Summa Theologiae*. Vol. 2: *Existence and Nature of God (Ia. 2–11)*. Edited by Timothy McErmott, OP. . London: Blackfriars, 1964.

Augustine. *The Confessions*. Translated by Henry Chadwick. New York: Oxford University Press, 1991.

Balthasar, Hans Urs von. *Karl Barth: Darstellung und Deutung Seiner Theologie*. Köln: Verlag Jakob Hegner, 1951.

_____. *The Theology of Karl Barth: Exposition and Interpretation*. San Francisco: Ignatius Press, 1992.

Barr, James. *Biblical Words for Time*. London: SCM, 1962.

_____. *The Semantics of Biblical Language*. Oxford: Oxford University Press, 1961.

Begbie, Jeremy S. *Theology, Music and Time*. Cambridge: Cambridge University Press, 2000.

Beinert, Wolfgang, and Francis Schüssler Fiorenza. *Handbook of Catholic Theology*. New York: Crossroad, 1995.

Beintker, Michael. *Die Dialektik in der "dialektischen Theologie" Karl Barths: Studien zur Entwicklung der Barthschen Theologie und zur Vorgeschichte der "Kirchlichen Dogmatik."* Beiträge zur evangelischen Theologie. München: C. Kaiser, 1987.

Boethius. *The Theological Tractates & The Consolation of Philosophy*. Translated by S. J. Tester, H. F. Stewart, and E. K. Rand. Cambridge, MA: Harvard University Press, 1973.

Bradley, Raymond, and Norman Swartz. *Possible Worlds: An Introduction to Logic and Its Philosophy*. Indianapolis: Hackett, 1979.

Brunner, Emil. *Natur und Gnade: zum Gesprach mit Karl Barth*. Zurich: Zwingli-Verlag, 1935.

_____. *Natural Theology: Comprising "Nature and Grace."* Translated by Peter Fraenkel. London: Centenary, 1946.

Busch, Eberhard. *Karl Barth: His Life from Letters and Autobiographical Texts*. Translated by John Bowden. London: SCM Press, 1976.

Calvin, John. *Institutes of the Christian Religion*. Edited by John T. McNeill. Philadelphia: Westminster Press, 1960.

Copi, Irving M. *Introduction to Logic*. New York: Macmillan, 1972.

Crombie, Ian M. "Eternity and Omnitemporality." In *The Rationality of Religious Belief*, edited by William J. Abraham and S. W. Holtzer, 169–84. Oxford: Oxford University Press, 1987.

Cullmann, Oscar. *Christ and Time: The Primitive Christian Conception of Time and History*. London: SCM Press, 1962.

Deutsch, David, and Michael Lockwood. "The Quantum Physics of Time Travel." *Scientific American* (1994): 68–74.

Dillard, Annie. *The Writing Life*. New York: Harper & Row, 1989.

Dorner, Isaak August. *Divine Immutability: A Critical Reconsideration*. Minneapolis: Fortress Press, 1994.

Duchrow, Ulrich. "Der sogenannte psychologische Zeitbegriff Augustins im Verhältnis zur physikalischen und geschichtlichen Zeit." *Zeitschrift für Theologie und Kirche* 63, no. 3 (1966): 267–88.

Edwards, Jonathan. *The "Miscellanies" (Entry Nos. a–z, aa–zz, 1–500)*. Edited by Thomas A. Schaffer. New Haven: Yale University Press, 1994.

Frei, Hans W. "The Doctrine of Revelation in The Thought of Karl Barth, 1909 to 1922: The Nature of Barth's Break with Liberalism." PhD diss., Yale University, 1956.

Green, Clifford. "Freedom for Humanity: Karl Barth and the Politics of the New World Order." In *For the Sake of the World: Karl Barth and the Future of Ecclesial Theology*, edited by George Hunsinger, 95–108. Grand Rapids: Eerdmans, 2004.

Green, Garrett. "Challenging the Religious Studies Canon: Karl Barth's Theory of Religion." *Journal of Religion* 75 (October 1995): 473–86.

Griswold, Daniel M. "Time." In *The Westminster Handbook to Karl Barth*, edited by Richard Burnett, 201–11. Louisville: Westminster John Knox Press, 2013.

Härle, Wilfried. "Der Aufruf der 93 Intellektuellen und Karl Barths Bruch mit der liberalen Theologie." *Zeitschrift für Theologie und Kirche* 72, no. 2 (1975): 207–24.

Harnack, Adolph. *What Is Christianity?* Gloucester, MA: Peter Smith, 1978.

Hartshorne, Charles. *Anselm's Discovery: A Re-Examination of the Ontological Proof for God's Existence*. LaSalle, IL: Open Court, 1965.

———. "The Formal Validity and the Real Significance of the Ontological Argument." *The Philosophical Review*, 53, no. 3 (1944): 225–45.

———. "Introduction." In *Saint Anselm: Basic Writings—Proslogium, Monologium, Gaunilon's On Behalf of the Fool, Cur Deus Homo*, translated by Sidney Norton Deane, 1–19. LaSalle, IL: Open Court, 1962.

———. "John Hick on Logical and Ontological Necessity." *Religious Studies* 13, no. 2 (1977): 155–65.

———. "Kant's Refutation Still Not Convincing: A Reply." *Monist* 52, no. 2 (1968): 312–16.

———. "The Logic of the Ontological Argument." *Journal of Philosophy* 58, no. 17 (1961): 471–73.

———. "Rationale of the Ontological Proof." *Theology Today* 20, no. 2 (1963): 278–83.

———. "Ten Ontological or Modal Proofs for God's Existence." In *The Logic of Perfection and Other Essays in Neoclassical Metaphysics*, 28–117. LaSalle, IL: Open Court, 1962.

———. "What Did Anselm Discover?" *Union Seminary Quarterly Review* 17, no. 3 (1962): 213–22.

Hartshorne, Charles, and William L. Reese. *Philosophers Speak of God*. Chicago: University of Chicago Press, 1953.

Hegel, Georg Wilhelm Friedrich. *Hegel's Philosophy of Nature*. Edited and translated by M. J. Petry. Vol. 1. New York: Humanities Press, 1970.

Heidegger, Martin. *Being and Time*. San Francisco: Harper & Row, 1962.

Helm, Paul. *Eternal God: A Study of God without Time*. Oxford: Oxford University Press, 1988.

Heppe, Heinrich. *Die Dogmatik der evangelisch-reformierten Kirche, dargestellt und aus den Quellen belegt von Heinrich Heppe*. Edited by Ernst Bizer. Neukirchen: K. Moer, 1935.

———. *Reformed Dogmatics Set Out and Illustrated From the Sources*. Edited by Ernst Bizer. Translated by G. T. Thompson. London: Allen & Unwin, 1950.

Hunsinger, George. "Election and the Trinity: Twenty-Five Theses on the Theology of Karl Barth." *Modern Theology* 24, no. 2 (April 2008): 179–98.

———. *How to Read Karl Barth: The Shape of His Theology*. New York: Oxford University Press, 1991.

———. "*Mysterium Trinitatis*: Karl Barth's Conception of Eternity." In *Disruptive Grace: Studies in the Theology of Karl Barth*, 186–209. Grand Rapids: Eerdmans, 2000.

Jenson, Robert W. "Does God Have Time? The Doctrine of the Trinity and the Concept of Time in the Physical Sciences." *CTNS Bulletin* 11 (1991): 1–6.

———. *God after God: The God of the Past and the God of the Future, Seen in the Work of Karl Barth*. Indianapolis: The Bobbs-Merrill Company, 1969.

———. *Unbaptized God: The Basic Flaw in Ecumenical Theology*. Minneapolis: Fortress Press, 1992.

Jordan, Robert. "Time and Contingency in St. Augustine." In *Augustine: A Collection of Critical Essays*, edited by R. A. Markus, 255–79. Garden City, NY: Anchor Books, Doubleday & Co., 1972.

Jüngel, Eberhard. *Barth-Studien*. Oekumenische Theologie, vol. 19. Zürich Gütersloh: Benziger Mohn, 1982.

———. *God's Being Is in Becoming: The Trinitarian Being of God in the Theology of Karl Barth*. Translated by John Webster. Edinburgh: T. & T. Clark, 2001.

———. *Gottes Sein ist im Werden: verantwortliche Rede vom Sein Gottes bei Karl Barth: eine Paraphrase*. 4th ed. Tübingen: Mohr Siebeck, 1986.

———. *Karl Barth: A Theological Legacy*. Philadelphia: Westminster Press, 1986.

Kasper, Walter. *The God of Jesus Christ*. New York: Crossroad, 1992.

Kenny, Anthony. "Divine Foreknowledge and Human Freedom." In *Aquinas: A Collection of Critical Essays*, edited by Anthony Kenny, 255–70. Garden City, NY: Doubleday-Anchor, 1969.

Kneale, Martha. "Eternity and Sempiternity." *Proceedings of the Aristotelian Society* 69 (1969): 223–38.

Kneale, W. C. "Time and Eternity in Theology." *Proceedings of the Aristotelian Society* 61 (1961): 87–108.

LaCugna, Catherine Mowry. *God For Us: The Trinity & Christian Life*. San Francisco: HarperSanFrancisco, 1991.

Lancaster, Sarah Heaner. "Three-Personed Substance: The Relational Essence of the Triune God in Augustine's De Trinitate." *The Thomist* 60, no. 1 (1996): 123–39.

Larson, Duane Howard. "The Temporality of the Trinity: A Christian Theological Concept of Time and Eternity in View of Contemporary Physical Theory." PhD diss., Graduate Theological Union, 1993.

Leftow, Brian. "Response to '*Mysterium Trinitatis*: Barth's Conception of Eternity." In *For the Sake of the World: Karl Barth and the Future of Ecclesial Theology*, edited by George Hunsinger, 191–201. Grand Rapids: Eerdmans, 2004.

———. *Time and Eternity*. Ithaca, NY: Cornell University Press, 1991.

Manzke, Karl Hinrich. *Ewigkeit und Zeitlichkeit: Aspekte für eine theologische Deutung der Zeit*. Göttingen: Vandenhoeck und Ruprecht, 1992.

Marsh, J. *The Fulness of Time.* London: Nisbet & Co., 1952.

McCormack, Bruce L. "Election and Trinity: Theses in response to George Hunsinger," *Scottish Journal of Theology* 63, no. 2 (2010): 203–224.

_____. *Karl Barth's Critically Realistic Dialectical Theology: Its Genesis and Development, 1909–1936.* New York: Oxford University Press, 1995.

_____. "A Scholastic of a Higher Order: The Development of Karl Barth's Theology, 1921–31." PhD diss., Princeton Theological Seminary, 1989.

Moltmann, Jürgen. *Theologie der Hoffnung.* München: Chr. Kaiser Verlag, 1965.

_____. *Theology of Hope: On the Ground and the Implications of a Christian Eschatology.* London: SCM Press, 1967.

Morris, Thomas V., ed. *The Concept of God.* New York: Oxford University Press, 1987.

Neville, Robert Cummings. *Eternity and Time's Flow.* Albany, NY: State University of New York Press, 1993.

Oblau, Gotthard. *Gotteszeit und Menschenzeit: Eschatologie in der Kirchlichen Dogmatik von Karl Barth.* Neukirchen-Vluyn: Neukirchener Verlag, 1988.

Ogden, Shubert M. *The Reality of God and Other Essays.* New York: Harper & Row, 1966.

Padgett, Alan G. *God, Eternity, and the Nature of Time.* New York: St. Martin's Press, 1992.

Pike, Nelson. *God and Evil: Readings on the Theological Problem of Evil.* Englewood Cliffs, NJ: Prentice-Hall, 1964.

_____. *God and Timelessness: Studies in Ethics and the Philosophy of Religion.* London: Routledge & K. Paul, 1970.

Placher, William C. *Narratives of a Vulnerable God: Christ, Theology, and Scripture.* Louisville: Westminster/John Knox Press, 1994.

Roberts, Richard H. *A Theology on Its Way? Essays on Karl Barth.* Edinburgh: T. & T. Clark, 1991.

Robinson, John A. T. *In the End, God . . . : A Study of the Christian Doctrine of the Last Things*. New York: Harper & Row, 1968.

Schleiermacher, Friedrich. *Der Christliche Glaube nach den Grundsätzen der Evangelischen Kirche im Zusammenhange Dargestellt*. Edited by Martin Redeker. Berlin: Walter de Gruyter, 1960.

_____. *The Christian Faith*. Edited by H. R. Mackintosh and J. S. Stewart. Edinburgh: T. & T. Clark, 1986.

Spieckermann, Ingrid. *Gotteserkenntnis: Ein Beitrag zur Grundfrage der neuen Theologie Karl Barths*. München: Chr. Kaiser, 1985.

Streetman, Robert F. "Some Questions Schleiermacher Might Ask about Barth's Trinitarian Criticisms." In *Barth and Schleiermacher: Beyond the Impasse?*, edited by James O. Duke and Robert F. Streetman, 114–37. Philadelphia: Fortress Press, 1988.

Stump, Eleonore, and Norman Kretzmann. "Atemporal Duration: A Reply to Fitzgerald." *Journal of Philosophy* 84 (1987): 214–19.

_____. "Eternity." *Journal of Philosophy* 78 (1981): 429–58.

Torrance, Alan. "The Trinity." In *The Cambridge Companion to Karl Barth*, edited by John B. Webster, 72–91. Cambridge: Cambridge University Press, 2000.

Torrance, Thomas F. *Belief in Science and in Christian Life: The Relevance of Michael Polanyi's Thought for Christian Faith and Life*. Edinburgh: Handsel Press, 1980.

_____. *Christian Theology and Scientific Culture*. New York: Oxford University Press, 1981.

_____. *Karl Barth: Biblical and Evangelical Theologian*. Edinburgh: T. & T. Clark, 1990.

_____. *Reality and Scientific Theology*. Edinburgh: Scottish Academic Press, 1985.

_____. *Space, Time, and Resurrection*. Grand Rapids: Eerdmans, 1976.

_____. *Theological Science*. New York: Oxford University Press, 1978.

———. *Theology in Reconciliation: Essays towards Evangelical and Catholic Unity in East and West*. Grand Rapids: Eerdmans, 1975.

Toulmin, Stephen, and June Goodfield. *The Discovery of Time*. New York: Harper Torchbooks, 1965.

Welch, Claude. *Protestant Thought in the Nineteenth Century: Vol. 1, 1799–1870*. New Haven: Yale University Press, 1972.

Welker, Michael. "Barth und Hegel: Zur Erkenntnis eines methodischen Verfahrens bei Barth." *Evangelische Theologie* 43 (1983): 307–28.

Westphal, Merold. *Suspicion and Faith: The Religious Uses of Modern Atheism*. Grand Rapids: Eerdmans, 1993.

Williams, Robert R. "Introduction." In Dorner, *Divine Immutability*, 1–38.

Wolterstorff, Nicholas. "God Everlasting." In *God and the Good*, edited by Clifton J. Orlebeke and Lewis M. Smedes, 181–203. Grand Rapids: Eerdmans, 1975.

Yates, John C. *The Timelessness of God*. Lanham, MD: University Press of America, 1990.

Index

actualism, 75, 120, 149
analogy, 11, 13, 39n53, 87, 108, 118-20
Anselm of Canterbury, 9, 42n63, 47n80, 50-63, 64, 67, 76, 99n33, 105n48, 115, 203
anticipation, 29-30, 33, 229, 245
appropriations, doctrine of divine, 188, 220, 222-25
attributes (or perfections), of God, 24, 39, 51, 70, 72-75, 94, 148, 172, 201-4
Augustine, 3, 9, 22-40, 44, 45n73, 47n81, 47n82, 49, 50n89, 62, 74n168, 79, 115, 122, 198, 203, 245

Barr, James, 17n31, 18-19
Begbie, Jeremy, 245, 247
Beintker, Michael, 122n10, 125-26

biblical interpretation, 17-19, 24-25
Boëthius, and Boëthian, 9, 39, 40-51, 60, 62, 64, 67, 68, 69, 84, 95, 100, 101, 115, 148, 166, 197-98

Calvin, John, 126-28, 130-31, 144, 145
causality, 73-75, 148
chance, 41
change, 25-27, 30-31, 33, 39, 56, 63-65, 78-79, 91-92, 112-13, 167n19
christocentrism, 158, 160
Christology, 11, 16, 93n21, 150-54, 156, 158-168, 174, 186, 193, 200, 224
constancy, of God, 26-27, 202-4
creation, 1, 25-28, 39, 49, 111, 143, 162, 164, 173-74, 187-190, 192, 204, 211, 214,

215, 218, 219, 220-21, 222-26, 230, 234, 237, 248
crisis, 122, 125, 132, 141, 156
Crombie, Ian, 97
Cullmann, Oscar, 17n31, 18, 91

dialectic, 118-21; of God's freedom and love, 172; of time and eternity, 7-8, 12, 122, 124-25, 128-33; of revelation, 12, 123, 155-56, 170-74, 202, 212n26; dialectical inclusion, 11, 220, 236
dipolar theism, 98-100
dispensationalism, 135, 141-42
distention, 29-31, 240, 245
Dorner, Isaak, 69, 74n171
Duns Scotus, John, 90
duration, 30, 35, 37-38, 44-47, 58, 64, 68-69, 74, 80, 85, 101-2, 104-5, 148, 203-07, 210, 214, 238, 241

Edwards, Jonathan, 111-12
Einstein, Albert, 3
election, doctrine of, 162, 174, 218, 220, 223-25, 229, 234, 237
eschatology, 2, 128, 130, 134, 136-42, 154, 219-20, 223-225, 234

foreknowledge, divine, 41-47, 107-8
free will, 41-43, 60, 92-93, 107-8
Frei, Hans, 118

general revelation, 169
Gerhard, Johann, 187
God: as unchangeable, 31, 63, 64, 67; freedom of, 12, 115-16, 127, 164-65, 167, 172-73, 202-4, 212, 214-15, 229; omnipresence of, 112-13, 148-49, 202, 207, 215, 243-44; simplicity of, 13, 43, 46, 51-52, 56, 60, 64-65, 69-70, 94, 107, 111

Hartshorne, Charles, 84-85, 90, 91, 93, 98-100, 112, 115
Hegel, Georg Wilhelm Friedrich, 49, 76-81, 88, 90, 113n61, 115, 116, 137
Heidegger, Martin, 3, 31n30, 36n44, 37, 244
Heppe, Heinrich, 44, 68, 146-48
hope, 2, 10, 134-35, 139, 219, 220
Hunsinger, George, 8, 11, 13, 18n32, 48, 62n131, 75n174, 87-88, 90n12, 102n38, 115, 119-20, 132, 142n57, 149, 163,

164n12, 170, 179, 184, 192n96,
    214, 218n43, 230
Härle, Wilfried, 151

incarnation, 2, 26, 92, 93, 111,
    150, 152-53, 162n7, 164-67,
    169, 200, 211-13, 219-21,
    223-26, 229, 233, 234, 237,
    248
infinite qualitative distinction,
    124-26, 132

Jenson, Robert, 4, 5, 7n12, 84, 87,
    89n11, 90, 91
Jordan, Robert, 32
Jüngel, Eberhard, 4, 165n16

Kant, Immanuel, 131
Kasper, Walter, 175, 177n56, 180
Kierkegaard, Søren, 124, 125
Knowledge: divine, 51, 92, 108-9,
    112, *see* foreknowledge, divine;
    human, 12, 51, 65-66, 70, 124,
    130-31, *see* revelation
Kretzmann, Norman, *see* Stump,
    Eleonore

Lancaster, Sarah Heaner, 35n41

Leftow, Brian, 40, 45, 46, 57-58,
    85, 91n14, 98, 100, 105-13,
    115, 142n57, 167n19, 241,
    243n5
Lombard, Peter, 40

Manzke, Karl-Hinrich, 12
memory, 23, 29-30, 33, 229, 245
modalism, 177-79
Molinism, 107
Moltmann, Jürgen, 4
music, 245-48
mystery, of God, 12, 72, 170-74

obedience, 172-73, 190
objectivism, 120, 134, 153, 214
Oblau, Gotthard, 13, 19n36,
    31-32, 36n42, 123, 141n56,
    227
Ogden, Schubert, 112
omnipotence, 74-76, 79, 112, 202,
    207, 215
omnipresence, 112-13, 148, 149,
    202, 207, 215, 243-44
ontological argument, 99

Padgett, Alan, 7n14, 17n31,
    93n20, 96-98, 110
particularism, 75, 120, 132, 134,
    153, 163, 169-70
perfections, of God, *see* attributes

perichoresis, 10-11, 179-80, 188, 218-20, 222-25, 233-34, 235-39
permanence, 33-34, 39, 46, 49
personalism, 120, 149
Pike, Nelson, 74n171, 109-10
Polanus, Amandus, 187, 203
Pseudo-Dionysius the Areopagite, 34

redemption, doctrine of, 71-73, 143, 187-89, 190, 192, 215, 218-25, 233-34, 237
revelation, 11-12, 129-30, 134, 142, 156, 158-59, 166, 168-74, 178, 181-86, 193; time of, 36-37, 165-68
Roberts, Richard, 7-8, 12

Schleiermacher, Friedrich, 11-12, 68-76, 147, 148, 182-85
Schmid, Heinrich, 147-48
science, 14-17
sempiternality or sempiternity, 26, 35, 44n70, 45n73, 47, 80, 84-85, 203
simplicity, divine, 13, 46, 51-53, 56, 60, 64-65, 69, 94, 107, 111
simultaneity, 26-27, 33-34, 38-39, 43-44, 47-49, 54-58, 68, 101-108, 113, 148, 166, 168, 197, 203, 208, 228, 238
Stump, Eleonore, 1n1, 5n10, 13n23, 44n71, 45, 85, 86, 92n18, 95, 100-105, 110, 115, 241

Thomas Aquinas, 63-67, 68
time: contingency of, 32, 96-100; lost (also, empty, fallen, wounded), 37, 162-63, 165-68, 198, 226-27, 230; modality of, 90-91, 94-100; of revelation, 165-67, 198; tensed and thenseless theories of, 88, 109-10; true (also, genuine, real), 165, 167-168
Torrance, Alan, 177n58
Torrance, Thomas, 4, 15, 165
Toulmin, Stephen, 3

von Balthasar, Hans Urs, 118, 119

Welch, Claude, 183
Welker, Michael, 76-77
von Balthasar, Hans Urs, 118, 119
    Welch, Claude, 183 Welker, Michael, 76-77 Wolterstorff, Nicholas, 92

www.ingramcontent.com/pod-product-compliance
Lightning Source LLC
Chambersburg PA
CBHW071152070526
44584CB00019B/2766